PENETRATION

The New Battle for Mind Space and Shelf Space

Marcel Corstjens

ISBN: 9780956468413

Acknowledgments

Many authors have inspired and fertilized my thinking, but in the context of this book, I would like to single out two of them, Andrew Ehrenberg and Daniel Kahneman. One a statistician at heart and the other a psychologist, they have strictly nothing in common, but their work has shaped many of the ideas in this book.

With the persistence of the true scholar, more than anyone else in marketing, Andrew Ehrenberg applied the scientific method to problems in the field. Although not always understood or appreciated, he successfully established the notions of double jeopardy and brand salience in the field. Marketing is as much a science as it is an art, and Professor Ehrenberg clearly excelled in this dimension.

The second, but more recent, influence on my work is Daniel Kahneman. This remarkable scholar is the only psychologist ever to win the Nobel Prize in economics. His notions of fast and slow thinking and the theories on which they are based are echoed throughout my book. Intuition dominates marketing's conventional wisdom, but as so often in the past, the truth is not always what common sense would suggest. I show in this book many instances in marketing where slow thinking is required and fast thinking is wrong.

Over the years many executives and academic colleagues have significantly influenced my views about marketing, strategy and retailing. I am particularly grateful to a number of them, both from academia and the business world, for finding quality time in their overloaded schedules to generously provide thoughtful and in-depth comments on specific chapters of the book: David Aaker, Fridjov Broersen, Willem Brandt, Greg Carpenter, Mike Dawson, Philiep Dedrijvere, Lou Lievens, Jeffrey Merrihue, Bruno Monteyne, Scott Neslin, Paul Polman, Rajiv Lal and Nils Van Dam.

The contribution from Stefan Van Rompaey and Andree Pages for the detailed editing of every single chapter with great aplomb was invaluable.

A special word of thanks to Judy, my wife, for her support and her suggestions on the content, the title and the design of the cover of this book.

CONTENTS

PART III. Improving Shelf Space

Part IV. Last but *Not* Least

Flawed Marketing Thinking: An Appetizer

Yet another marketing book? You must be kidding, no? And it doesn't even have 'social', 'digital' or 'disruption' in the title... What can possibly be the point of this?

Yes, I can already hear you thinking aloud. And I agree, there is no need whatsoever for another book on conventional marketing wisdom – another book on how to develop a marketing strategy by selecting target markets and creating an offering that presents a differential advantage for the selected target group; another book on how to implement such a strategy by an effective and efficient use of all marketing-mix instruments, old and new. There is also no need for more pontification on the importance of brands and the fostering of relationships with customers to maximize the ROI of a company's product and service offerings. Plenty of books are already doing a great job of these things

This book intends to offer another view of marketing, one based on facts. It got its inspiration from the path-breaking book by Daniel Kahneman, *Thinking, Fast and Slow*. The intuitive framework of conventional marketing wisdom (thinking fast) has proved most helpful on many marketing issues, but it has its limitations. On some issues, we need to do some slow thinking and reframe our conventional marketing views.

Three Conventional Wisdoms

Just for starters, let me show you three examples of conventional marketing thinking that are intuitive, elegant, logical and believed to be true by most marketing professionals – but are nevertheless wrong, and therefore wasteful and dangerous.

1. 'Brands are Lovemarks.'
Are brands in and of themselves really that important to consumers? Nowadays we see a flow of evidence emerging that questions long-held notions of what a brand actually is for the consumer, how the consumer behaves towards brands and what is important to make brands grow.

What is actually happening
Consumers are polygamous with regard to brands and retail banners. They are *not* in love with fast-moving consumer goods (FMCG) brands. They don't think about them all the time. In the mind of the consumer, most of these brands are not as differentiated as marketers would like to think. Some are more memorable than others; some are very popular and have achieved top-of-mind awareness; some are even relevant for several consumer consideration sets. Nevertheless, what makes the difference above all between more successful and less successful brands is their degree of penetration in the consumer population.

How does this change managing brands and banners?
Conventional wisdom holds that for a new product, consumer penetration is needed to generate trial, but that focus should then gradually shift towards making those new consumers loyal to the brand, making them buy more of it or buy it more frequently, to drive profitability.

In actuality, what is needed over a brand's life cycle are three things: consumer penetration, consumer penetration and consumer penetration. Why? Because if we don't focus on penetration it will suffer and decrease, and because loyalty and purchase frequency are difficult to increase. There is also evidence that brands with the highest penetration tend to command higher consumer loyalty and higher purchase frequency. Let's focus less on building loyalty and creating deeply emotional relationships with consumers for our FMCG brands or our retail banners, and instead invest in making brands and banners memorable and relevant to the consumer, and if possible make them enter several consideration sets (purchase occasions for brands and shopping trip types for retailers). Those actions will drive penetration.

In sum, what really makes a difference in increasing consumer penetration are two essential parameters:

- *Mind space:* Memorability, relevance, presence in several consideration sets
- *Shelf space:* Presence at the point of sale (including e-commerce and its corresponding 'shopping lists'), omnichannel availability, in-store activation

What counts less: building loyalty, increasing purchase frequency, trying to get an advantage by focusing on small segmented target markets that are then supposed to remain very loyal to your brand and buy it all the time (monogamous brand choice).

2. 'Retailers are oh so powerful!'
This wisdom holds that big retailers wield so much power over their suppliers, the brand owners, that they dominate play in the consumer goods industry. Actually, this is a myth. Retailers are relatively poor; they work very hard in their complex businesses. Brand owners, the allegedly oppressed, are rich as measured by whatever financial criteria and over whatever time period one chooses.

What is actually happening
Retailers do indeed have vertical power, but their lack of horizontal power mitigates this vertical power. The outcome: what retailers painstakingly obtain from brand owners, they pass on to the final consumer in the form of price reductions and other promotions. Retailers are the modern-day Robin Hoods: they take some wealth from the rich brand owners and redistribute it to the consumer. They are philanthropists. Really!

How does this change managing brands and banners?
It is important for brand owners and retailers to understand their predicament and to find ways to reduce this 'value leakage' of retailers. For brand owners, it is not particularly

useful to give more margin to retailers, as this is like giving drugs to drug addicts. Brand owners should try to find ways of collaborating with their retailers to create sustainable value for them by offerings services and other goodies that will not be passed on directly to the final consumer. For retailers, it is important to create more distinctiveness for their offerings in such a way that their lethal business model of high fixed costs and low margins can be transformed into a less price-driven business model, where shoppers are willing to pay for the services offered by the retailer. In this context, retailers should move away from trying to be good at everything (assortment, store quality, service, loyalty systems, prices and promotions, etc.) and aim to be outstanding in some well-chosen dimensions that are relevant for the consumer and the shopper, accepting to be second-rate in others.

3. 'Innovation: Bigger-Better-Faster!'
The biggest consumer goods companies spend about $1 billion or more a year on R&D and have done so for a number of years under the motto 'You need to invest big in R&D to get big and valuable R&D outputs and to get them fast'. Actually, the evidence seems to show that for fast moving consumer goods companies, a more modest approach to R&D produces better results.

What is actually happening
It seems logical: You need to spend big to get big results. However, in consumer goods industries there are many reasons why this does not appear to be true. The company that produces the best results with their innovation approach is Reckitt Benckiser. They spend significantly less than the big guns (80% less), yet produce better results. They are more realistic in their R&D endeavours, thinking in terms of marginal improvements research which can then be turned into profitable and successful upgrades of their existing megabrands.

How does this change managing brands and banners?
Consumer goods companies should adjust their expectations and change their approach to R&D investment. They should outsource their research investments and buy in potentially useful patents, setting their sights on pragmatic, modest improvements from R&D which can then be turned into market successes. Such an approach also works for big retailers who have the resources to follow a 'marginal improvements' approach over what is currently on the market for their private-label offerings.

A Guided Tour Down My Marketing Lane

Every company and most brands pursue profitable growth, and in order to achieve this, penetration in the consumer/shopper population is key. To enhance and sustain consumer penetration, brands and banners need to build mind space (awareness) and shelf space (availability). We'll highlight the different roads to take. Here is the framework of the book.

PART I. The Importance of Consumer Penetration

Chapter 1. Getting Out of the Marketing Comfort Zone
We begin by highlighting the need for marketers to reorder their priorities. Suppose you were given the following three options to grow your brands or banners:

1.   Increase consumer/shopper loyalty, or
2.   Increase purchase frequency, or
3.   Increase consumer penetration.

All three lead to profitable growth, but which one would make the biggest impact? Well, it is not making your consumers/shoppers more loyal to your offering that will generate the strongest growth. Neither will getting them to buy your brand more frequently. Growth isn't about grabbing more money from your loyal customers; it's about attracting new ones. What you should focus on is increasing the number of consumers who buy your offer, making your offer more popular. Although laudable objectives, loyalty and purchase frequency are not easy to improve. Moreover, loyalty and purchase frequency do not differ that much between winners and losers – consumer penetration does. To improve your chances of increasing penetration, you need to work on two drivers: mind space and shelf space. Although not independent of each other, they need to be activated by different marketing and sales investments.

'Rule numero uno: The popularity of your consumer offer beats everything.'

PART II. Improving Mind Space

Chapter 2. Innovation for Brands
Brand innovation stimulates mind space and therefore brand penetration. Innovation can be achieved by two major vehicles: research and development (R&D) and consumer and shopper insights. R&D has generally been poor in FMCG companies; it could be improved substantially via a new approach and a more modest set of achievable objectives. Innovation isn't just about R&D; it is in at least equal measure about generating insights into consumer and shopper behaviour. Both vehicles require new, penetrating ideas combined with flawless execution – easier said than done.

'Never stop asking why.'

Chapter 3. Marketing in a Digital World
Like any other industry, the FMCG industry will continue to be transformed by information technology: in distribution, communication and new product development, as well as in the generation of new consumer insights. Social media, e-commerce, consumer-generated content and Big Data are just a few examples of the innovations that allegedly will make the next 20 years the age where information and information

technology are the fuel for competitive advantage. The speed at which this transformation will take place varies between product categories, but even for those categories where the impact is currently lagging, once the transformation gets going, it will power ahead faster than one had imagined.

'Don't run too far ahead of your consumers, but be prepared.'

Chapter 4. Doing Good or Doing Well – or Both?

Another way of focusing on consumer penetration is to avoid losing customers. Indeed, there is a danger that consumers or regulators may disqualify your company and your offering. Environmental sustainability and the massive issue of obesity are fundamental areas where FMCG companies, both brand owners and retailers, have to act before they are forced to do so. Many companies claim they are better than the others on this dimension, but the obesity issue is a big gaping hole.

'Don't be defensive, but act before you get cigarettized.'

PART III. Improving Shelf Space

Chapter 5: The Robin Hood Syndrome

Brand owners are rich but have supposedly surrendered to the whims of the retailers. Retailers are powerful but poor. This paradox is the result of a number of dark powers operating at the retail level which reinforce each other: sameness, high fixed costs and small profit margins. This lethal potion has become a vicious circle for retailers.

'Retailers are a force for good in society.'

Chapter 6: The Retailer Distinctiveness Challenge

Brand owners have succeeded in creating salient and memorable consumer offerings, an acid test most retailers have flunked. Retailers have been very convincing with consumers, but they have convinced them of the wrong thing: that it's all about price, the lowest price, and the best promotions. Alternative solutions exist and need to be pursued with a passion, not just for retailers but for the whole industry.

'To be outstanding, dare to be bad.'

Chapter 7. What Drives Your Trade Partner?

The quality of the relationship between a retailer and a manufacturer depends largely on two critical factors: the degree of information available at the level of both trade partners and the market conditions in which they operate. The better players know what they want from their trade partners, and the better they understand the economics of these partners, the higher the probability that they will achieve their objectives.

How does the FMCG industry turn collaboration into win-win-win results? All three parties have to benefit: consumers/shoppers, brand owners and retailers. Is this possible in the real world? Yes, but maybe not for the reasons you think.

'I am all for win-win, as long as it means winning twice.'

PART IV. Last but not Least

Chapter 8. Getting the Job Done

Companies can innovate, have great insights, understand how IT can be a vector for growth, proactively develop a responsible attitude towards the issues that are important to society and work synergistically with their trade partners, but they can still not succeed if they don't emphasize the importance of flawless execution.

'Without great execution, your business would still be an idea.'

Executive Summary, Chapter Insights

Part I. The Importance of Consumer Penetration

Chapter 1. Getting Out of the Marketing Comfort Zone
1   'Brands are Lovemarks'? You can't be serious!
2   Of market penetration, consumer loyalty and purchase frequency, market penetration is by far the most potent driver to grow sales and market share, whether of your brands or your retail banners.
3   Light buyers are more important for brands or banners than you think. They tend to be the vast majority of your customers, and they are crucial to your profitability.
4   To increase household penetration, here are four useful drivers:
   a   Make every effort to be constantly present and relevant in the mind of the consumer.
   b   Try to become relevant for additional consumer consideration sets.
   c   Focus on your core products.
   d   Invest in optimal point of sale, in time and in space.

Part II. Improving Mind Space

Chapter 2. Innovation for Brands
1   Innovation is not just about R&D. Consumer and shopper Insights are equally important sources for innovation.

2   If your company only knew what your company knows. There are so many undiscovered and unleveraged insights in each and every company.
3   'Bigger, Better, Faster' is not a good recipe for R&D in the FMCG industry. Evidence shows that a strategy of Marginal Improvements in R&D is dominant.

Chapter 3. Marketing in a Digital World
1   There is tremendous hype on how the digital transformation will fundamentally change every industry. Managers should be careful not to get caught up in it, even at the risk of being seen as 'old hat'. The fact that recent research shows that good old TV advertising still has a significantly better ROI than digital communication is a good illustration.
2   Big Data opens up new sources for improving brand owners' and retailers' business models. However, this will take time, and the industry has to avoid trying to run faster than the consumer and the shopper it is trying to better satisfy. Price obfuscation at retail being a case in point of getting carried away by technical sophistication while consumers are left behind, confused.
3   The best insights, algorithms and decision rules (e.g. for price, promo, shelf space, advertising spend) based on optimised Big Data methodologies, will not be used if the manager does not understand them or if they seem counterintuitive. There will be rich pickings for organisations that manage to meld the skills of managers who feel they have the experience and marketing nous, with the insights from IT driven analysts who often dismiss these traditional managers as irrational dinosaurs.

Chapter 4. Doing Good or Doing Well – or Both
1   If 'doing good' and 'doing well' were generally synergistic, there would be no reason not to follow the most socially responsible path.
2   If the food industry – manufacturers and retailers – does not act on the obesity issue, Big Food will become the new Big Tobacco.
3   Focusing on making food products tasty, convenient, cheap *and* healthy will not solve the obesity problem. Two actions that would improve the situation are (i) in the short run, to substantially tax bad foods and subsidize good foods; and (ii) for the longer term, to educate consumers from a very young age about healthy eating.

Part III. Improving Shelf Space

Chapter 5. The Robin Hood Syndrome
1   Although retailers are powerful, they stay relatively poor.
2   Retailers' vertical power is diluted by their lack of horizontal power, turning them, against their own will, into 'Robin Hoods'.
3   Like giving more drugs to addicts, giving more margin to retailers is to be avoided.

Chapter 6. Retailers' Distinctiveness Challenge
1   Location and penetration are still key in retail. They are not everything but they are a pretty powerful start.

2   The race for distinctiveness is the Achilles heel for retailers: they try to be good at everything that could make them distinctive and end up as mediocre. They have to have the guts to dare to be bad on some dimensions to be able to be outstanding on specific, chosen dimensions that count for the shopper.

3   Creating a distinctive retail proposition based on a business model driven by the store manager and thereby excelling locally is too often dismissed or overlooked by retailers.

Chapter 7. What Drives Your Trade Partner?

1   The root cause of conflict between retailers and manufacturers is not the lack of trust between them, but the lack of distinctiveness between retailers.

2   To improve the way retailers and manufacturers interact, both parties must make an effort to deeply understand how the other party generates its profits. This will reveal the levers needed to bring the interaction to a more productive level.

3   Yes, win-win is possible, but it is not enough. Why is it possible? Because manufacturers and retailers want different things. Why is it not enough? Because we need win-win-win: the consumer/shopper also has to win.

Part I
The Importance of Consumer Penetration

Chapter 1
Getting Out of the Marketing Comfort Zone

The illustrious advertising man and current chairman of Saatchi & Saatchi, Kevin Roberts, was famous for his notion that brands arouse deep emotional connections in consumers, inspiring loyalty beyond reason. According to Roberts, brands are owned by people who love them, hence they are 'Lovemarks'. And he is certainly not the only one with this conviction.

'Brand loyalty is much the same as true love. Whilst some people experience love at first sight, most of us recognize that there is a path to purchase that unfolds much the same as the development of a romantic relationship.'[1] Thus began an article I found in my inbox the other day, written by an enthusiastic marketer at a brand design agency, describing the stages of the brand–consumer relationship in romantic terms:

Today's consumer is looking for much more than a brand, he is looking for an experience, an emotional connection that significantly improves and adds value to his life...Brand love is the ultimate status for a brand to achieve. Your consumer sees you as an extension of himself and you are viewed as an essential, much utilised member of the wider family...[T]he consumer and the brand are onto a lifetime journey together, with the brand working at its very hardest and the consumer finally appreciating the brand's mega ability to impact and better lives, to make a real difference in the world and forever rule the consumer's heart.

Touching, isn't it? Actually, a lot of brand managers and marketing executives would agree with the above statements, even going as far as comparing their job to that of a marriage counsellor.

Are you one of them?
If you are, let's agree to disagree, then. This book uses a more fact-based take on marketing. This difference must be emphasized from the beginning, for marketing is often seen as an art rather than a science. Marketers stress the importance of 'gut feeling' and creativity, of originality and intuition. They love the idea of performing magic. Without wanting to minimize the impact of a hilarious TV commercial or truly smashing billboard,

[1]Marianne Madsen, 'When a Man (Consumer) LOVES a Woman (Your Brand).' Accessed at www.designboard.com/news_brandloyalty.

I think there is more to marketing than the glamour of the ADDY Awards or the Cannes Lions Festival. This book is based on facts – figures, statistics, observed regularities. Sound boring? Think again. It's a fascinating business, really.

Beware of Marketing Assumptions

Let us start with a rather provoking thesis: In practice, marketers often operate on 'automatic pilot'. This is a normal consequence of what we call experience and it is a very good thing. One learns over time from successes and failures in the marketplace. While this may be great in many situations, sometimes it can lead to lazy thinking. And if marketing is to be fact based, it should never be built solely on armchair assumptions and common sense.

Consider the history of science. For ages, people believed the earth was a flat disk – they were afraid they would fall off if they steered their ships too far out to sea. And this was not just the superstition of less educated folk. Even the great Aristotle argued that the earth must be stationary, for one cannot feel the earth move and one does not feel any wind caused by its movement. This was just common sense, and it took a lot of effort and time for science to correct this conventional wisdom. It took the best thinkers of the Renaissance to challenge the dominant paradigms and blind faith of established organisations, men such as Galileo in astronomy, Luther in religion, Vesalius in anatomy, Paracelsus in medicine, Descartes in philosophy, Newton in physics, Brunelleschi in painting, and Columbus and Vespucci in cartography. New insights often have a hard time overcoming barriers of so-called 'reasonable belief' and 'common sense'.

We left Ancient Greece and the Renaissance behind us long ago. But even today, in the twenty-first century, unproved common sense abounds in many areas, and marketing is no exception. The assumption that people 'love' brands, for example; the idea that brands should strive for deep and meaningful relationships with their buyers; the concept of loyalty, as if people's behaviour towards brands is comparable to their married life; the notion that brands function as cults, giving meaning to people's lives – these are no more than visions or impressions for which no scientific ground can be found. The truth is, people want relationships with their family and friends, not with a brand.

As Stephen Jay Gould wrote in his book *Ever Since Darwin*, 'Science is not "organized common sense"; at its most exciting, it reformulates our view of the world by imposing powerful theories against the ancient prejudices that we call intuition.'[2]

Now, if we want to practice marketing as a fact-based discipline, we'll have to be open minded and search for repeated patterns, define laws that explain and predict those patterns, empirically test them, and put the pieces together into a theory that might well go against our common beliefs. In this book, we want to get managers out of their comfort zone and show them that the world in which they operate is not always as they think it is. Sometimes marketers need to adjust their experience and learn new models and concepts about the consumer goods industry.

To be clear, marketing executives should not feel singled out for insult or attack by this rather confrontational introduction. The dominance of prejudices and intuition in our thinking is inherent in the way the human brain works, as was demonstrated by psychologist Daniel Kahneman in his book *Thinking, Fast and Slow*. Kahneman discerns two different modes of thought, which he terms System 1 and System 2. System 1 thinking is fast, intuitive, effortless and automatic. It operates with no sense of voluntary control. System 2 is slow, and requires focus and attention. It's the thinking you need, for example, to solve a non-trivial multiplication problem.

When you see the question *2 x 2 = ?*, you don't need to think, the right answer pops up immediately, reflexively. It just happens. This is an instance of fast thinking, or System 1.

On the other hand, what if you see *17 x 24 = ?* To solve it, you have to think for a minute. Unless you are a skilled math teacher, at first you will only have a rough idea of the possible solution – maybe quickly see that the answer won't be less than 300 or more than 500 – but it will take effort to figure out the exact answer. This is what Kahneman calls slow thinking, or System 2. Slow thinking takes you through a sequence of steps. In this particular case, you will recall the method you learned at school to solve multiplication problems, and then you will have to implement it, which takes some effort, keeping the figures in your memory and working towards the result. Kahneman notes that this process of slow thinking even causes physical reactions, like your muscles tensing up or your blood pressure rising. System 2 thinking is really work.

Kahneman points out that although we identify with System 2 (the conscious, reasoning self), we are actually using System 1 thinking most of the time. We run on automatic pilot, which is not a bad thing in itself, for life would be impossible if we needed to think deeply about every action we make and every decision we take. But System 1 has its limitations and often tricks us into preconceptions – Kahneman's book is full of entertaining examples of biased intuitive thinking.

The problem with marketing is that very often it seems to be based on System 1 thinking, confirming prejudices instead of seeking new insights. This book wants to emphasize the importance of System 2 thinking in order to generate marketing insights and improve decision-making. Throughout the book, we will show many examples of how System 1 produces the wrong ideas, frameworks and solutions. In this chapter we will focus on how a fundamental bedrock of marketing thinking is flawed and leads to wrong decisions.

Popular Brands and the Polygamous Consumer

Consider the conventional wisdom that good marketing is about specifically focusing on carefully selected target customers. Your brand should offer these target customers a product or service that is perceived by them to be meaningfully different from and sustainably superior to competing products, a product that even exceeds their needs and expectations. The result of this approach, conventional theory says, will be that this target group will like your product, buys it and becomes loyal to your offering. If you manage to build a deep relationship with your consumers and if your offer is right, they will reward you with their loyalty. In other words, you have to target the right group of consumers for your brand and offer them a convincing reason to prefer your offer over competing brand offers. Ultimately, they will love you and keep buying your product.

In the case of FMCG products, the actual reality is not quite like that, partly because products are not that different – blind tests often prove this – and partly because most consumers are not really that involved with your products. Just look at divorce rates these days. Do you really think people who don't even stay loyal to their spouses will stay loyal to a brand of soft drink or coffee? As we will show, statistics prove that brand loyalty is a highly overrated concept, and that goes even for so-called cult brands like Harley Davidson. Harley drivers have an unbreakable relationship with the brand – so the story goes – so strong that some even get a tattoo of the logo. The facts? As Byron Sharp shows, on average Harley Davidson buyers buy other bikes twice as often as they buy Harleys – they buy Harleys about a third of the time, which seems to be a very normal metric for many consumer goods[3].

In reality, even though there are millions of brands vying for their attention or love, people think and care relatively little about most brands. That certainly goes for most FMCG categories. Typically, consumers have a small repertoire of popular brands from which they choose when the need occurs. Consumers tend to be polygamous in terms of their behaviour towards brands.

Granted, there are exceptions. In the case of cigarettes, for example, there is a physical addiction to the product and many consumers are brand loyal. Nespresso coffee capsules provide another example. Brand loyalty is high when there is a lock-in for a specific brand – in this case, the need for patented refills that work with a specific machine. However, even here, once the system becomes open, the consumer becomes more polygamous. This is happening to Nespresso right now, as every retailer now carries their own private-label alternative refills that can be used in the machines.

Don't confuse heavy users with loyal users
If consumers are polygamous, the traditional approach of selecting a target market (as specific as possible) and articulating the differential advantages of your product for that market is not really as productive as one would think. To illustrate, there are many examples where we see a clear disconnect between the desired target group (what most people expect a brand's buyer group to look like) and the reality. In real life, the socio-

demographic make-up of most brands' consumers is actually extremely 'average', showing the same breakdown as the average category consumers.

Based on research from Bain & Company, here are some striking examples: For instance, contrary to popular belief, Coke Light and Coke Zero have an almost identical gender breakdown in their consumer basis. Snickers is bought as much by women as by men. Families without kids buy M&M's and Kinder Bueno candy bars as often as those with kids. You may think craft beers are really something for richer or higher-educated men, but this is not the case. In addition, private-label products are as popular with rich people as with poor people, and people who don't have dandruff buy Head & Shoulders as often as people with dandruff.

Certainly, some undeniable biases do exist. Very expensive luxury brands will skew towards higher-income consumers because the very poor simply can't afford them, but the biases are surprisingly small and never go beyond the obvious. The point is that marketers often confuse heavy users with loyal users, portraying the heavy users of their brand as their 'core' consumer group. In reality, their heavy users tend to be identical to those of competing brands; they are just heavy users of the category.

Bain & Company once did a small study on brand loyalty in lingerie. They simply asked women to open their drawer at home and report back how many different brands they had. Almost all reported 3 or 4 different brands. Or consider the question of whether brand loyalty extends across different categories, in sports apparel, for instance. Nike and Adidas would of course love to have you buy your entire outfit from them. In practice, that's not at all what consumers do. Just walk into any fitness club and look around – most people's shoes, socks, trousers and T-shirts are all from different brands.

Why successful niche brands are so rare

It is time to look beyond the easy-going armchair reasoning. Just forget the nice and consistent stories told by overpaid snake oil salesmen and marketing gurus. Their rhetoric does nothing but reflect common sense, with a few well-chosen examples to fit their 'theories'.

We can find a more scientific, fact-based approach in the theory of Andrew Ehrenberg, a statistician turned marketing professor. Between the 1970s and the '90s, he developed an empirical theory by which he could explain the distribution of market shares over brands in many consumer goods product categories. Ehrenberg was a scientist who used large amounts of data to test hypotheses about the outcomes of consumer behaviour in relation to brands and the resulting market shares of those brands. He found his constant by extensive empirical testing of a statistical model (the Dirichlet distribution) which could predict brand choice behaviour over time, across many product categories.

What he found out exactly was this: if you rank brands in a stable product category from the largest to the smallest in terms of their market share, you will find a monotonic

[3] Byron Sharp, How Brands Grow (Oxford: Oxford University Press, 2010).

relationship between this rank order and the rank order of the brands by penetration (the number of different people buying the brand in one year); by frequency of purchase (how many times on average those purchasers buy that brand over a year); and by loyalty (the percentage of the purchases devoted to that brand).

Furthermore, of all the variables highly correlated with brand market share, one stands out by a mile: market penetration. Table 1 of data from Ehrenberg and Scriven's famous gasoline example illustrates how market share is driven by penetration, rather than by frequency or loyalty; what's more, greater penetration comes with more loyalty. Ehrenberg showed that the difference between big and small brands is driven mainly by penetration – that is, how many different people buy the brand in a given period of time. Simply put, big brands are bought by more people, more often. This is a fundamental law of marketing, as solid as the law of gravity in physics. It's all about making your brand popular with consumers who consume products in the category.

Yes, there are also differences in purchase frequency and loyalty between big and small brands, but they are less pronounced than the penetration variation. The implied causation goes from penetration to loyalty and frequency of purchase. As with so many things in this world, the big brands have an advantage. Smaller brands have fewer customers and those customers buy the brand slightly less often.

Table 1. Performance of the top six US gasoline retailers

BRANDS	MKT SHARE	PENETRATION	FREQUENCY	LOYALTY
A	25	60	4	50%
B	15	50	3.7	48%
C	10	30	3.5	46%
D	5	20	3.3	42%
E	2	10	3.1	41%
F	1	8	2.8	38%

Source: ASC Ehrenberg, MD Uncles, and GJ Goodhardt, 'Understanding brand performance measures,' *Journal of Business Research,* 2004, 57(12):1307-52.

In the real world, it is a rare occurrence that smaller brands, with a smaller market share, have more loyal customers than the market leader. This goes even for so-called 'cult' brands like Harley Davidson. In fact, Ehrenberg does away completely with the notion of successful niche brands, those combining relatively low sales and low penetration figures with remarkably high loyalty scores. Such brands are very rare! Small brands have two things against them: fewer people buy them and they buy them less frequently. Ehrenberg called this the 'double jeopardy' phenomenon. So, put boldly, when a manager says they have decided to 'niche' a brand, Ehrenberg would respond that this is merely a euphemism for the fact that they are losing market share… The consequences of this theory are clear. Instead of trying to make loyal buyers buy more and/or buy more frequently, marketers should focus on building penetration, by making more people buy their brand. Increase the brand's popularity: this is the mission for brand marketers.

Double jeopardy is caused by the fact that in stable markets, as most FMCG markets are, brand share depends mainly on brand availability, both mental and physical. If market share of brands were driven by the unique differentiation of brands for specific target markets, the double jeopardy phenomenon would be rare. In reality, it is a pretty accurate characterization of stable markets.

Ehrenberg's theory did not prove very popular in traditional marketing circles, both managerial and academic. Maybe this is understandable, given the fact that his core message doesn't really help marketers develop a creative ad or compelling brand message. But recently, his predictions have been confirmed and further developed by Bain & Company analyses of the buying habits of nearly 100,000 shoppers across the globe[4], based on data collected by Kantar Worldpanel. The study's message is that the best way to ensure growth for your brands over time is to grow the number of people who buy it. The simple rule for success that brands should follow is to increase household penetration. Bain found out that leading brands across dozens of categories in markets all around the world have one thing in common: they significantly dominate their categories in penetration. On the other hand, loyalty and purchase frequency do not vary that much across brands.

Table 2 overleaf shows the penetration, purchase frequency and repurchase rate (loyalty) of market-leading brands in China, one of the many countries covered by the Bain & Company study. The data show that leading brands in every category outperform their competitors by a wide margin in penetration, while the differences in terms of frequency and loyalty are of a much smaller order of magnitude. Penetration makes the difference, every time, in every category – and according to the Bain and Country study, in every country.

Actually, the double jeopardy effect is not restricted to the world of FMCG brands – it is just as valid for retailers. A recent study by Kantar Worldpanel on the UK retail food market illustrates the impact of penetration on market share for Tesco and its competitors. Figure 1 shows the relationship between market penetration and annual spending per shopper. It seems impossible for retailers to increase loyalty without increasing penetration. Smaller retailers combine lower penetration with lower annual buyer spend,

[4] Guy Brusselmans, John Blasberg, and James Root. 'The biggest contributor to brand growth.' Bain Brief, 19 March 2014. Accessed at www.bain.com/publications/articles/the-biggest-contributor-to-brand-growth.aspx.

regardless of their market positioning. The law is valid across formats, for hard discounters such as Aldi and Lidl as well as higher-end retailers such as Marks & Spencer (M&S). Penetration drives market share. This puts a different spin on the enormous investments retailers make developing ever more sophisticated loyalty schemes.

Table 2. Performance of Category Leaders vs. Average of Top 20 Competing Brands

PRODUCT CATEGORY	#1 BRAND	PENETRATION RATE	PURCHASE FREQUENCY	REPURCHASE RATE
BEER	TSINGTAO	4.4*	0.8	1.0
BABY DIAPER	PAMPERS	4.9	1.4	1.4
RTD TEA	JDB	3.1	1.2	1.4
CHOCOLATE	DOVE	5.1	1.5	1.7
FABRIC SOFTENER	COMPORT	13.1	1.3	1.5
CSD	SPRITE	4.5	1.3	1.5
PERSONAL WASH	SAFEGUARD	6.4	1.8	1.9
COLOR COSMETIC	MAYBELINE	4.5	1.2	1.5
TOOTHPASTE	DARLIE	2.4	1.4	1.3
CHEWING GUM	EXTRA	6.8	1.7	1.7

RTD= ready to drink; JDB= Jia Duo Bao; CSD= carbonated soft drinks.
*For example, the leading beer has a penetration rate 4.4 times higher than the average of the top 20 brands in its category, a purchase frequency 0.8 times higher and the same repurchase rate.
Source: Bain & Company analysis of data gathered by Kantor Worldpanel. Bain Brief, 19 March 2014.

The double jeopardy effect is not monolithic. Europanel, a partnership between GFK and Kantar, recently released research based on 10,000 FMCG brands across 16 countries, which showed that the effect of household penetration on a brand's market share depends on the annual number of purchase occasions of the product category. More purchase occasions create more opportunities to switch. For example, in categories with rare purchasing (averaging less than 5 occasions per year), each additional penetration point adds .75% volume share. In categories averaging more than 10 purchases per year, increasing penetration by 1% adds less than half that in terms of volume share. Opportunity fosters promiscuity!

The profitability paradox

Another phenomenon follows directly from Ehrenberg's theory. In conventional marketing thinking, the profits of mass-market brands don't originate from the mass market but from the brand's most loyal buyers, a small proportion of buyers who account for a large share of the brand's sales volume. This suggests that since loyal buyers are very profitable per buyer, marketing should target them tightly and focus marketing spending accordingly.

However, Ehrenberg shows that focusing only on heavy users will actually reduce the size of the brand, as it will lose a huge amount of its less loyal users, who are also crucial to generating profitability. What marketers should do is increase the brand's popularity in a broader sense, in order to concurrently increase the number of heavy users. Brands

Figure 1. Penetration of retail supermarkets in the UK and annual household spending at retailers, 2014. Vertical axis: Average annual household spending, €. Horizontal axis: Household penetration of UK supermarket retailers, %. Source: Kantar Worldpanel 2014.

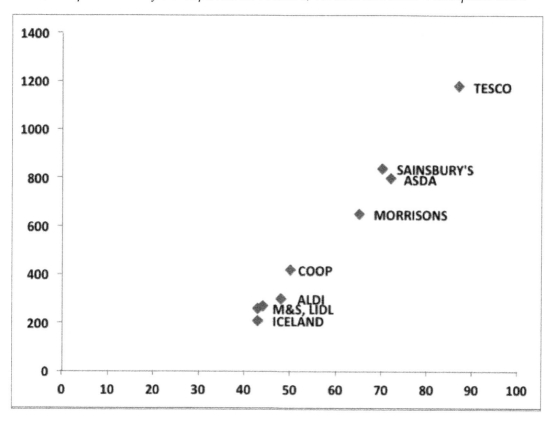

have a large number of light users, who actually generate the lion's share of a brand's profits. Marketers know that market share is crucial in generating profits. Leading market share, which generates the revenue leverage for the brand, does not originate just from the heavy brand buyers, but from all its buyers.

A 2002 study by Ned Anschuetz showed the typical empirical distribution of a large brand's buyers (see Table 3). About 80% of the brand's buyers bought it once or twice a year (light users), and 20% bought it more frequently (more loyal users). This distribution has since been researched across many brands and product categories, and the same regularity shows up every time: a large percentage of light users and a small percentage of heavy or strongly loyal users.

The point of these results is not that this distribution was desired by the makers of this or any brand, but that it is simply what happens to brands as a result of buyers' polygamous behaviour and – of course – the fact that all brand managers are doing their best to market their product to consumers. The profit implications of the above buyer profile of brands illustrates what Anshuetz termed the 'profitability paradox'.

Table 3. *Buyer distribution of a major brand*

FREQ OF PURCH/YEAR	% BUYERS	% VOLUME BOUGHT	VOLUME BOUGHT PER BUYER
1	59.9	29.6	1.8
2	21.2	21	2.5
3	9.3	12.6	3.8
4	4.5	8.3	5.0
5	2.3	6.6	6.2
6	1.2	4.8	7.3
7	0.7	2.1	8.6
8	0.4	3.3	10
9	0.2	1.8	11.2
10+	0.2	9.9	13.7

Source: N Anschuetz. 'Profitability and the 80/20 rule.' Journal of Advertising Research, 2002, 37(6):51-56.

The profitability paradox states that although loyal consumers are far more profitable, the least loyal consumers also contribute significantly to a brand's total profits. The paradox is illustrated by the data in Table 4, in which the group of very light buyers (those buying the product once a year) account for over 40% of the brand's profits, simply because there are so many of them. This is not the exception but the rule. Why is this? Well, empirically one can observe that brands, even the most successful ones, have masses of light users. So, should the brand focus on increasing the brand loyalty of these light buyers to increase profitability?

Table 4. *Number and percentage of households driving one brand's profits*

BUYING FREQ	# HOUSEHOLDS	$ PROFIT CONTRIBUTION	% OF HH	% PROFITS	$ PROFITS/HH
1	7,277,819	12,954,517	59.9	41.9	1.78
2	2,571,048	6,363,343	21.2	20.6	2.48
3	1,135,746	4,216,457	9.3	13.6	3.71
4	551,951	2,732,155	4.5	8.8	4.95
5	282,887	1,750,364	2.3	5.7	6.19
6	149,992	1,113,687	1.2	3.6	7.43
7	81,424	705,333	0.7	2.3	8.66
8	44,973	445,235	0.4	1.4	9.90
9	25,172	280,352	0.2	0.9	11.14
10	14,237	176,187	0.1	0.6	12.38
11	8,121	110,553	0.1	0.4	13.61
12	4,665	69,281	0	0.2	14.85
13	2,696	43,371	0	0.1	16.09
14	1,566	27,126	0	0.1	17.33
15	913	16,953	0	0.1	18.56
TOTAL	12,148,035	30,917,464	100.0	100.0	

Source: Anschuetz, Journal of Advertising Research, 2002, 37(6):51-56.

Increasing the brand loyalty of these light buyers sounds very sensible. However, trying to make polygamous consumers monogamous is a very difficult job. So what marketing managers should do is to increase brand popularity overall (the number of people buying the product) in order to increase the number of buyers, both heavy and light. A marketing approach to actively discard light buyers would be disastrous for the brand's profitability. Allowing more water in will lift all boats.

There's a hole in your bucket

The Bain study mentioned above identified another phenomenon: while penetration may be the biggest contributor to brand growth, it also happens to be a leaky bucket. Following individual consumers over time, Bain analysts found that as many as 50% who bought the brand in year *t* did not buy it in year *(t+1)*. Even some top brands experienced churn rates of nearly 50%. This remarkable leak is a long way from classical marketing theory, implying as it does that brands need to invest constantly to re-earn penetration over and over again.

Great statistician, poor marketer?

The first name that comes to mind when you think of marketing would probably be that of Philip Kotler – and certainly not Andrew Ehrenberg. The author of the highly successful textbook *Marketing Management*, there is no denying that Kotler was a great synthesizer, but he was not an originator of insightful marketing theories or paradigms like Ehrenberg was. Even if the latter's name was honoured by the University of South Australia when it formed the Ehrenberg-Bass Institute of Marketing Science, Professor Ehrenberg never became a marketing celebrity, and his 'double jeopardy' theory never made the headlines or won great popularity in the marketing community. One of the reasons he did not make the impact he deserves is probably because the theory is explicitly counterintuitive, definitely belonging to Kahneman's System 2 thinking. What Ehrenberg pontificated, based on his extensive statistical analyses, wasn't particularly helpful for marketing executives in developing campaigns for their brands.

Ehrenberg's theory became easy to ignore during the late '80s and early '90s, when new data sources became available to marketers to answer more relevant managerial questions about how much to invest in advertising, promotions or distribution. Instead of having to wait for the bi-monthly Nielsen sales data, they would dive into timely detailed panel scanner data that allowed them to run statistical marketing-mix models estimating the effect of price, promotion, advertising and other variables on sales and market share. This became the standard approach, as marketing academics and practitioners alike felt closer to these marketing-mix response models than to the stochastic modelling of Ehrenberg's theory, even if he argued that the negative binomial distribution pattern sufficed to explain the ins and outs of market share and brand switching data.

And there's another point: maybe, for a scientific theory to gain ground, it takes not only a bright scientist, but also a shrewd marketer. Ehrenberg was clearly the former, but not the latter – an important disadvantage in a highly competitive academic world.

Actually, the problem may not be as bad as it looks at first sight. For heavy buyers, the leakage is not so bad. The lion's share of the leakage happens with light (infrequent) buyers, and for most brands there are many of these. There is not a lot a company can do to prevent this leakage: light buyers buy infrequently and they buy from a repertoire, but your brand's turn will show up again. And there is more good news: brands have a lot of growth potential if they look at penetration of the overall population of consumers who consume the category, instead of limiting themselves to narrow target segments or subcategories and purchase occasions.

So if you are really into romantic brand-marketing metaphors, think of it this way: why would a brand want to 'marry' a small group of consumers when it can 'flirt' with hundreds of thousands of them? What's more, these consumers don't want to marry one brand anyway – they are by nature polygamous. In their quest for true love, brands may overlook the charm and excitement of a passing crush. Master the game of seduction. If consumers are polygamous, your brand should be too. Don't get mad, get even.

The Key to Growth

Every year, Kantar Worldpanel publishes its influential Brand Footprint ranking, revealing how consumers around the world buy FMCG brands. Based on panel data from 412,000 households across 35 countries, the ranking uses a new metric called Consumer Reach Points to calculate how many households brands are reaching and how frequently shoppers purchase them. The measure is a straightforward indication of a brand's strength. The essential message from the most recent (2015) Kantar study confirms that consumer penetration is the key driver of the power of brands. Increasing the number of households buying the brand in one year is the secret to success in FMCG, as Table 5 and Figure 2 illustrate, echoing what Andrew Ehrenberg and Bain & Company have stated before.

Table 5. Distribution of household penetration over brands

% OF BRANDS	% HOUSEHOLD PENETRATION
2	80 +
5	60-80
9	40-60
19	20-40
19	10-20
15	5-10
32	UNDER 5

Source: Kantor Worldpanel, 2015.

In fact, Kantar Worldpanel identifies four principles ruling brand growth in FMCG that are fully in line with the theses we develop in this chapter:

1   Increasing brand penetration is pivotal to brand growth.
2   Make your brand accessible to as many shoppers as possible.
3   Work to retain and attract light or occasional buyers.
4   Your buyers don't belong to you.

Figure 2. Relationship of household penetration, purchase frequency, and volume growth for brands. Penetration drives volume growth.

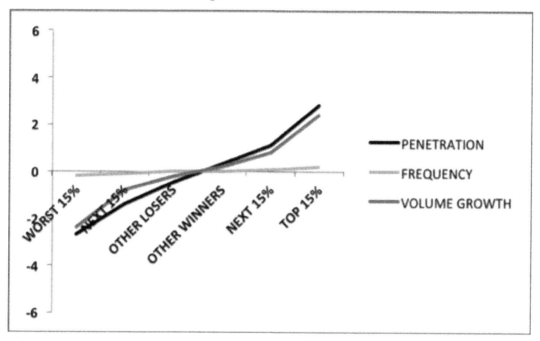

Source: Kantar Worldpanel, 2015.

Increase consumer penetration

The double jeopardy phenomenon has profound implications for marketers. What should they do now? Well, they should probably not be obsessed about becoming 'intimate' with their consumers, at least in FMCG categories, and instead should work relentlessly at their brand's penetration, year in, year out. In order to grow consumer penetration rates, brands need to work predominantly on four parameters.

The first is top-of-mind awareness. Not surprisingly, this is a key determinant of brand share. No rocket science here: make sure your brand comes to mind first when consumers consider a purchase in your product category. A means to achieve this top-of-mind position is through memorable, wide, consistent and frequent communication. Send out a consistent message over time, using exciting copy that gets noticed and talked about.

Coca-Cola has never stopped doing so, even though they have been the most popular FMCG brand in the world for ages. Why? Because in addition to a loyal fan base, Coke also has many light, polygamous consumers. So the brand makes sure they are in consumers' consideration sets as frequently as possible.

A second factor is relevance. Develop your communication and product options in such a way that the brand will be relevant in several product categories or consumption occasions. The ice cream brand Magnum can be a delicious 'big eat' as well as a small bite-size snack. Cadbury chocolate can be a present (Cadbury Roses), a treat for kids (Cadbury Creme Egg), a snack for the family while watching television (Cadbury's 'big night in' bite-size varieties), and so on. Red Bull is an alternative not only to other energy/sports drinks (Lucozade, Monster, Gatorade), but also to soft drinks (from Coke all the way to Brazilians' Schin) or coffee (from Nespresso to Starbucks) or iced tea, and it can even be an alternative to granola bars like Nutri-Grain. The more occasions or needs for which the brand can be made relevant, the more consideration sets the brand will enter, and the more penetration will likely increase. With penetration comes loyalty, and together they drive market share and ultimately profitability.

Third, brands should focus on their core. Often, companies launch too many new products in too many versions. Sometimes one gets the impression that much so-called innovation takes place because the brand managers, marketing and sales people in a company get bored with the product before the consumer does. But more product launches mean less resources for building top-of-mind brand awareness of existing products. The almost compulsive drive for new versions within brands is often fuelled by the need for growth for brands that seem to have run out of steam. The resources spent on versioning could be used more productively to blow new life into the core product. Avoid the usual escape into drifting away from the core. It is like taking aspirin for an illness that needs surgery.

The fourth and last parameter is availability. Make sure the product is available where the consumer typically buys or might buy the brand, make sure in-store merchandising is perfect, and avoid out-of-stock situations. 'Eighty percent of success is just showing up,' as Woody Allen once said. Be present. Execution is key here.

What brands should do primarily is to remove any obstacle that could prevent people from buying their product. Forget about cultish consumers who stay extremely loyal to your brand. Get real – consumers are humans, doing human things. They need your detergent to clean their clothes, they'll buy your drink when they are thirsty, and they'll look for a snack to offer their kids after school. Marketing issues may disrupt brand managers' sleep every now and then, but do you really believe that consumers lie awake at night thinking about the FMCG brands they may or may not buy tomorrow?

Make better marketing decisions
Thus far, we have put into question one of the main tenets of marketing, the belief that brands should aim for deep relationships – yes, even love – with consumers; the idea that

brands should be built to generate passion and loyalty from shoppers; the notion that successful brands are like cults that add meaning to people's lives.

Empirical research and statistical evidence point in a different direction. Basic exchange relationships are the most prevalent form of relationship in the commercial space, especially in low-involvement product categories. This doesn't have to be a bad thing. Why are brands trying to move beyond them?

We conclude with the words of Byron Sharp, that marketing is not about building passionate relationships, but largely about building mental and physical availability. It is about the battle for mind space and shelf space, to quote the subtitle of a book I coauthored with Judith Corstjens[5].

This first chapter has aimed to give the reader an appetite for what is to come in the rest of the book. Instead of rehashing the lessons from marketers' System 1 thinking, from intuition- and experience-based models of how the world of marketing works – in other words, instead of being just another marketing book – this book will focus on prevailing ideas, concepts and models that are part of the pedigree of many marketing and sales managers, to demonstrate that they are not as solid as they think. Every chapter will take on one or more of these common marketing beliefs, and adopt a more scientific, fact-based approach in order to separate what is real and what is make-believe. This book is not intended to provoke merely for the sake of provoking, though. On the contrary, it is intended to help marketing people reconsider some of their postulates and develop an improved set of ideas, models and frameworks to aid in their decision-making.

---

[5] Marcel and Judith Corstjens, *Store Wars: The Battle for Mindspace and Shelfspace* (Chichester: J. Wiley & Sons, 2005).

Chapter Insights

1 'Brands are Lovemarks'? You can't be serious!

2 Of market penetration, consumer loyalty and purchase frequency, market penetration is by far the most potent driver to grow sales and market share, whether of your brands or your retail banners.

3 Light buyers are more important for brands or banners than you think. They tend to be the vast majority of your customers, and they are crucial to your profitability.

4 To increase household penetration, here are four useful drivers:

    a   Make every effort to be constantly present and relevant in the mind of the consumer.

    b   Try to become relevant for additional consumer consideration sets.

    c   Focus on your core products.

    d   Invest in optimal point of sale, in time and in space.

Part I
Improving Mind Space

Chapter 2
Innovation for Brands

The fact that companies need to innovate is a truism. The world of consumer preferences, technology and competitive offerings on the market is continually in motion. Existing brands erode, while at the same time opportunities arise to create winning new brands and consumer propositions. What is less of a truism in the field of innovation in the world of FMCG are the following three observations:

1 Innovation is often associated exclusively with R&D.
Consider this quote by Paul Bulcke, CEO of Nestlé: 'We want to enhance the quality of people's lives through nutrition, health and wellness, and we want to drive that with science-based innovation.'

As important as research and development (R&D) may be, it is not the only driver of innovation. Insight into the consumer and the shopper is definitely another potent driver. And then there is execution, because a product can only become a success if it is launched flawlessly on the market. So the successful combination of consumer/shopper insights and R&D, which generates consumer propositions, requires the confluence of

a discovering new ground-breaking consumer/shopper insights;
b developing productive R&D that builds on these insights and generates tangible new consumer/shopper propositions; and
c flawless implementation when bringing the new proposition to market or upgrading the existing product proposition.

The case of Cialis from Eli Lilly illustrates how innovation can be mainly driven by powerful consumer insights even in the pharma industry where R&D is a dominant force. The case illustrates how seemingly small insights can lead to huge sales success. Coming to market years after its successful competitor, Viagra, Cialis needed to find significant product advantages, but on the two most important product benefits according to physicians – efficacy and safety – the newcomer could not make a difference. The longer duration of action (36 hours vs. 4 hours for Viagra) was not considered important by physicians; these erectile dysfunction pills were aimed at a more senior population, for whom 4 hours was plenty, rather than a few exceptional younger testosterone-driven sexual athletes who would want continued support for 36 hours. The tables turned when the Cialis team adopted a broader perspective on the issue. The brief time window offered by Viagra increased pressure on women to have sex with their partner within a few hours, causing stress in the relationship. Cialis could offer a 36-hour window, reducing the level of stress in the relationship, and the brand was positioned as a 'couple product' as opposed to a male product. The approach worked: by 2011, sales of Cialis had overtaken Viagra.

The example of McDonald's in Singapore also shows how insights can lead to innovation for existing brands and products. When McDonald's entered Singapore, a vertical and dense metropolis with a ubiquitous take-away food culture, local management decided to explore home delivery, using motorbikes with temperature-controlled containers to enhance the quality of the delivered food. After the initial launch, home delivery sales increased so rapidly and increased overall sales so positively that it drew the attention of senior management in the United States. Would the quality of the McDonald's experience suffer? What would the effect be on the McDonald's brand? The potential sales success seemed small compared to the considerable risks, some argued. But consumer satisfaction was high, and the success of home delivery in Singapore exceeded all expectations. So home delivery continued, and these sales now account for nearly 12% of all McDonald's sales in Singapore.

2   Innovation is thought of as bringing new products to the market.

Of course this is true, but innovation is also about innovating for existing brands. No matter how powerful the brand is, over time it will inevitably erode and lose its relevance. There is only one remedy: innovation is needed to upgrade and improve the brand and keep it top-of-mind in the consumer population. Chapter 1 discussed how important churn rates are, even for strong FMCG brands. Brand innovation, through new consumer/shopper insights and R&D, is an absolute must to win these consumers back on the next occasion by keeping the brand relevant and memorable, thanks to new features, for example. Nike's Pegasus running shoe illustrates the point. The style has seen over 30 different iterations – every year a new version with new features and performance attributes is released. The result? It's been Nike's most popular running shoe for the past 30 years.

3   Innovation is considered futile when markets become mature.

You know the story: "Everything has been tried, unsuccessfully mostly, so let's cut our losses and stop wasting money on innovation." In large markets like the US and Western Europe, FMCG product categories are often labelled as mature, or even saturated, especially when compared with the sometimes astonishing growth rates in markets like telecommunications, e-commerce, biotechnology and pharmaceuticals. However, in several established, so-called mature food categories, we have recently seen some remarkable cases of new brands and products building successful businesses from scratch by combining R&D and consumer insights. The coffee market, for example, after being asleep for many decades, was completely turned upside down by the consecutive arrival of newcomers Starbucks and Nespresso. The amazing success of Nespresso, after a rather long and expensive incubation time at Nestlé, is living proof that the combination of consumer insight and R&D can bring even a seemingly comatose category back to life.

Indeed, the observation that a sizeable segment of consumers are willing to pay for professionally prepared coffee, although they could cheaply and easily make it at home, opened a new road towards growth. It must be said that a smart and well-executed advertising campaign for Nespresso in Europe featuring a popular actor helped a lot, too.

It is a nice case of 'bringing class to the masses', comparable to what P&G did with its Crest Whitestrips teeth-whitening system. Before, such whitening was normally done professionally in clinics, but Whitestrips enable people to do this by themselves, at home, for a lot less. The same is true for the German cleaning systems company Kärcher, which made a professional industrial product into a big success for the home market.

In the US, the mature yogurt category was shaken up by a new brand with a new proposition, the launch of Greek yogurt by Chobani – developed by a Turkish entrepreneur, no less. Within a few years, Greek yogurt had conquered almost 50% of the category.

Invest in Two Core Competencies

Clearly, companies have no choice but to keep innovating. Lego provides a notable example. From 1993 to 1998 the toy company went through a stagnant period where it had reached the end of a natural growth cycle. Tripling the number of new toys didn't increase sales, while costs went up significantly. Many firms would have said, "We don't have the money or the time to innovate. We have to concentrate on survival." But Lego didn't do that. Given the industry they were in, they really had no choice. In a toy market that is viciously competitive, with fickle customers who have rapidly changing tastes, you have to renew your product line every year or two. Lego had to innovate. So what they did after 2003 was to go back to their core product, the brick, focusing more on the police stations and the firetrucks and the other things that not only were what their fans wanted, but were also very profitable. Eventually fans returned to the brand.

Talk of innovation features prominently in the 'Letter from the CEO' in annual reports of any FMCG company. It seems as if the more innovation, the better, with no decreasing returns to scale… But is this really true? Judging by the results of recent product innovation, the record of FMCG companies is abysmal. For example, only 10% of new FMCG products launched in the US reach $7.5 million in their first year, according to the market research company IRI. And in Western Europe, only 15% of new products launched survive their second year, according to a recent Kantar survey.

So how can FMCG companies improve innovation? To develop new products and keep existing brands relevant in this changing and challenging world, companies should invest in two core competencies: 1) generating and leveraging powerful insights (about consumers, shoppers and retailers); and 2) producing effective R&D/technology outputs. Both of these competencies are potent forces to create and sustain brands that generate profitable growth over time: just look at Apple, Nespresso or Starbucks – these brands have thrived over time by excelling in both consumer insights and R&D. A brand does not have to excel in both competencies, but lacking both is a sure recipe for failure. Unilever's Dove is a purely insight-driven megabrand, and the Chiquita banana brand illustrates that even a brand with high awareness cannot generate profitable growth, because they are poor in both insight and R&D.

The Italian confectionary manufacturer, Ferrero, illustrates what it means to win by being outstanding in both consumer insight and technology. The company is world-class at creating and developing brands: just think of Nutella, Tic Tac, Kinder, Mon Chéri… Their great inspiratory, Michele Ferrero, was constantly obsessed by two things: the consumer and machinery. Ferrero was an ardent advocate of consumer focus groups, eager to test ideas for new products on them and to learn from their feedback. At the same time, he was an engineer at heart, deeply involved in the development of the machinery needed to produce the products, preferring to develop sophisticated production methodologies, as technical difficulties in production would make it harder for competitors and retailers to copy his products.

The Importance of Insights Versus Information

In discussing this first driver of growth, it is important from the outset to note that insights are fundamentally different from information. The fact that a brand's market share has gone down during the last quarter by 10% is important information, but it is not an insight. To illustrate the difference between information and insights, take the experience of Vitaly Komar and Alexander Melamid, two émigré Russian artists living in America who were inspired by the power of marketing in capitalist societies to make a fortune in the world of art. Instead of producing paintings as expressions of their own artistic interpretations of an event or emotion, the two decided to would ask consumers in different countries what they would like to see in a painting that hung in their living room. They convened scientifically determined samples of consumers from their target markets and asked them specific questions about the content, colour scheme and style of the painting they would like to have. Working with professional market research companies, they determined what these consumers would like. Unfortunately, despite being grounded in a rigorously scientific market research study, the paintings were a commercial flop. The information they gathered as the basis of these paintings was not insightful. Yes, the interviewees had answered all the questions (the market research companies ensured they met the defined quotas), but the questions were not particularly relevant. Interviewees didn't think in an analytical way about paintings, yet the premise of the market research was that they did. The outcome of the research was useless.

Conversely, one of the biggest success stories Coke ever had came from a single penetrating observation, that the quantity of in-home consumption of Coke was directly proportional to in-home inventory. If people had more Coke in their fridge on Friday evening, more would be consumed over the weekend, especially in households with children. However, this would not have been transformative had it not been coupled with

Figure 3. America's most wanted painting, as determined by Komar and Melamid.[6]

an imaginative and far-reaching execution plan that went beyond the obvious approach of launching larger sizes and maximizing availability. Through this insight about consumption, Coke had identified the important distinction between marketing categories that are 'expandable' (e.g. soft drinks and confectionery) and 'non-expandable' (e.g. diapers). For Coke, consumer promotions do everything they do for Pampers, but they also increase the total consumption of Coke without taking sales from other brands, hence expanding total soft drink sales. This is not the case for Pampers, for which promotions may switch brand choice or build a home inventory, but do not increase overall consumption of diapers. Hence, Coke promotions are potentially more valuable to both retailers and Coke than those on Pampers, a fact that could be leveraged with retailers to obtain more prominent and more frequent promotional slots than had previously been the case.

What Coke had that Komar and Melamid didn't was a consumer insight. Vitaly and Alexander's market research, although providing mountains of accurate data, had failed to provide any insights into the mind of the buyer of commercial art, insights that Andy Warhol and Roy Lichtenstein can be credited as having had without the benefit of any scientifically based market research. The Coke manager who spotted the causal link between inventory at home and consumption did not have a mountain of data but had an insight into the soda-drinking habits of consumers. That same Coke manager also had two attributes essential in turning an observation into a marketing insight: the tenacity to convince the business to change its tack, and the ability to develop an execution plan that

[6] For more on the project, visit 'Komar & Melamid: The Most Wanted Paintings on the Web.' Accessed at http://awp.diaart.org/km.

was uniquely derived from the core idea. It is the combination of breakthrough idea and radical execution together that makes marketing insights such important contributors to any company's profitable organic growth. It is not enough to have a brilliant and perceptive new idea: without impactful execution, the results will be marginal. Too often, the power of the new idea tends to be overestimated and the importance of execution underestimated.

The 'paradox of choice', first discussed by Barry Schwartz, and its corollary, 'feature fatigue', a phrase coined by Roland Rust, are other examples of perceptive, penetrating and unexpected ideas that rock conventional wisdom[7]. Schwartz had noticed that presenting more product choice and options was not always a good thing for consumers. Feature fatigue is an illustration of this paradox. The problem arose in the consumer electronics industry: technologists and engineers found it was inexpensive to add features to an electronic apparatus, while marketing people felt that the availability of more features with no additional cost created more value for prospective buyers. The outcome, as we now know, is that a significant percentage of consumers are overwhelmed by the feature complexity and become turned off rather than on, just like the equipment. The paradox that some people would rather pay more for a universal remote control that does far less than the one that comes for free with the equipment was thus explained. Interestingly, in food retail, the remarkable international success of hard discounters Aldi and Lidl may not be due just to low prices, but also in part to this paradox of choice: many shoppers are uncomfortable with the enormous choice offered by big box retailers like Tesco, Kroger and Carrefour, as well as by the amount of time taken up by a shopping trip. They are happy to turn to smaller, low-cost retailers with a limited but well-chosen assortment where a shopping trip takes only a fraction of the time spent at a big box retailer.

'"Break" – the most important part of breakthrough'

Now, if the impact of insights on organic brand growth is decisive, how can brand owners make sure their marketing teams become more creative and generate crucial insights? Unfortunately, there is no cookbook for great insights. It is not feasible to develop a conceptual framework for creativity. As the famous English poet T.S. Eliot stated, 'There is no method but to be very intelligent.'

In his 1942 book *Capitalism, Socialism and Democracy*, Joseph Schumpeter popularised the idea of creative destruction, the notion that radical innovation was inevitably accompanied by a process of transformation to the detriment of the incumbents. This same notion applies equally to the innovation in understanding represented by a marketing insight: if it doesn't challenge the status quo, then it probably isn't very new, penetrating or perceptive. Therefore, an organization has to be courageous and reward rather than penalize their people for challenging the 'holy cows' of the business in their search for insights. Indeed, insights are rare beasts. The nuggets of information that may spark an insight have always been needles in haystacks, but the search has been compromised by the double whammy of an exponential increase in the size of the haystack, coupled with a recent tendency to label all pieces of straw as being

---

[7] Marianne Madsen, 'When a Man (Consumer) LOVES a Woman (Your Brand).' Accessed at www.designboard.com/news_brandloyalty.

potential needles.

Learning about successful innovations by other brand owners may ignite that much needed spark of inspiration. An interesting case at Boots, the British drugstore, shows the value of observing shopping in person. Perceptive store managers in town-centre stores noticed that shoppers, especially at lunchtime, shopping for top-up or a quick bite for lunch, would go to the checkout till as soon as their basket was full. The basket being small, they tested in some stores the effect of increasing its size. The positive impact on average transaction size was significant. The anomaly of 'Why do shoppers plan to buy only what they can carry?' was explained by the insight that many shoppers clearly have a flexible mental shopping list that is cut off as soon as it becomes inconvenient for them to continue. This was confirmed when ambitious marketing people went one step further and increased the basket size in a few test stores by another 50%. Results were disappointing because many shoppers didn't pick up the relatively large shopping basket for a quick shop and bought only what they could carry in their hands. Even the sales benefit that came from those who picked up the larger basket was lost as they created checkout queuing problems at the stores' busiest time.

Successful innovations at Heinz have been based on true consumer insights, allowing the brand to address new consumption occasions. The launch of individual foil condiment packets, for example, came from the insight that serving individual portions from a big bottle takes time and portions are not always fully used. Small packets for individual usage, especially in restaurants and on the go, provided a solution. The development of the plastic squeezable bottle was built on the insight that the viscosity of ketchup makes it difficult to pour. A squeezable bottle makes it easier to propel the ketchup out of the bottle and to measure. The creation of the upside-down bottle was based on the insight that consumers store their ketchup bottle upside down to get the ketchup out more easily and to get as much as possible out of the bottle. Lastly, the more recent Dip & Squeeze packets came from the insight that consumers hate the mess that comes with the foil packet, and that they need to squeeze ketchup onto a plate before they can dip in it. The Dip & Squeeze packet makes it more convenient to use ketchup on the go and addresses new 'dipping occasions'.

The Importance of Improving R&D Performance

The second critical driver to create new brands and keep existing brands relevant to consumers is to generate new technical advantages through the outputs of product R&D. Possibly because food companies in particular did not believe for a long time that R&D would contribute much to their success, the output of the R&D effort in the FMCG industry has been rather poor. However, although there are relatively few examples of successful R&D/technology-driven products in the industry, we may see their importance increase in the near future.

This is so because successful R&D/technology outcomes will be helpful in making new products' claims more credible and more sustainable. Credibility is an essential quality in a world with so much information available to consumers, shoppers and retailers. Moreover, patents are powerful barriers to copiers, including other brand owners as well as retailers' private labels. Consider today's challenges for FMCG brand owners, coping with securing sustainable resources, adjusting to changing health issues in the market due to an obese and aging population, working in the transparency of the e-world – there are many indications that patent platforms will become more and more valuable

Innovation overload

While real innovation is important, innovation for its own sake is often overdone. Brands should not innovate for innovation's sake. The failure rate of new products is astounding, but no wonder, given the enormous number of stockkeeping units (SKUs) in an average supermarket. In my local 5000 sqm Sainsbury's, I can choose from 142 pasta sauces, 53 fabric conditioners, 27 mayonnaises, 227 deodorants... Logically, only a small percentage of these generate significant sales. Products need to differentiate in order to stand out from so many competitors. This rotation survey in Table 6 shows the average number of SKUs sold per week per store in the US and Europe:

Table 6. SKU Rotation

	US	EUROPE
0	45	55
1	14	5
2-5	24	11
6-9	8	8
10+	9	20

Source: AC Nielsen

Isn't it amazing to see how many products aren't even selling one SKU per week? The overload of products is due to the fact that retailers, afraid of disappointing shoppers, have difficulty making clear choice. After all, some consumers have a strong preference for special SKUs, and if they cannot find them, they will buy their full basket at another retailer. It is also due to the fact that retailers tend to buy what their suppliers sell to them, instead of what the consumer really wants. And brand owners will offer great deals, as they are obsessed with 100% distribution and reducing shelf space for competitors. But the overload is equally driven by many marketers' predilection for new product development.

The innovation race sometimes leads to hilarious consequences. In his presentation on 'the Seven Deadly Sins of Innovation', innovation expert Mat Shore makes fun of marketers

> **Innovation overload cont.**
> who love innovation a bit too much. For example, the razor blade category has seen intense
> competition with brands adding more blades to their shaving systems: first two, then three
> or four, until Gillet Fusion came to market with a five-blade technology. Paradoxically, the
> brand was forced to add a sixth blade, an extra 'precision trimmer' on the back, for areas
> that are 'hard to reach'. Indeed, with its five blades, the razor has effectively become too
> big to shave the area under the nose. Another example is BIC's new Cristal For Her pen,
> designed to fit a woman's hand, with an elegant pink design. The product has rapidly
> become the most sarcastically reviewed product on Amazon.com.

and necessary.

Now try to think of a major new product in the FMCG industry that was the result of a breakthrough R&D project. Can you? Of course, the FMCG market does show some fine examples of product innovations contributing to brand growth. La Vache Qui Rit owns an exclusive technology to miniaturise and package melted cheese, allowing the brand to successfully position a new product as a snack or appetizer. The success of LU's La Paille d'Or biscuits relies on an exclusive technology to produce a very thin wafer. Gillette's Fusion differentiates itself by its delicate shape, the angle and fixing of the blades, the quality of the steel. These are all very nice, but who would call them breakthrough innovations?

R&D isn't stunted for lack of trying. Many CEOs pontificate about the importance of R&D to create 'good' growth:

- 'We know from our history that while promotions may win quarters, innovation wins decades.' – *Bob McDonald, P&G CEO*
- 'The main growth engine is innovation.' – *Paul Bulcke, Nestlé CEO*
- 'We have invested in and spent behind our brands and innovation, and that has given us the growth. That's quality growth.' – *Paul Polman, Unilever CEO*

And not only do they talk R&D, they all have a chief R&D officer on their executive board and they put their money where their mouth is: In 2014, Nestle spent €1.371 billion on R&D, P&G spent €1.5 billion and Unilever spent €0.955 billion. Unfortunately, the output of their R&D investments in the past (at a level similar to that of 2014) have been disappointing, to put it mildly.

Unilever's success with Dove, for example, had very little to do with R&D. Its breakthrough did not come from a revolutionary moisturizing technology – even though it was a credible, skin-friendly soap brand from the beginning. As long as Dove was positioned on the functional USP (US) of keeping the skin moist, it remained only relatively successful. The brand only really took off after Brazilian marketer Sylvia Lagnado, observing growing criticism of the 'model zero' images in advertising, saw an opportunity and went for a positioning under the 'internal beauty' umbrella. It was a risky move that took some guts, but it worked, partly helped by a first-mover advantage and the spontaneous endorsement by Oprah Winfrey on her famous show. Clever and courageous? Definitely. But not built on R&D.

How can one actually assess the quality of the R&D output generated in a particular company or in a particular industry? One way of measuring this output is to assess the number of patents generated by a company's R&D investments. The problem with merely counting patents, however, is that their economic value is not uniform. This is why many recent studies using patents as an indicator of R&D productivity weight patents by their number of citations. While this measure of patent citations may reduce the non-uniformity problem of patent count, it has a serious truncation bias. Because it takes time for citations to occur, older patents may have more citations than newer ones, even though the latter may be more innovative.

To measure R&D productivity, I use the market impact of R&D investments, by estimating the effect of a 1% increase in R&D investments on the output of a company. This measure of R&D elasticity, the research quotient (RQ), was recently developed by Anne Marie Knott[8]. It calculates the return companies and/or sectors generate from their R&D investments, relative to the returns from their investments in labour and capital. Based on the concept of production functions in microeconomics, the RQ approach shows how changes in R&D expenditure affect the company's output (i.e. sales), enabling measurement of the input elasticity of each of the three production factors: labour, capital and R&D. For example, if the estimated elasticity for R&D were 0.20, it would mean that a 1% increase in R&D investment for that company (or sector, or economy) would produce a 0.2% increase in its output.

Say a company like Unilever, with annual sales of around €50 billion and R&D investment of €1 billion, has an R&D elasticity of 0.2%. This would mean that an increase of €10 million (1% of €1 billion) in their R&D budget would produce incremental sales of €100 million (0.2% of €50 billion). At a net profit margin for Unilever of 15%, the incremental R&D investment of €10 million would generate €5 million incremental profits (€15 million - €10 million). Therefore, if Unilever's R&D elasticity were .2%, it would indicate that its R&D is very effective and should probably be increased.

We need to point out that this elasticity, or RQ, is the outcome of two processes: R&D and marketing. Indeed, an R&D investment might create a great innovative new product, but if it is marketed poorly, the market impact will be below par, and vice versa. This nature versus nurture issue is intrinsic to market impact studies of any investment. At the end of the day, companies invest in R&D to generate a return – and this return will be generated by the performance in the market of the product that is the result of the R&D. It would be unlikely to justify great R&D output with poor market impact as simply the fault of poor marketing.

Sometimes, maybe; but on average I would argue no. Certainly, top FMCG companies are known for their marketing pedigrees.

So, how do FMCG and food & beverage companies perform in terms of R&D elasticity? Using the most recent data available from the EEC, I selected a number of industries to compare their respective R&D productivities (see Table 6).

	CONSTANT	LABOUR*	CAPITAL**	R&D***	Rsquared*****	Sample size
All companies	-.08 (.10)****	.60 (.02)	.38 (.01)	.12 (.015)	.89	1899******
FOOD & BEV companies> 1 billion euro in sales)	2.40 (.40)	.40 (.08)	.46 (.10)	-.04 (.06)	.90	52
FMCG companies> 1 billion euro in sales	2.93 (.43)	.31 (.08)	.46 (.09)	.06 (.06)	.84	78
BIG PHARMA companies> 5 billion euro in sales	2.58 (.85)	.59 (.10)	-.05 (.10)	.16 (.06)	.80	24

Table 7. Results from regression analysis of EEC R&D elasticities

- *Labour is measured by the number of employees per company in 2013.
- **Capital is measured by the capital expenditures of the company in 2013.
- ***R&D is measured by the R&D investments of the company in 2013
- **** Standard error of the estimated coefficient. For the coefficient to be statistically significantly different from zero, the ratio of the coefficient and its standard error should be 2 or larger. Coefficients statistically significantly different from zero are underlined. Those not underlined do not statistically differ from zero, i.e. their value is due to randomness.
- *****R-squared basically measures how well the model fits the data. An R-squared of .90 shows that the three variables (labour, capital and R&D) in the model explain 90% of the variance in output. Actually, the very high values of R-squared show that the model fits the data extremely well.
- ******Although the report contains data on 2500 companies we only had full information for all the variables above for 1899 companies.

The one result that shouts out from this analysis is the shocking performance of R&D in the food and FMCG industries (i.e. food and non-food FMCG manufacturers). The relevant coefficient for food is -.04, which means that given the data in the sample of companies, when food and beverages companies increase their R&D investments by 1%, their sales will not be influenced (the coefficient of -.04 is not statistically different from zero). For the FMCG industry (which includes non-food manufacturers), the figure is slightly better (.06), but still very poor and not statistically significantly different from zero.

[8] Anne Marie Knott, The trillion-dollar R&D fix,' Harvard Business Review, May 2012, 76-82.

We can conclude, based on the data for 2013, that a 1% increase in R&D investment by the companies in the food, beverage, tobacco, personal care and household care sectors does not produce any increase whatsoever in sales! Compared to other sectors, the FMCG industry performs towards the bottom of all industries. Across all industries (for the large sample of 1899 companies), an increase of 1% in R&D investments produces an increase in output of .12%, statistically significantly bigger than zero. For Big Pharma, the figure is 0.16.; this is not surprising, because large pharmaceutical companies are relatively productive with their R&D investments.

There is no denying that FMCG performs poorly in R&D. Over the last 10 years, the CEOs of FMCG companies have kept communicating in an almost emotional way about the importance of generating good growth via R&D investments, emphasizing their 'bigger, faster, better' credo. But what has it led to? Not a lot.

Granted, a lot of the money spent on R&D in FMCG companies is aimed at finding cost reductions and improving packaging. This is often not very sexy, but useful and needed. When they do generate patents, the end result does not get the 'wow' factor from consumers and from outside observers. Unilever, for example, spent considerable time and effort turning Knorr bouillon cubes into a jelly form. Technically not an easy task, but they did it. The company also invests in removing preservatives from food products while not reducing taste and still keeping a reasonable shelf life, as consumers frequently have an issue with preservatives. Now this is all very nice, but is it sustainable for the long term? Some reverse engineering will help competitors copy these results without infringing patents.

In the chocolate category, Barry Callebaut recently boasted of inventing a chocolate that melts only at higher temperatures. Sounds nice enough, but digging a little bit shows that Cadbury had already claimed this at the end of 2012, and Nestlé also seems to have it. Moreover, higher melting points seem aimed at selling the stuff in warmer climates; however, one reason chocolate is such a much-loved product is that it melts in your mouth at body temperature. I can imagine stuffing your mouth with non-melting chocolate makes the product less tasteful. In countries where the taste for chocolate has still to be acquired, this is not a great asset. I think these examples are very typical for what R&D comes up with in the FMCG industry.

What should FMCG brand owners do? One possible reaction would be to reduce R&D investments. Another would be to think about doing R&D differently, as we will show in the next paragraphs.

Patents as potent platforms
If the performance of FMCG companies in terms of R&D output has been poor, we must ask why. After all, most of them find R&D important and have it high on the agenda. Maybe talent is an issue. If top researchers got job offers from Genentech, Google or Unilever, how many would chose Unilever? Or is it a question of budgets? The big FMCG players spend between $1 and $2 billion a year, which is less than most Big Pharma

players, but Genentech in its top years didn't spend much more, and they created top cancer drugs such as Herceptin, Tarceva and Avastin. Clearly, FMCG manufacturers' poor R&D output is not about critical mass in spending, but rather about how that money is spent. As R&D becomes more important, how can FMCG companies leverage this spending to develop successful new products?

Are marketers prejudiced against R&D?

Some years ago, I was invited to New York by Unilever for a two-day brainstorming session on revitalizing Hellmann's, the mayonnaise brand. Present were 15 other people: 10 Unilever executives and 5 'outsiders' – people from agencies, consultants... It was great fun, with presentations from the Hellmann's team, the advertising agency, the design agency, and the Unilever R&D team that had worked on things that might be interesting for the brand.

Now, Hellmann's was not an original Unilever brand, but had come to the company when they acquired Bestfoods. Even though Hellmann's was a solid brand, it was not the reason Unilever had bought Bestfoods. Instead, Unilever wanted to build their position in Germany, where Bestfoods was strong; they wanted to get the Knorr brand; they wanted to turbo-charge Unilever's foodservice business; and they wanted to bring in the more entrepreneurial spirit that characterized Bestfoods. Hellmann's was a brand they didn't fully understand, but it was big, extremely profitable, and had stood the test with private label over time. However, the Unilever foods executives felt there was even more in the brand if it could be updated and made more relevant for modern consumers. Just the stuff marketing people love to discuss.

The first day began with interesting presentations from both Unilever's Hellmann's marketing team and the agencies. Then, at the start of the afternoon, the Unilever R&D people – more development people than basic researchers – made their presentation. I thought it was wonderful, full of innovative ideas, like making fruits taste like other fruits, pears like strawberries, for example. It didn't take a rocket scientist to see opportunities for things to be done with Hellmann's. However, after lukewarm applause at the end of this presentation, the group immediately went back to the previous brainstorming sessions about the 'brand key' and the personality of Hellmann's. The R&D stuff was never brought up again . I was amazed and disappointed. Why had it not caught on?

In my opinion there were two key reasons. First, the presenters were pretty boring, lacking motivation and inspiration: 'Here are the tests we have done and here are the results. If it interests you guys, we 'd be happy to discuss it further with you; we'll be around for the rest of the afternoon.' And second, there was – and still is today – this preconceived idea that R&D is of no great use for food products. There is an assumption that all the easy stuff has been done, and money has been invested, but there will be no great outcomes in terms of new products or product improvements. R&D may work for non-food – as chemistry might be relevant for cosmetics or detergents, for example – but not for food. Marketers just don't believe in R&D, or at least not enough, it seems.

Table 8. Annual R&D Spending, 2014

Nestlé	€1.4 billion
Unilever	€1.0 billion
P&G	€1.5 billion
L'Oreal	€0.9 billion
Reckitt Benckiser	€0.2 billion

Source: Company Annual Reports, 2014

One option may be to buy relevant patents developed by companies from other industries that are more effective and efficient in R&D, and enter those patents in the FMCG's development process to create new products. Traditionally, FMCG companies are weak in research, but they can probably do an excellent job in development. They can then use the output of such research as a platform to create new brands or improved versions (with better margins) of existing brands.

So, how can FMCG companies get their hands on good patents? Unlikely as it may seem that companies would be willing to sell their great patents, there are interesting possibilities. A promising hunting ground could be the pharmaceutical industry. Pharma companies have very high hurdle rates to progress options in their research funnel, as their R&D investments to do so are considerable and they need to perform extensive and expensive clinical trials. As a consequence, they often possess patents, complete or intermediate, that don't meet their hurdle rates even if they do contain promising features. Indeed, some of these patents, being below the acceptance level for Pharma, might be powerful for FMCG, taking into account the consumers' concerns about health and obesity, for example. Of course, FMCG brands should not try to treat diseases, but developing healthier food products does sound like a sensible idea, doesn't it? To make such an approach work, FMCG companies need to invest in attracting hard-to-find talented people who combine two crucial characteristics: they need to be top-notch and well-connected researchers with a deep understanding of what promising patents are and where to find them, and they also have that rare quality that enables them to 'market' those new patents within the FMCG company to developers, marketers and, especially, the senior executives who hold the purse strings.

Another option is to have a different R&D philosophy. The case of Reckitt Benckiser (RB) is illustrative. As Table 8 shows, the company spends only a modest budget on R&D, compared to its main competitors, P&G and Unilever. Still, RB has shown remarkably profitable growth over the last few decades, outperforming its peers by wide margins (see the 'Good strategy, good execution' section in Chapter 8). How did they do this? Part of it is due to their approach of focussing on continuous, small product improvements, based on incremental insights about consumer needs, instead of pursuing big breakthrough innovations. Starting from their star brands, they constantly search for small improvements the consumer would like to have and for which she would be willing to pay a little bit more. What they have done with their dishwasher detergent power brand, Finish, illustrates their approach. A few years after launching the original Finish, a pure detergent dishwasher product, RB launched Finish 2-in-1, which added a rinse agent; this was followed a few years later by Finish 3-in-1, which added a salt component, and more recently by their current 4-in-1 Finish, which includes a glass-protection component. The successive new features that RB researched and introduced were based on learnings from straightforward consumer research on improving convenience in product use. No rocket science indeed, but solid insights coupled with outstanding execution. And each of these apparently small improvements grew volume as well as margin. RB's small ideas, coupled with outstanding execution driven by great 'pay for performance' incentive schemes for their people, have produced unrivalled performance.

Where is the sense of urgency?

Maybe it is high time for the FMCG industry to develop a sense of urgency regarding R&D. One should note that a group of businesses that are sometimes called the GAFA companies (Google, Amazon, Facebook and Apple) had a collective R&D budget of over $30 billion in 2014. Facebook's R&D spending in recent years has been colossal; they spend more in R&D as a percentage of their sales than the big pharmaceutical companies.

Without any doubt, these companies will be crucial players in the FMCG industry in years to come. They will take up activities in the fields of distribution, communication and even production, act as supporting players in the supply chain and maybe even as substitutes for existing retailers and/or manufacturers. It is expected that Amazon will overtake Walmart, currently the world's biggest retailer, in sales in a few years' time. Just imagine how the opportunities created by Big Data and artificial intelligence, coupled with the GAFA companies' huge R&D investments, may bring an entirely new set of outstanding competitors into the FMCG industry. Shouldn't it be a frightening idea for retailers to see that a company like Amazon spent $15 billion on R&D in 2014? That is more than the cumulative spend of the top 20 retailers in the world...

And it doesn't end there. Google is currently backing a new health-focused company called Calico, led by former Google board member and current Apple chairman Arthur D. Levinson, who is also ex-chairman of Genentech and himself a top-notch researcher. Calico wants to do research in health and pharma in order to combat aging and age-related health issues. They believe that thorough analysis of the genomes of people who live to be 100 years old and are relatively healthy will allow them to solve the puzzle of human aging. And they have very, very deep pockets. The link with food, health and obesity is obvious. If they get serious about it – and they undoubtedly will – where will that leave Nestlé, Unilever and the others?

Chapter Insights

1 Innovation is not just about R&D. Consumer and shopper insights are an equally important source for innovation.
2 If your company only knew what your company knows. There are so many undiscovered and unleveraged insights in each and every company.
3 'Bigger, Better, Faster' is not a good recipe for R&D in the FMCG industry. The evidence shows that a strategy of marginal improvements in R&D reaps more success.

Chapter 3
Marketing in a Digital World

We are living in a time of exponential change – all of it driven by the connection of a bunch of digital technologies. Cloud, mobile, social, Big Data and analytics, and robotics are fundamentally forcing us to reimagine and reorganize all aspects of our lives. We are moving rapidly to a state where digital is becoming the default. Even though these technologies started invading our lives more than 20 years ago, we have hardly begun to see the enormous impact they may have on the availability of information, buying behaviour, marketing, communication and retailing, R&D, production, and logistics. This evolution goes well beyond the mere possibility of selling online or sending personalized promotions to individual consumers and shoppers. Automated shopping lists? Intelligent packaging? Parcel delivery by drones? 3D printing at home? We have seen nothing yet! Above all, we are gradually witnessing the emergence of a new breed of consumers: extremely well informed, constantly connected and highly volatile, the limit of which we will see in a few years when the millennials become the dominant force in the market.

In this context, we need to investigate how the digital revolution will impact the way brands and retailers pursue penetration-driven organic growth. Will brands continue to be at the apex of marketing thinking? Will marketers keep their jobs? Will advertising agencies become a concept of the past? Will physical stores disappear? Will cities become overly congested with vehicles carrying out home deliveries of goods and services to individual households? Or will self-driving cars change our shopping habits and delivery options? John chambers, CEO and chairman of Cisco, predicts that because of internet-based technologies as many as one third of companies will disappear in the next 10 years because they will be unable to adjust to this new reality.

Although there are still some doubting Thomases about the quantum leap change digital technology will provoke, facts are stubborn, and when one observes the disruption GAFA have already brought about today, the writing is on the wall. Remember, the average age of the GAFA companies is just over 20 years. And by the way, the digital revolution is not limited to the GAFA frontrunners, consider recent start-ups and industry disrupters like Uber, Airbnb, Pinterest, Instagram and Alibaba, to name just a few. Remarkable. Frightening. Be prepared for major changes!

Table 9. Industries GAFA is disrupting

	8	é	f	a
TELECOM & IT	FIBER	APPLE SIM	WHATSAPP	CLOUD DRIVE
HEALTH	CALICO	HEALTH KIT	MOVE	MARKET PLACE
RETAIL	SHOPPING EXPR	iBEACON	F BUY BUTTON	GROC DELIVERY
ENERGY & UTILITIES	SMART HOME	SOLAR POWER	ORG PROJECT	FULFILLMENT BY AMAZON
MEDIA/ENTERT	PLAY	ITUNES	OCULUS	TWITCH
FINANCIALS	WALLET	APPLE PAY	F-TO-F PAYMENT	AMAZON PAYM
TRAVEL& LEISURE	CAR	CARPLAY	MESSENGER + UBER INTEGRATE	MEDIA APP FOR CONNECTED CARS

Source: FaberNovel, 'GAFAnomics: New economy, new rules.' 25 Nov. 2014.[9]
GAFA=Google, Apple, Facebook, Amazon.

Of course, the specific impact of technology, and in particular the internet, on marketing and sales in the FMCG industry depends on the time horizon one adopts. What we consider as science fiction today may well be reality ten years from now. In this chapter I will adopt a realistic three-to-five-year perspective, which is what I expect to be the half-life of this book. Even if we are not sure how information technology will change the industry, I would advise anyone involved, 'Be prepared.' As economist Rudi Dornbush used to say: 'Change always takes longer to start than one anticipates, but once it starts, it moves faster than one anticipated.'

In this chapter, we will examine the expected impact of the digital transformation on three dimensions that shape consumer and shopper penetration:

1 *The way consumers will select brands and form their brand consideration sets.* How can brands conquer mind space in the digital age? Could it be that the availability of online information is turning consumers into 'prosumers' and that traditional marketing and advertising will become obsolete?

2 *What the consumer will be confronted with at the point of purchase.* How can brands occupy shelf space in the context of multichannel retailing and new consumer journeys? How likely is it that in the FMCG industry, e-commerce will become the dominant route to the consumer and stores will disappear in large droves? Should FMCG brand owners and retailers focus their efforts towards building their online business?

3 *The impact of Big Data and artificial intelligence.* How can availability of information help drive consumer and shopper penetration? Will information become the competitive advantage, allowing for targeted marketing and highly personalized shopping experiences? Will Big Data, turbocharged by sophisticated analytics and artificial intelligence tools, be able to take management decisions and do it better than biased (or is it 'experienced') managers possibly can?

[9] Accessed at www.slideshare.net/FaberNovel/gafanomics.

Marketing: From the Bowling Lane to the Pinball Machine

E-commerce will no doubt have a significant impact on today's FMCG industry, but one should not get carried away and look at today's facts. Table 10 compares the 2014 market capitalization, sales, and inventory statistics of the four largest retailers in the world, two 'e-age' and two 'old age'.

Table 10. A comparison of the largest 'e-age' and 'old age' retailers, 2014

$ billion	ALIBABA	AMAZON	WAL-MART	CARREFOUR
MARKET CAPITALIZATION	172	256	214	24
SALES	76	89	485	76
MCAP/SALES	2.3	2.9	0.45	0.3
INVENTORY	0	8	45	7

Source: 2014 Company Annual Reports, and Bloomberg 2015.

How many times have I heard and read that Alibaba has become the biggest retailer in the world? This is wrong on two counts. First, they are not your typical retailer. This is how the *Financial Times* defines them: 'Alibaba Group Holding limited is a China-based online and mobile commerce company in retail and wholesale trade, as well as cloud computing and other services.' And second, even if we were to stretch our definition of retail, Alibaba is not the biggest. Wal-Mart is bigger both in terms of sales and market capitalization. And Wal-Mart is definitely no frontrunner in the e-commerce space – by no stretch of the imagination.

Judging by how much they are willing to pay for every dollar of sales, investors do seem to believe that e-tailers are the future. The point is that e-tailers have a radically different business model. Alibaba is worth seven times more than Carrefour, with the same sales and no inventory... In the same vein, Uber is the largest taxi company in the world even though it owns no vehicles. Airbnb is the largest accommodations provider without owning any real estate. And Facebook, the world's most popular media owner, doesn't create any content. Surely the world is changing...

Not only will the business models of retailers change, but the ownership of goods is also expected to evolve into a more fluid world where consumers will rent instead of buy goods and services that they need for only short periods of time or special events. According to Matt Truman of TrueCapital, the driving factor is the low cost of connectivity between consumers – and between consumers and providers of goods and services. How many of you own a power drill? Did you know that the typical owner of a power drill uses it for only 12 to 13 minutes over its entire lifetime and that the lion's share of cars sit idle for 23 hours a day? No wonder collaborative consumption has plenty of space to play in. A move towards a 'shared economy' driven by millennials, where consumers will own less and rent more, seems inevitable.

Similarly, consumers are becoming more self-centred because technology allows it. While most of us still remember opening maps before planning a journey, trying to find our place on the map, today's consumers don't need to work out their place in the world: the blue dot on their smartphone tells them exactly where they are – and they're always right in the centre. This is the final Copernican revolution: the world (r)evolves around 'me'.

So where does this bring us with respect to marketing in the digital age? For a long period of time, marketing in general and advertising in particular were seen as ideal tools to influence people's perceptions and preferences, to entice them into buying specific products and brands. Marketing would select relevant target markets for their products and communicate the competitive advantages of their offer. If this did not produce the desired response from the target market, the message might be fine-tuned and communication amplified and repeated in order to achieve the coveted level of reach and frequency. This old-school view, according to such marketing scholars as Itamar Simonson (see later in this chapter), is gradually becoming obsolete.

Consumers in a not so distant past based their perceptions, preferences and buying behaviour on information provided by brands and other influencers, as well as on their past experiences with a brand or product. Today, however, consumers have abundant information from all over the world at their fingertips. Apart from visiting the brand's website, they have easy access to product reviews by other users, comparison websites, and test results from consumer organizations. The influence of these sources may jeopardize traditional communication efforts by marketers, even if the information provided online doesn't always prove to be reliable, as there is no referee on the internet to sanction false information.

Most people wouldn't think about booking a hotel room without first checking user reviews on a site like Booking.com. The heavy communication investments by hotels to reach potential customers may lose some of their bite when the traveller can easily find out if the hotel is located on a busy street or near a peaceful park, or if other guests thought the staff was friendly and the breakfast delicious, or not. All this information – and lots more – is readily available. No advertising campaign can ever compensate for user complaints about uncomfortable beds or dirty bathrooms. What's even worse, the damage of negative social media reviews strongly outweighs positive contributions. [10] As an answer to these developments, some companies post their own positive reviews on TripAdvisor and the like, or have specialized service providers do that on their behalf, the same way they might buy Facebook 'likes' or Twitter followers.

Brands must also learn to engage with consumers through new digital and social channels, without appearing intrusive. The point with marketing in today's age is that we are moving towards multiway communication. Along with communication from the brand owner to consumers and shoppers, marketers now have to deal with uncontrolled communication from consumers to other consumers, from people outside the target market to people in the target market, and so on. How can brand owners manage this

[10] Marcel Corstjens and Andris Umblijs , 'The Power of Evil,' Journal of Advertising Research, 2012, vol 52,p433-449.

multilateral game? More profoundly, the question becomes, Is brand ownership moving into the hands of consumers faster than ever before?

As a result of this new digital and social reality, marketing has moved on from a bowling game to a game of pinball. In bowling, the player aims at the pins (consumers) and skilfully throws the ball (message) hoping for a 'strike'. If not all pins get knocked over, the player continues with a second ball, then a third. With a pinball machine, the ball (message) goes in all sorts of directions, expected and often unexpected, and you have to be extremely skilful to hit the ball with the paddles and keep it bouncing around inside the machine to keep scoring. Only the most proficient players will score high-value shots and get 'extra balls', while most other players end up in 'tilt'.

An example? Unilever brand Dove's 'Real Beauty' campaign has become the victim of parody commercials in which guys instead of girls test their own self-image. How should Unilever cope with social media's alleged criticism of the company's inconsistencies in the respective positioning of their power brands, Dove (internal beauty for women) and Axe (young men looking at young women as sex objects)? Those spontaneous and uncontrollable events can become a horrible nightmare to brand owners, who find themselves in a catch-22 situation: if you react, you give even more visibility to the problem, but if you decide to ignore the whole situation, it may backfire.

So, should marketers forget about old-fashioned television advertising and move their investments into digital media, especially with a view to millennial consumers becoming more and more important? Well, the truth is actually more nuanced. Recent research published by MarketShare, the marketing measurement consulting company, shows that over the last five years (2010-2014) the effectiveness of TV marketing still outpaces that of digital media by far (Figure 4). The study concludes that across a number of industries, TV has the highest relative efficiency in improving KPIs. Thus, in spite of changes in consumer habits over the last few years TV effectiveness has not diminished. Other recent academic studies point out a positive synergistic effect between traditional (TV) and new digital media in terms of their effectiveness. It's still early days, but marketing managers need to be careful not to throw the baby away with the bath water. The power of mass communication via traditional media like TV cannot be underestimated in the context of driving penetration in the market. Digital media have a powerful advantage in their ability to tailor their messages to individual consumers. Unfortunately, this may not be an effective method to drive penetration. It would be wise to keep track of the actual effectiveness of media investments via proper statistical analysis and adjust the investments gradually in the direction of where one gets the most bang for the buck.

Amid the barrage of dizzying claims about the reach and impact of ad-tech platforms, it is useful to remain cool and objective. In a recent *Ad Age column*, Sean Cunningham reported that in the US on a monthly basis, millennials spend 101 hours with TV content versus 23 hours with Facebook[11]. In 2015, young people are not abandoning TV for all things social media and digital.

[11] Sean Cunningham, 'It's Not a Video Revolution – It's a TV Evolution.' Ad Age, 24 April 2015. Accessed at http://adage.com/article/digitalnext/a-video-revolution-a-tv-evolution/298241/

Figure 4. Media effectiveness: relative lift factors, by sector (CPG=consumer packaged goods).

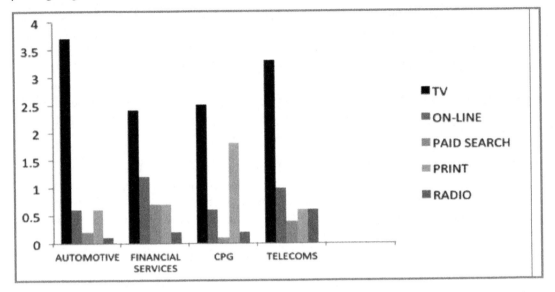

Source: MarketShare, 'Evaluating TV Effectiveness in a Changed Media Landscape,' 2015. Accessed at www.marketshare.com/insights/article/evaluating-tv-effectiveness-in-a-changed-media-landscape.

Personally, I believe that ultimately content will dominate medium. A good story will catch consumers' attention, whether shown in an ad on TV or as a video on YouTube or Facebook, etc....

Information overload?

Even if e-commerce and web-based communication in themselves still represent a relatively small percentage of total FMCG retail sales, the influence of the web on the consumer decision journey may be changing consumers' shopping behaviour and brand choice.

In his 2014 book, *Absolute Value: What Really Influences Consumers in the Age of Perfect Information*[12], Professor Itamar Simonson of Stanford University makes a useful distinction between three forces that impact purchase decisions: priors (P, past experience and information); marketing (M, brand messages); and opinions and information (O, mostly gathered from the internet). In his view, because of the internet and the impact of social media, the influence of O is expected to increase strongly, while the impact of M is likely to be substantially reduced. Simonson states that the sacred trio of 'Brands, Loyalty and Persuasion' will have to give in to product information abundantly available through social media and other channels. The implications for marketing and retailing could be important. According to Simonson, product (or service) performance becomes more important than brand image.

[12] Palo Alto, CA: Stanford University Press, 2014.

His insights, however, seem to be most relevant for high-priced, high-involvement categories, like cars, personal computers and smartphones. After all, what does 'performance' really mean in the case of a chocolate bar, a carbonated soft drink or a breakfast cereal? Does laundry detergent A really wash whiter, and will shampoo brand B make your hair shine significantly brighter? If online comparisons and reviews were that influential, we would already have seen some dramatic shifts in buying behaviour, wouldn't we?

While it seems pretty logical to check reviews before booking a restaurant, or to compare technical details when you want to buy a new smartphone or car, it remains to be seen if consumers will make the same kind of effort when shopping for groceries. Many food categories are typically 'low involvement' categories where the consumer is less driven by information (see Table 11, based on an idea from the Foot, Cone & Belding advertising agency).

Specific brands from the same product category can have different positions in the table. Ford Mondeo or Volvo would be in the top left quadrant, and Audi and sports cars would be in the top right hand. Also, some brands or categories are located more towards the centre of the square. Diapers are probably in the middle of the horizontal axis towards the higher part of the table. Itamar Simonson's ideas apply mostly to products in the top quadrants and less to products in the bottom quadrants. As most FMCG brands are in the bottom half of the table, marketing and prior experiences are still crucial to typical grocery products.

Table 11. Consumer Behaviour for different type of Products

	RATIONAL	EMOTIONAL
HIGH INVOLVEMENT	Real Estate, Medication, Washing Machine, PC, etc... **INFORMATION**	Luxury goods: Porsche, Perfume, etc... **PRESTIGE**
LOW INVOLVEMENT	Mustard, Tissues, Toilet paper, Milk, Bread... **HABIT**	Soft Drinks, Chocolates, Cheese, Beer, Pastries... **PLEASURE**

On the other hand, we need to keep an open mind – peer recommendations may gain significant impact in the future for low-involvement products, even for FMCG. Just look on YouTube, where some bloggers have a larger audience than most brand owners. Zoella, a London girl blogging mostly on clothing and make-up, has 8.6 million subscribers who follow her weekly shopping adventures. Indeed, 'haul videos' are a remarkable phenomenon where people share the unpacking of their shopping bags with the world.

And they aren't restricted to fashion or decoration. Grocery hauls show housewives sharing meal plans and smart grocery shopping advice, helping each other to feed their families in a healthy way while saving money at the same time. These videos get tens of thousands of views and should not be ignored by marketers.

There is little doubt that online information is becoming more relevant, even for FMCG brands. Shopping apps inform consumers not only about price differences and promotions, but also about origin, ingredients, additives, allergens and nutritional values in food products. For example, since the obesity issue is gaining in importance, consumers will be interested in finding out how fattening and damaging for their health certain products are. This information will be progressively more available on the web and through specific smartphone apps. At the point of purchase, shoppers can scan a barcode and get an immediate reading as to whether this is a red, orange or green product.

Product information in everyone's pocket

In Germany today, smartphone app and web platform Barcoo delivers a range of essential information on FMCG products: opinions, nutritional values, a 'traffic light' evaluation (red for unhealthy), price comparisons, a product description and consumer reviews. Barcoo claims to be the biggest product guide in Europe. What's amazing about the app – but also alarming to a degree – is that it is almost completely based on 'user generated' content, which means brand owners have little control over the information published about their products. "We cannot guarantee 100% accuracy," admitted co-founder Benjamin Thym in an interview with Storecheck magazine. "We always disclose our sources, we use a control system that checks data entered by our users and we limit allergen information to non-critical allergens – we don't include nuts allergy, for example."

Some personal care products and high value non-food product categories will probably be more impacted by product information availability. Marketing will have to take these new sources of information into account. As an example, the diaper category may be deeply influenced by additional info available, since this is a 'high involvement' product category.

Likewise, all sorts of real-time retailer comparisons are becoming available on the internet: price, service, effective promotions… This may seduce some retailers into sophisticated management of prices in order to improve their price image. Such an approach may bounce back on them and hurt them (read our comments on price obfuscation and individualized promotions further on in this chapter).

One should be careful though in exaggerating the influence of information, especially online information: sometimes there is just too much of it, and too much information kills information. That is the 'paradox of choice'. Moreover, there is a lot of doubt about the reliability of data on the internet. Price comparison websites, for example, are under criticism for a lack of accuracy, which is logical given the number of daily price changes and the many possibilities for brand owners and retailers to make one-to-one price offers. Making price comparisons between retailers perfectly transparent is science fiction, and shoppers are aware of that. Yes, the world has become more transparent, but not completely…

Even if it is a completely different ball game, there is no reason to expect that digital marketing communication will change the fundamentally polygamous consumer behaviour observed so far, certainly not in low-involvement FMCG categories.

How brands engagte with consumers through social media

With threats come opportunities. The digital world offers chances for brands to interact with consumers through what is called storytelling, content marketing and user-generated content. These are new ways of creating 'buzz' around a brand, bypassing traditional advertising and aiming at younger people who don't watch much television. Just think of the way Unilever built the emotionally loaded Dove brand via promotional videos on YouTube. Another example is Red Bull Media House. The energy drink has its own production company that produces sensational videos of extreme sports and breath-taking stunts. Young people love it. Red Bull produces content that is valuable to its audience, thus building top-of-mind awareness.

Engaging with consumers through social media can lead to new insights and even to new forms of co-creation. Brands can outsource aspects of their new product development to their users: let them choose a new taste, give ideas for an attractive packaging design or come up with a catchy bass line. Perhaps one of the most successful co-creating initiatives was Walkers Crisps' 'Do Us a Flavour' campaign. The potato snacks manufacturer asked the public to develop a new crisps flavour, present it on Facebook and try to win as many votes as possible. The response was huge (more than a million votes in the UK), the winning flavours became an instant sales success and the campaign was rolled out to many different markets.

The trend towards storytelling and user-generated content poses some fundamental questions about the business model of the advertising industry. Check out MOFILM, a crowdsourcing platform for filmmakers to develop their careers by connecting them with iconic brands. Who needs an expensive agency when you can have access to talented volunteers from around the world at a fraction of the cost?

There was a time when big brands had big ideas. Michelin, the tire manufacturer, created the Michelin guide for restaurants, long before there was television, and P&G created the idea of soap operas to sell their soap and personal care products. Brands have been rather tame in the last 30 years, but maybe the internet will be the impetus for breakthrough ideas.

The Point of Purchase: Retailing Reinvented

During recent years we have witnessed the rise of pure play online grocery e-tailers like Ocado in the UK or Peapod and Amazon Fresh in the US. At the same time, virtually all grocery retailers are moving toward a hybrid omnichannel approach. Some of them (Tesco, Ahold, Kroger) are doing this faster and better than others, but they are all trying to get there. Table 12 offers a closer look at these different strategies, showing that the choice between them rests on three critical assumptions.

Table 12. Pure play versus brick and click assumptions

PURE PLAY ON-LINE	BRICK AND CLICK OMNI-CHANNEL
1. Online retail will become a **dominant** route to the consumer in the grocery industry (or at least it will become a large business, far bigger than what is projected today).	1. Online will be a significant business, but for the foreseeable future people will keep doing the majority of their grocery shopping in **stores**.
2. There are significant **learning effects** in online operations, both in terms of 'economies of scale' and 'learning by doing over time', and both will generate important first mover advantages. New and smaller players will have a hard time becoming competitive and late entrants will not be able to catch up with focused and experienced online grocery retailers. Furthermore, focusing on one business model will be more effective and efficient.	2. You need to cover all the different channels where the consumer is likely to shop. Actually, being present in a variety of channels will work in a complementary way, and there will be little risk of cannibalization. You can capture most of the economies of scale as well as add more economies of scope by being present across many channels simultaneously.
3. Avoiding brick and mortar stores' huge **CAPEX** and the subsequently high fixed costs of operating physical stores, will lead to superior online retail profitability.	3. The main economies of scale are generated by the bargaining power with suppliers. Costs of goods sold account for 70% or more of retailers' sales. Operating an omni-channel retail business will increase the sales of the retailer and therefore lower % COGS.

Are these pure players' assumptions realistic? The future will tell, but there are serious doubts. Considering the importance of two critical dimensions for grocery products, 'research for shopping' and 'actual purchases online', the graph below shows that the grocery sector is far behind other sectors in the consumer goods market. By and large, consumers do not tend to research FMCG products on the internet before and during shopping, and for all the hype on home delivery for grocery products, e-commerce still accounts for a market share of far less than 10% – but it is growing rapidly, with specific markets (South Korea and the UK) leading the way. When the supermarket innovation was introduced in Europe in 1960, it took less than 20 years to dominate grocery retailing. The e-commerce model has been introduced now for about 15 years and has only made marginal inroads in the sector. Still, this evolution forces retailers to allocate substantial investments for the development of new distribution channels without any guarantee of a rapid return on investment.

Figure 5. Relative importance of online shopping across product categories.

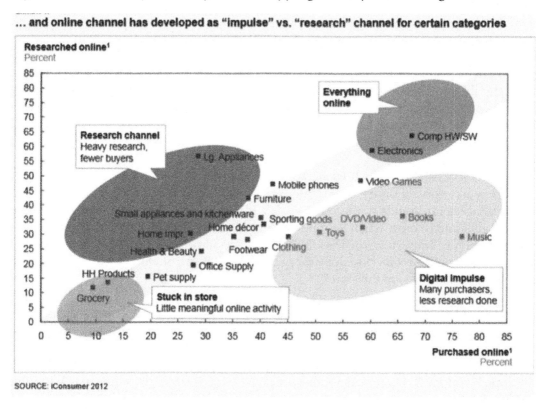

SOURCE: iConsumer 2012

For grocery retailers, e-commerce presents one of the most fundamental challenges since Piggly Wiggly opened the first self-service supermarket in Memphis, Tennessee. For many years, retail was about three things: location, location and location. The typical growth strategy of retailers consisted of rolling out real estate in a race for space. Technology is creating a new reality: the option to have retail without stores. E-commerce takes location out of the equation. Retailers need to develop a new business model and those that opt for an omnichannel strategy, will have to excel in two completely different worlds, bricks and clicks, each with their own specific business rules.

E-tailing means retailing reinvented. It is a very different trade. Instead of organising aisles, shelves and displays, retailers have to learn to work with web pages, pop-ups and banners. Most of all, they will need to deeply understand the new digital shopper journey. Walking a cart through the supermarket or browsing product lists on a website are two radically different things indeed. The challenges are countless.

For example, will e-commerce make the market even more transparent and price sensitive for consumers, as they will have all prices and promotions available at their fingertips? Will it have an impact on the basket share of brands versus private labels? It turns out that currently the share of big brands on e-commerce is larger than in-store. Maybe that is because it is the better-off who shop on the internet. Internet shopping seems to be used primarily to save time, and less to save money. Maybe this will change later, as new shopper segments start to use home shopping for FMCG products.

Virtual category management will become a new skill for retailers and brand owners. How can one organise an assortment of 20.000 SKUs – or even more, as there are no physical real estate constraints – in a clear and orderly way on a website or a smartphone app, to create a smooth and logical browsing experience for online shoppers? In what order should one present product categories and individual products? Will brands get the chance to enhance their visibility online, as they do in-store? Retailers will have to develop digital alternatives for traditional sales tactics like displays, coupons, on-pack promotions, shelf talkers, and cross-selling or cross-merchandising.

An important question will be how e-commerce will influence impulse purchase product categories, like confectionary, soft drinks and snacks. There is a real danger of losing important sales for brands in these categories. It will be a challenge to develop creative ways to generate interest when shoppers are ordering on the internet. Physical contact will remain very important for these products. The same goes for fresh produce: will shoppers trust online retailers to deliver vegetables and meat, or will they prefer to choose those items themselves, in the store?

To date, in most countries around the world, the general feeling is that with respect to e-commerce, FMCG brands and retailers are still in the experimental phase and that no one has yet found the definitive model for an online store. The degree of development of online grocery retail varies considerably across countries due to exogenous factors. In the developed world, UK, Japan and South Korea have a relatively high degree of penetration of grocery e-commerce partly because real estate in these countries is very expensive and because there is a high concentration of populations in large cities. It is also interesting to note that in China e-commerce has a relatively high degree of penetration in retail. It seems as if Chinese retailers are leapfrogging the race for space for traditional supermarkets and hypermarkets by accelerating the race for digital retail space, even in the grocery sector.

In the differing e-commerce models, some common elements deserve special attention. Shopping lists, for example, will become a crucial part of the shelf space of the future. All webshops offer their online shoppers the possibility of creating online wish lists and shopping lists for recurring items. Especially in the grocery area, shopping lists are a big thing. As a key reason to shop online is to save time, people tend to stick to their lists. This means that brands will have to fight to get on the shopping list. A new battle for virtual shelf space has begun.

Another interesting evolution is the emergence of the subscription model. Since consumers tend to buy a basically similar set of grocery items every week, it seems logical to offer them a 'subscription' that delivers high-volume goods automatically at given times: milk, coffee, soft drinks, pet food, breakfast cereals... Retailers (or brand owners) can offer substantial discounts as they are assured of a guaranteed volume during an entire year. The current subscription business seems to work for odd categories: pet food, socks, male underwear, condoms, things people need and don't want to shop for.

What's more, subscriptions needn't be limited to routine shopping. Subscription services already offer weekly 'surprise' vegetable bags, for example, or meal kits with recipes. Some people like to outsource their decision-making, as they get tired of answering the daily question 'What are we going to eat tonight?' A remarkable example is HelloFresh.com, a weekly recipe-kit delivery service that is expanding rapidly – the Berlin-based start-up now delivers almost nationwide in the US and is expanding into Europe (UK, Germany, Austria, the Netherlands, Belgium) and Australia. How does it work? Consumers choose three recipes each week, and HelloFresh delivers the fresh ingredients to the door, for around 10$ per person per meal. They guarantee a nutritious home-cooked meal in less than 30 minutes and claim to source at local, family-owned purveyors. Comparable meal kit delivery services are Blue Apron, FreshDirect and Plated.

Subscriptions increase shopper loyalty, and so does the membership model. Amazon Prime, which is now more than ten years old, offers its paying members benefits like free two-day shipping, unlimited streaming of movies and videos (Amazon Instant Video), and one free borrowed e-book per month from the Kindle Owners Lending Library. EBay is testing a Prime-like service called eBay+ in Germany, promising free, fast shipping and returns, while Wal-Mart is preparing to roll out a service offering unlimited free shipping for $50 per year, half the cost of Amazon Prime.

Table 13. UK grocery retailers' share of wallet

	share of wallet of average shopper at	share of wallet of average shopper at	Share of wallet of average shopper who shops also online at	Share of wallet of average shopper who shops also online at
	In store	On-line	In store	On-line
TESCO	28.8	2.0	30.9	16.1
ASDA	19.5	0.7	21.1	11.9
SAINSBURY	20.5	0.8	25.2	10.5

Source: Kantor Worldpanel, 2014.

And what about the impact of e-commerce activities on retailers' total sales? There is evidence today that presence in different channels has a synergistic and not a cannibalistic effect on sales. Data show that shoppers who shop at the same retailer in-store *and* online give the retailer a bigger share of wallet. A 2014 case study by Kantar Worldpanel, 'Accelerating the Growth of e-Commerce in FMCG', showed that offline Tesco customers spend 29% of their annual shopping budget at Tesco, while for offline *and* online Tesco shoppers this rate goes up to 46%.

Fewer stores, higher costs?

There is little doubt that e-commerce does hold some exciting opportunities for retailers to enhance their business in the future. Does this mean that grocery retailers should bet 'the farm' on e-commerce? Maybe not just yet. When Ocado, the pure play online UK retailer, was preparing for its IPO, one financial analyst opined: 'It's a zero at the start and a zero at the end, with nothing in between.' The e-tailer actually had a successful IPO, but has failed to fulfil its early ambitions.

E-commerce still represents only a small market share in groceries today. But a further growth of e-commerce may indeed confront physical stores with declining sales figures and lower profitability, since the total FMCG market is not expected to grow significantly in the developed world. What will retailers do with their 20th-century portfolio of physical stores in the digital 21st century? Most of these physical assets will prove too big for the new reality. In November 2014, Goldman Sachs asserted that in the UK, 20% of existing big stores should be shut. It's reasonable to expect a shift towards a new equilibrium where bricks and clicks will co-exist, each with their own strongholds: maybe e-commerce in 'boring' and heavy product categories, and brick and mortar stores for more exciting categories, including impulse purchases, fresh produce and prepared meals. This could lead not only to fewer stores, but also to smaller stores, because there would be less need to display the complete assortment on the shelves. As a consequence, retailers (and their landlords) will have to find solutions for the superfluous square meters of shop floor.

Return on investment is becoming a big challenge here. If the retailer goes for an omnichannel approach, will the end result not be more costs for a flat top line, in the aggregate? The FMCG market doesn't grow that much in mature markets, but retailers are forced to invest in upgrading their physical stores while simultaneously developing new websites, apps, distribution centres and logistical processes for their online activities. The costs of running an omnichannel business model might be difficult to recover for retailers. Their economic value added (EVA) might be dubious.

This is what is called a prisoners' dilemma. Retailers know that investing in omnichannel is, for many of them, a losing game at the moment (in terms of profitability), but if they decide not to invest while their competitors do, they end up even worse off. To illustrate, consider the difficult situation of British retailer William Morrisons. The company was lagging behind on e-commerce while its bigger competitors all took important steps. Under pressure from financial markets, they felt the need to catch up quickly and decided to partner with online pure player Ocado instead of taking the time to organically build their own e-commerce business. This was manna from heaven for Ocado, but it proved a bit of a misfit for Morrisons, especially since Ocado already had a buying agreement with upmarket retailer Waitrose, while Morrisons is positioned more as a value retailer.

How do the economics of on-line FMCG retail currently look? The conventional typology of online grocery retail distinguishes three distinct business models (see Table 14):

1 In-store picking and delivery from the store
This is typically a good starting point for an online business: although picking costs tend to be high, there are relatively few incremental costs. At some point the online business might become too big to be handled efficiently by the store's capacity. That is when the retailer might add dark stores.

2 Dark stores and home delivery
Here, the picking occurs in purposefully built 'stores' (actually dedicated e-commerce distribution centres not open to shoppers), while delivery to the shopper is organized from this 'dark store'. Since these dark stores are specifically designed for online retail, they tend to have low picking costs. On the other hand, as they are located farther away from customers, delivery costs are significant and capital costs tend to be high. Ocado can be seen as a large dark store online retail operator.

3 The 'drive' model
This is a fulfilment centre with remote pick-up points. Although there are various submodels for the drive online approach, they tend to be the least economical for the retailer. Still, the drive model has a number of appealing features, which might explain its early success. There are some lessons to be learned from the French market leader E.Leclerc. In its drive channel, this retailer offers a relatively small assortment online (less than 7,000 SKUs) that consists of about 50% brands and 50% private label products with almost no cheap budget lines and lots of fresh produce.

The prices are low compared to its online competitors, though not necessarily the lowest in the market. Leclerc operates an efficient supply chain concept where so-called 'master drives' act as DCs servicing several collect points within a distance of 10 km. Ironically, those standalone collect points are now gradually becoming small commercial centres, adding a convenience store, a flower shop, a bread machine... maybe this is the food retail model of the future: a collect point for 'routine' groceries ordered online, in combination with a relatively small inspirational supermarket offering fresh produce and food specialties. Once again, the return on investments will need to be demonstrated.

The question is, who will pay for the on-line + delivery service? Consumers (higher prices)? Suppliers (lower margins)? Retailers (lower margins)? Shareholders (lower profits)? It is interesting to observe that looking back at the history of FMCG retail, retailers have been outsourcing services to the consumer in exchange for lower prices. E-commerce is going the other way around: the retailer takes care of more activities (more service). Will the consumer be ready to pay for that?

In practice, retailers tend to charge the same prices for products online as in the physical store. Actually, many studies advise that to be successful, the omnichannel strategy has to be seamless, which means online stores carry not just the same prices everywhere, but also the same promotions. Moreover, delivery charges tend to be low, or even free. It is hard to imagine how this can be a sustainable business model. Can retailers go on using one channel to subsidize another and not charge a fair price for their services? After all, most FMCG retailers charge higher prices in their convenience stores than in their hypermarkets or in wealthier areas with higher real estate costs.

Recent studies by analysts at Bernstein have drawn clear conclusions regarding the profitability of the various online grocery retail business models in the UK (see Figure 6).

Although the profitability of the three business models varies considerably, the UK online grocery retail is reasonably profitable for omnichannel grocers because it is seen by households as a premium service for people with above-average income who order above-average shopping baskets online. Although the margin it delivers is smaller than that for normal in-store sales, it is reasonable because it has some good features (particularly the in-store picking model):

- People seem to be willing to pay for a delivery charge (depending on time of delivery and size of order)
- Online shoppers start from a shopping list and are less driven by promotions
- No cost of in-store checkout (significant cost for retailers in-store)
- Less shrinkage (no stealing from shoppers)
-

Last but not least there is a societal aspect to the question. Research at a number of large retailers shows that the most inefficient process from an energy and environmental perspective is that of the shopper driving to and from the store. Currently, that seems to be the most wasteful part in the entire supply chain. Home delivery, drives, pick-up points and probably many more business models to come will get goods to shoppers while reducing energy and environmental waste. We haven't seen the final solutions, but this

Figure 6. Profitability of UK online grocery retail business models. Source: Bernstein, E-commerce Long-View Conference, 2015.

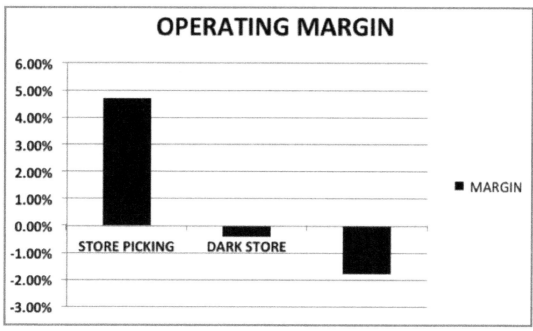

Source: Bernstein, E-commerce Long View Conference, 2015.

Table 14. Cost comparison of different business models for online grocery retail

	IN-STORE PICKING	DARK STORE	DRIVE
Picking Cost	HIGH	LOW	LOW
Delivery Cost	LOW	HIGH	MEDIUM
Idle Time Cost	VERY LOW	LOW	HIGH
Overhead	MEDIUM	HIGH	HIGH
Capital Cost	MEDIUM	HIGH	HIGH

Source: Bernstein, E-commerce Long View Conference, 2015.

aspect may become a crucial piece of the puzzle, as the institution that takes care of and controls the final mile could end up having a lot of power in the entire supply chain. It might be an innovative retailer, a collective retailer organization, an existing logistics company or a new Uber-like structure that solves the problem in terms of convenience and cost for the shopper, cost efficiency for the retailer and environmental friendliness.

Caught in a red ocean

In sum, e-commerce will no doubt have an impact on FMCG retailing, albeit with important differences depending on the product categories. In non-food retail the dominance of e-commerce will continue. Grocery retailers entering the non-food online retail business will face huge, experienced and efficient competitors like Amazon. It will take deep pockets, scale, and strong and persistent efforts to succeed.

In the FMCG categories, there is more uncertainty. How big will e-commerce become? Which business model will prove to create the most value for shoppers and retailers? Overall, progression is real but from a small base. For some categories, though, a breakthrough may be imminent: real commodity products, heavy to carry; products that are bought regularly… Furthermore, one should consider what will happen to e-commerce in the grocery industry once the millennials start to dominate, in just a few years' time. This new generation of digital natives was virtually born with a mobile in their hands. We may expect a quantum change for the FMCG industry in terms of consumer preferences and shopper behaviour. It remains to be seen how and when they will want their goods available at arm's length and how much they are willing to pay for the service.

What should retailers do now? One of the key issues with omnichannel for retailers is that if one competitor invests in an additional channel, there are two options for the other retailers: either it works and they will do the same, or it doesn't work and the first mover loses his investment. Typically, to minimize the possible first-mover advantage of a competitor, the other retailers will copy as soon as they can. This results in higher costs for every competitor – and little advantage. Once more, retailers get caught in a red ocean, which is the price they have to pay for a lack of differentiation in the eyes of the consumer. Therefore, it seems sensible to make defensive investments in e-commerce: don't go overboard, but develop the capability, and then when it takes off (maybe unexpectedly) be ready to capitalize on the opportunity. Don't overinvest in technology, because technology changes fast and those that invest heavily early on may find themselves stuck with obsolete tools. Furthermore, retailers will need to re-evaluate their real estate portfolio, as hypermarkets will inevitably end up being too big.

Should Brands Become Retailers?

While digital technology offers brands the opportunity to communicate directly to consumers, it also offers them the option to sell directly. Who needs retailers when you can open your own webshop? In the fashion industry for example, we have seen a fairly dramatic shift from brands selling their products through traditional multi-brand retailers to the emergence of mono-brand flagship stores and webshops. Brands like Esprit, Tommy Hilfiger and s.Oliver, who initially built businesses through traditional multi-brand outlets, have set up their own distribution channels and started competing with their b-to-b customers. The multi-brand fashion boutique is becoming an endangered species. Would a comparable evolution be possible in the FMCG sector?

Should Brands Become Retailers? cont.

In the health and cosmetics sector, companies like Avon and Amway succeeded in building penetration without being present in physical retail stores long before the e-commerce revolution. In food, at least one brand has succeeded in doing something similar. When Nestlé launched Nespresso, it decided to bypass the traditional supermarket and start selling directly, online and in dedicated flagship stores, like a fashion brand would do. And it worked. Nespresso has become one of the world's top brands and is a goldmine for Nestlé, even though the volumes sold remain relatively small compared to the tons of ground coffee sold through the supermarket channel. The brand is in full control of every aspect of its marketing and sales strategy. And there's no need to negotiate with demanding supermarket buyers… One can imagine that this makes a lot of FMCG colleagues quite jealous. Is this model reproducible for Nestlé's other products and other FMCG products as well?

There are precedents. Consumer goods giant P&G has opened webshops in the US (www.pgshop.com) and in Germany (www.pgshop.de) where consumers can order anything from diapers to cosmetics and detergents. The launch of these shops was rather low-key, and P&G emphasized that its purpose was not to compete with supermarkets, but to better understand the wishes and the buying behavior of its consumers. P&G also partnered with Amazon and took a 1% share in British online retailer Ocado to learn about e-commerce. Those sound like productive ideas.

It is clear that supermarkets will not be happy if more big brand multinationals open their own webshops. So in order to maintain good relationships with their retailers, brands should consider their online moves carefully. In terms of sales, they may have more to lose than to win, for it is highly unlikely that consumers will give up the comfort of 'one stop shopping' in the supermarket (whether it be clicks or bricks) and start ordering their groceries at hundreds of different brand webshops. A brand has to offer something very special to convince consumers to shop directly with them. Apparently, Nespresso does that.

Still, we can cite at least two worthwhile reasons for brand owners to have a webshop: the first is the learnings they may draw from direct contact with consumers; the second is the improvement of the brand owners' best alternative to a negotiated agreement (BATNA) vis-à-vis retailers. The big challenge lies in the physical delivery of all those internet orders. One can hardly imagine every brand owner going directly to the final consumer's home. For some categories, brand suppliers may outsource physical delivery to specialized logistics companies (at home and/or at convenient locations – e.g. the office, special stations). This could work for recurring weekly or monthly orders for pet food, water, shaving utensils, and other products for which the consumer is not so keen to go to a store. Maybe it will take a totally new intermediary to crack this problem. If so, we are back to where wholesalers and retailers started: as logistics conduits for brand owners…

Big Data – From Folk Wisdom to Technology Driven Insight?

Never before have marketers had access to such colossal amounts of data from various sources: data from consumer research and demographical statistics, from cash registers and loyalty cards, from websites and smartphones, from YouTube, Facebook, Twitter and so forth. Today there is also an impressive arsenal of analytics available to make these Big Data 'sing'. For some, Big Data analytics will be the holy grail of marketing and sales, the ideal tool to predict consumer behaviour with unprecedented accuracy while at the same time reducing managerial bias based on limited data-based experience and intuition. Big Data should allow for real one-to-one conversations with consumers, for perfectly targeted bespoke offers, for flawlessly composed assortments in stores and on-line, and for discovering deep uncovered insights about consumers and shoppers.
As consumers, we all know marketers aren't there yet. Not by a long stretch. Most of us receive a stunning number of utterly useless and inappropriate sales messages from banks, grocery stores and even Amazon: loan offers you don't need, diaper offers when your kids are already in their teens, propositions for books you're totally uninterested in…

The hype on Big Data doubles every year, but maybe the information technology tools at our disposal nowadays aren't yet as sophisticated as we would like to think. Remember the disappearance of Malaysian Airlines flight MH370 from Kuala Lumpur to Beijing on 8 March 2014. We are already 18 months on and, despite the analysis of satellite data, the use of extremely precise GPS tracking and new, sophisticated sonar devices, only today by pure accident are we discovering something about the whereabouts of this huge machine. (Of course, sophisticated data analysis has allowed the international search team to narrow down the area in which the aircraft might have come down to a 60,000-square km strip of ocean, 650km long and 93km wide, and to discover two previously unknown volcanoes.) What has all the sophistication brought us?

Four hurdles to overcome for Big Data success
A number of hurdles need to be overcome for Big Data to become the holy grail of marketing, sales and retail.

First, Big Data, coupled with its sophisticated analytical complement, is still predominantly about prediction and less what it would like to be about: explanation and causation. Data science is mostly about correlational analysis and pattern recognition, aiming at generating great predictive power by using enormous data sources. Do its results help a manager make better decisions? Maybe. However, managers are mostly interested in explanation and causation, 'Why did this happen?' and 'If I do this, what will happen, and why will that happen?'

An interesting illustration was the crowdsourcing competition by Netflix in 2009, offering a prize of $1 million to anyone who could improve their movie recommendation algorithm by 10%. The company paid the winning team but never implemented their solution. According to Netflix, the 'additional accuracy gains that we measured did not seem to justify the engineering effort needed to bring them into a production environment.' In fact, the winning algorithm was loaded with variables that just had no face validity to be in the model (e.g. 'the number of characters in the title of the movie'), but were kept in because they improved the model's predictive power. This is a danger with Big Data: prediction is not explanation.

Second, there is an issue with statistical significance. Because Big Data is based on a huge number of observations, virtually every variable used in the models will be statistically significantly different from zero – i.e. important. However, how do we deal with very small effects that are statistically significant? In 2012, Facebook and Cornell university set up an experiment to study 'emotional contagion', using a huge sample size of 689,003 Facebook users (Table 15). By manipulating messages in these users' News Feeds, the study tested whether exposure to specific positive or negative emotions led people to change their own behaviour. Two parallel experiments were conducted, one in which subjects' exposure to friends' positive emotional content in their News Feed was reduced, and one in which their exposure to friends' negative emotional content was reduced. And indeed, the study saw a change in the emotional content of status updates by the users. More negative feeds led to more negative updates and vice versa.

Table 15. Cornell and Facebook study of emotional contagion

PARAMETER TESTED		- REDUCED		+ REDUCED
GROUP TYPE	CONTROL	EXPERIMENTAL	CONTROL	EXPERIMENTAL
Positive words %	5.25	5.30*	5.27	5.12
Negative Words %	1.75	1.69	1.74	1.77

- reduced=exposer to friends' negative emotional content reduced;
+ reduced=exposure to friends positive emotional content reduced.
*When negative emotional content in subjects' News Feed was reduced, their status updates had a slightly higher % of positive words (5.30 vs. 5.25), as well as a slightly lower % of negative words (1.69 versus 1.75).
These differences were statistically significant because of the huge sample sizes in the study.

Source: Kramera, Guillory, and Hancock, 'Experimental Evidence of Massive-Scale Emotional Contagion Through Social Networks, PNAS, 111(24) June 17, 2014.

Now, these results may seem interesting and informative, but what do they really mean? Even though the effects are statistically significant, they are tiny. In the words of Tal Yarkoni, from the University of Texas at Austin: 'Eliminating a substantial proportion of emotional content from a user's feed had the monumental effect of shifting that user's own emotional word use by two hundredths of a standard deviation. In other words, the manipulation had a negligible real-world impact on users' behaviour. Theoretically interesting, perhaps, but not very meaningful in practice.'

This is one of the key problems with Big Data. Using the example above, one can imagine an interest group getting on their '1984 Ministry of Thought' high horse, and theoretically there is some support for that, but practically speaking it is a washout, really.

Third, there is the question of how managerial intuition and Big Data 'insights' can be integrated. There are views which argue that the challenge of Big Data is that we need to learn to trust our judgment less, to relinquish the 'marketing guts' that we so admire in marketing legends like Leo Burnett — and that we like to think we see in ourselves — and learn to collaborate with machines. Rather than trying to use data to inform our judgment, we would do much better to put our energy into building improved models, but take their answers at face value.

But if managers only use Big Data' results to confirm their own intuition, there is no need for Big Data, is there? Is it possible to change managers' mindsets, knowing their bonus hinges on a conflict between what their intuition tells them to do and what Big Data proposes? After all, we like to think of ourselves as experts with an intuitive feel for the marketplace, don't we? We like being respected for our judgments and our special gift of insight. In the end, we will have to decide what's more important: our intrinsic feeling of self-worth, or winning in the marketplace based on unbiased technology-generated insights.

Fourth and last, there are ethical issues to address in this context. When Big Data is mentioned, Big Brother is never far away. The Facebook experiment on emotional contagion we mentioned has led to a heated debate: should a company be allowed to manipulate its customers to test their emotional states? The British newspaper *The Guardian* (July 1, 2014) was not pleased when it failed to get decent answers from the Facebook experiment researchers on relevant questions: 'Whoever we ask, nobody seems to know anything. Did the study have ethical approval? First the answer was yes. Then it was no. Then it was maybe. Then it was no again. Was it funded by the US Army? First the university said yes. Then it said no, without explanation. Why did the scientific journal not state whether the study was ethically approved, as required by its own policy? "Sorry," editor Susan Fiske told me, "I'm too busy to answer that question".'

A very well-known example of unapproved data mining is that of American retailer Target, a forerunner on data analysis, which used such mining to predict when ladies would sign up for baby registries, an important part of their business. Target was able to identify about 25 products that, when analysed together, allowed them to assign each shopper a 'pregnancy prediction' score (amongst others, unscented lotion, soap, cotton balls, and supplements like calcium, magnesium and zinc). The retailer started sending coupons for baby items to customers according to their pregnancy scores, until one day a father complained that his teenage daughter was receiving coupons for baby clothes and cribs, which he thought was very inappropriate. It wasn't very long, though, before he found out that Target was right and that there had been activities going on in his house he hadn't been aware of...

As long as Big Data simply allows for more attractive promotions, people don't seem to mind, but when data analysis discovers embarrassing truths we don't like to see uncovered, it's a different story. There is a striking analogy with the 'uncanny valley' hypothesis of robotics professor Masahiro Mori. He stated that as the appearance of a robot is made more human, people's emotional response to it becomes increasingly positive and empathic, until a point is reached where it starts to look and behave very much like a human, and the response quickly becomes that of strong revulsion.

An illustration: price obfuscation, a dangerous game

Not surprisingly, a huge target for Big Data is the management of pricing and promotions at retail. Advanced analysis is used by retailers to optimize price levels and promotional mechanisms, aiming for maximal shopper response as well as an optimal margin mix. A logical goal that is, however, not without danger.

Shopping at Waitrose at London's Canary Wharf, I stumbled upon two prawn offers. Waitrose 'essential' (budget line) prawns were £2.99 for 150g. Next to this were Waitrose 'normal' (own label) prawns at 4£ for 200g. Indeed, the essential prawns looked a lot cheaper at first sight, but actually, per kg the difference was 6p, hardly 0.3%! Is this what Waitrose hopes the shopper will understand? Moreover, the normal prawns were in promotion, 'Buy 2 for 6£', which made them 24.89% cheaper per kilo than the essential prawns. How many shoppers can figure all this out?

There is a science to using Big Data to manage retail prices. Sometimes cutting prices on products can improve margins. How? By cutting the price on a very high margin product, you drive additional volumes. While the margin on that item is lower than before, your overall margins might still go up, because you sell more of those still- higher-margin items in the mix. That goes some way to explaining the large number of price changes retailers carry out every week. Retailers gladly communicate that they have been cutting prices on a huge number of items. They are a lot quieter about price increases, though... Table 16 provides revealing 2014 figures for large UK retailers.

Own label products are another excellent source of margin management. These products are not directly comparable across retailers, different levels of quality justify different pricing levels, and...pack sizes can be amended to pass on hidden price increases.

And it gets even more sophisticated when we look at Figure 7, based on a recent study at the University of Warwick (Chakraborty, Dobson, Seaton and Waterson, 'Pricing in Inflationary Times – the Penny Drops,' 2012). The vertical axis shows the price change in pence, while the horizontal axis shows the direction of the price movement. To a chain that is predominantly making price cuts, a value of +1 is assigned. If for that price change a chain is predominantly raising prices, a value of -1 would be assigned. The four major retailers in the UK have been monitored: T(esco), S(ainsbury), M(orrisons) and A(sda). The graph shows there are more price reductions than price increases, but for 7p and more the increases dominate, meaning the increases are bigger in value that the decreases. Is this very clever, very naughty, or both?

Table 16. Year-on—year price changes for identical products at UK grocery retailers

	% PRICE INCREASES	% SAME PRICES	% PRICE CUTS
WAITROSE	29	56	15
TESCO	30	50	20
ASDA	27	50	23
MORRISONS	30	46	24
SAINSBURY'S	39	35	26

Source: mySupermarket.com, Bernstein analysis, 2014.

Figure 7. Proportion of price falls and increases and their respective magnitudes at UK grocery retailers. Source: Chakraborty, Dobson, Seaton, Waterson, 'Pricing in Inflationary Times – the Penny Drops,' 2012.

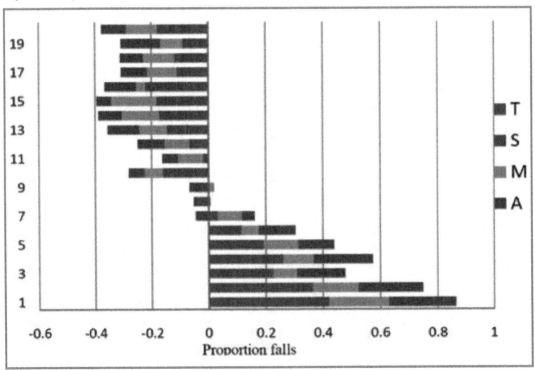

So although throughout this sample more prices fall than rise (at least for Tesco and Asda), average basket prices still rise. The price falls are much smaller than the price rises. Hence, the companies can claim they are engaged in a price war, lowering prices, without it actually hurting too much. Price 'mudification' is another term used for this type of pricing behaviour.

Of course, in one form or another, price obfuscation has always been part of the retail game. An item used to sell at $19.99; today this item is 10% cheaper, but contains 15% less stuff. This item is $99.99, but for today only, there's a 15% discount, and a 'stackable' BOGOF 50%, and a special 10% discount on any one item before noon…

The mechanisms abound, and most benefit from the fact that consumers are not great at math. One wonders what shoppers make of all these sophisticated price offers when the majority of them are uncomfortable with simple percentages. Will technology and Big Data weaken the ability of retailers to obfuscate prices or will they become even more sophisticated? Will the mathematicians who used to work for hedge funds cook up some 'out of this world' pricing schemes to optimize retailers' profits? In the last decade, online searching has aimed at normalizing prices online; high penetration of smartphones and related apps allow consumers to look up products and compare while they are on the move and shopping in-store. However, for consumers that have a hard time understanding percentages, how much help will this information bring? At the same time, of course, the hard discounters are offering everyday low prices…and they are easy to understand for every shopper.

Retailers have to be careful with their pricing games because, after a while, collectively, shoppers figure them out. For all their pricing sophistication and Dunnhumby's Big Data analysis, Tesco let their average price raise relative not just to hard discounters but also to Asda, and paid a huge price: they lost more than 50% of their market cap and their CEO and several senior managers were fired. Retailers can and should optimize prices, but they have to make sure they don't snow their shoppers with significantly higher prices than their competitors. Shoppers notice and react. That is why the retail business is so prone to price wars.

Revealing the potential
Notwithstanding the caveats expressed above, Big Data combined with advanced analytics, cognitive computing and artificial intelligence has tremendous potential, for both retailers and brand owners. Let's develop three striking examples: marketing-mix ROI, geographical retail pricing and multichannel retailing.

The road towards profitable marketing-mix decisions
Promotions are a very complex phenomenon. Even if they result in higher sales volumes, how do we know they really create value or profit? A lot of data and methodologies are needed to assess their profitability and desirability. A promotion causes a lift in sales, but a price discount is needed, along with vendor funding as a direct contribution. There are incremental marketing costs, supply chain costs, store labour costs. Sales may be cannibalized, and there is the 'pull forward effect' of reduced sales following a promotion. So, where is your real incremental margin? In order to measure all these effects for a multitude of products and SKUs across a large number of categories, extensive data and analytics are needed. Big Data and its complements will enable retailers and brand owners to make this analysis almost a routine job and save billions of dollars by reducing ineffective and unprofitable promotions.

Figure 8. The decomposition of the effects of price promotions.

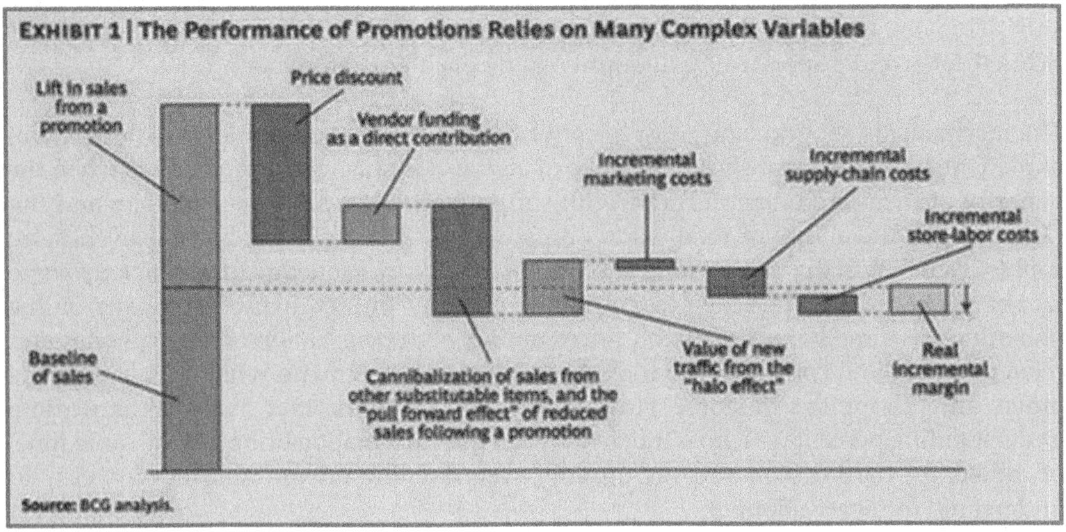

EXHIBIT 1 | The Performance of Promotions Relies on Many Complex Variables

Lift in sales from a promotion

Price discount

Vendor funding as a direct contribution

Incremental marketing costs

Incremental supply-chain costs

Incremental store-labor costs

Baseline of sales

Cannibalization of sales from other substitutable items, and the "pull forward effect" of reduced sales following a promotion

Value of new traffic from the "halo effect"

Real incremental margin

Source: BCG analysis.

Source: Souza, Jensen, Kaestner, and Potere, 'Making Big Data Work: Retailing,' BCG Perspectives, June 2014.

However, more data and better tools don't always guarantee better management. Ever since marketers have had the availability of scanner data, we have seen a huge increase in promotions. Individually, they might have been effective and profitable, at least in the sense of leading to sales growth in flat categories. But as a whole, what has been the effect on brand equity and consumer price sensitivity? Haven't marketers and retailers been producing price-promotion junkies?

Personalized promotions may be the answer. Indeed, Big Data makes real-time personalization possible. Retailers may offer different promotions and price levels to particular shoppers. After all, shoppers show significant differences in the prices they are willing to pay for one product, but when they visit a store, all shoppers receive the same promotional offers. Some shoppers are more sensitive than others to these promotions, which is how retailers discriminate between high- and low-price-sensitive shoppers in their stores. However, using Big Data, retailers can go much further and offer tailor-made prices and promotions to each shopper.

Well documented are the Big Data initiatives by American retailer Sears. A new open-source data-processing platform called Hadoop allows the retailer to perform daily analyses of marketing campaigns and target individual customers. The company keeps all its customers' history in minute detail. The system captures analyses and reports on customer activity at an individual level, across every SKU at all 4,000 store locations. As a result, Sears's loyalty card customers receive individual coupons tailored just for them. These offers are based on where shoppers live, how many products are in the local store, the products Sears thinks the customer will like and how much of a particular product the retailer wants to get rid of in that store.

Recently, Albert Heijn in the Netherlands introduced a new loyalty card that allows for a more personalized promotion strategy. Since the introduction of this new Bonus card, a smaller number of shoppers receive promotions, but these promotions prove to be more effective.

Consider this current market test from from market research company GfK in Germany, illustrating what personalizing promotions could do for a crate of beer normally sold at €19,50. Consumers show significant differences in the price they are willing to pay for the product; while beer lover Kurt is willing to pay 22,70 €, Jenni sets the bar at 18,75 € and bargain hunter Heike wouldn't pay more than 16,20 €. Table 17 shows what occurs when they all receive the same promotion of 17,00 €: there is lost revenue of 5,70 € when Kurt buys the discounted crate; of 1,75 when Jenni buys it; and even 16,20 € in the case of Heike, who doesn't buy it at all. That makes 23,65 € of lost revenue in total.

Table 17. Consumers' Idiosyncratic price points

Consumer	Kurt	Jenni	Heike
Willing to pay	22,70	18,75	16,20
Lost revenue at 17,00 € discount price	5,70	1,75	16,20

Source: Gfk Germany, 2014.

Table 18 shows a different picture if discounts are moulded to individual consumer preferences. The normal (vanilla) price will be set at the level of the person with the highest willingness to pay, i.e. Kurt at €22.70. There is no need to offer a promotion to Kurt, as he is willing to pay the full price anyway. To convince Jenni to buy, a an 18% discount, to €18,75, is optimal; and to convince Heike, a discount of 28%, to €16,20.

Table 18. Idiosyncratic Retail Pricing

Consumer	Kurt	Jenni	Heike
Optimal promotional price	No promotion	18,75 or a discount of 18%	16,20 or a discount of 28%

Source: Gfk Germany, 2014

But the dangers of such a Big Data–driven approach are not to be underestimated. First, the retailer would need to set normal shelf prices very high to be able to get as big a margin as possible from the shoppers with the highest reservation prices. These vanilla prices will make the store look very expensive, compared to EDLP discounters and other retailers that do not use Big Data to discriminate prices. Second, how will the shopper take the fact that he has to pay a much higher price than say his friend just because he likes the product more or because he is richer? One might argue that airlines do it, but they offer tangible differences in the product and service offerings (e.g. check-in privileges, lounges, leg room, luggage facilities, meals).

Another potentially big advantage Big Data offers brand owners and retailers alike is the opportunity to get serious about measuring the ROI of their marketing investments and to optimize the allocation of their marketing and sales resources to the various marketing-mix instruments. Most sizable companies have become adept at measuring the return on their investments in a wide variety of areas — whether production processes at a consumer goods manufacturer, logistics in a transportation firm, or R&D in a pharmaceutical company. Such has been less the case with marketing. In many companies, marketing has operated below the radar of traditional performance metrics because it has been viewed by non-marketers as a creative process that's not easily measured by the same type of objective metrics long employed to gauge the effectiveness of other, more systematic and mechanized processes. That's not to say marketers have been undisciplined when determining where and how to spend their money. On the contrary, marketing—like any other function—has always undergone a formal budgeting process operating within the financial constraints of the larger business. However, because most companies have found it difficult to fully quantify marketing's value to the organization in terms of cold, hard cash, other metrics have served as the best indicators of marketing's contribution to overall business performance: brand health, direct-marketing response rates and numbers of prospective customers reached by ads. This, in turn, has precluded marketers from basing their budgeting and investment decisions on a strong financial fact base.

Big Data now offers a basis for assessing the effectiveness of various marketing investments. Consider the following example reported in the *Harvard Business Review* ('Advertising Analytics 2.0,' March 2013), from a company, MarketShare, that specializes in measuring marketing effectiveness based on Big Data. As shown in Figure 9, in analysing the holiday communication campaign for a consumer electronics company, MarketShare found that online searches of the manufacturer's name spiked in direct response to TV advertising. Advanced analytics revealed that the company could have made far better use of cross-media effects on retail traffic. Although digital media accounted for only 15% of the budget, it accounted for almost 40% of the product's retail sales. This led to a reallocation of media investments and 9% more revenue for the same total budget.

Figure 9 part 1. Media effectiveness measurement.

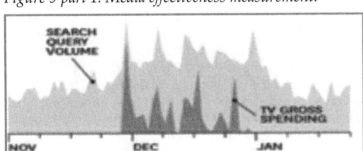

Source: Wes Nichols, 'Advertising Analytics 2.0,' Harvard Business Review, March 2013.

Figure 9 part 2. Media effectiveness measurement.

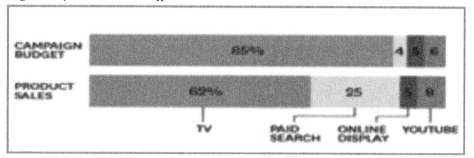

Source: Wes Nichols, 'Advertising Analytics 2.0,' Harvard Business Review, March 2013.

Figure 9 part 3. Media effectiveness measurement.

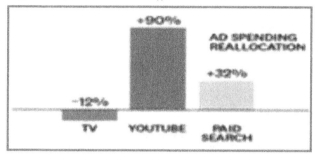

Source: Wes Nichols, 'Advertising Analytics 2.0,' Harvard Business Review, March 2013.

Detailed pricing zones across regions

Geographical retail pricing means that retailers change their prices to adjust to the local geographical characteristics of their stores' trading areas. Big Data and analytics allow them to construct far better and more profitable retail pricing structures than were possible before, when the data and analytics were not available. A study by Boston Consulting Group showed that analysing customer shopping behaviour led to better pricing across regions, while pricing zones before the geo-analytical approach largely mirrored state boundaries (BCG Perspectives, Making Big Data Work, June 2014).

The multichannel shopper

A third example shows how Big Data can turbocharge a company's ability to identify its most valuable customers. Are internet shoppers more valuable than brick and mortar shoppers, or vice versa? What about customers combining internet with catalogue and brick and mortar stores? Collecting multichannel data is far from easy, but very important. And it doesn't end there. Once a retailer has found out that multichannel shoppers are more profitable, how can they incite other customers to become multichannel shoppers, to increase their profitability? Or is it that the big customers are already multichannel? Even more data is needed to test for causality…

[13] 'State of the Industry Research Series: Big Data in Retail,' Edgell Knowledge Network, 2014.

Figure 10. Customer value and multichannel retail.

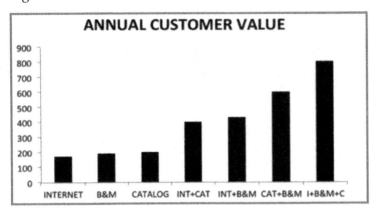

Source: S Neslin, 'Marketing Analytics in a Data-Rich Environment,' MSI conference, San Francisco, July 31-August 1, 2014. (Edited highlights)

Opportunities and pitfalls

Consider the specificities of the retail sector: you have thousands of stores; hundreds of thousands of product SKUs to be sourced, shipped and sold; tens of millions of customers; billions of transactions – retail is almost synonymous with Big Data. US retailers alone store more than 500 petabytes of data (one petabyte being 1000 terabytes). Meanwhile, at a micro level, every shopper signed up to a retailer's loyalty program is a walking data generator, closing dozens of transactions a year, online and offline, using multiple communication channels (web, mobile, email, kiosk, phone, social media). But are retailers ready to capture, process and analyse these growing data sets?

Only a few of them are. While 80% of retailers are aware of the Big Data concept, and 47% understand the impact of Big Data to their business, only 30% have executed a Big Data project and a mere 5% have or are creating a Big Data strategy[13].
There is no denying that Big Data helps create great opportunities in retail. A good example is Kroger, which state explicitly how Big Data is their secret weapon in the grocery wars. Dunnhumby, one of the Big Data experts in retail, has 120 analysts working full time on Kroger's business, sifting through 300 terabytes of data from 40 billion purchases made from 4 billion shopping trips by 42 million card-owners over two years. The results? Personalisation of communication and promotions has been driving incremental sales and profitability for over a decade. A Kroger pilot store in Cincinnati leverages data to serve up real-time coupons to consumers in different aisles of the store. The sophisticated Kroger mailing program reaches 11 million households, and 97% of the coupons are personalized.

On the flip side, Big Data and data mining will never replace managerial insight from passionate managers, from talented humans obsessed with the attitude 'Never stop asking why'. We can illustrate this with an example from Wal-Mart, the biggest retailer in the world, owner of the planet's largest retail data warehouse. Through data mining, the retailer discovered that in towns where a tornado is forecast, their stores sell up to seven times more strawberry Pop-Tarts than usual. But where's the insight? ABC News interviewed Steve Horwitz, an economist at St. Lawrence University in Canton, New York, who studied Wal-Mart's response to Hurricane Katrina, who told them: 'Over the course of their experience with hurricanes, Wal-Mart has learned that strawberry Pop-Tarts are one of the most purchased food items, especially for after storms, as they require no heating, can be used at any meal and last forever.' Horwitz noted that when a tornado is coming, consumers stock up on the following items:

1   Non-perishable food that can be eaten easily, without cooking such as Pop-Tarts & bread
2   Bottled water
3   Bleach, mops and other cleaning supplies
4   Flashlights/candles, etc.
5   First-aid supplies
6   Generators
7   Batteries

Now, do we really need the world's largest data mining tool to get to this? With Big Data, managerial judgment and insight become more important than ever. More information is not always a good thing. Someone has to figure out what is important and what is not. Sophisticated analytics applied to reams of data don't always lead to better decisions. Just look at what happened in the banking industry and the financial markets in 2008-2009.

The point is, sophisticated algorithms and analytical tools are a means to an end. They do not constitute a competitive advantage as such. They can help marketers take better decisions, but marketers should not take data-based decisions automatically. Companies still need skilled analysts to distinguish relevant from irrelevant data, and talented managers to take and execute the right commercial decisions. Analytics and marketing should not work in separate silos. Building mixed teams of people with analytical and commercial skills might be a great idea.

Putting the shopper first?

The rather staggering way in which Tesco took over the British retail scene during the '90s provided a lot of ammunition for Big Data believers. It wasn't called Big Data at the time, but in spirit it boiled down to a precursor of the Big Data approach. At the core of Tesco's success, they argued, was an unparalleled ability to understand the UK shopper. Tesco was considered to be the first retailer to put the shopper at the apex of everything they did, driven by Big Data. The introduction of the Tesco Club Card in 1995 proved to be a real game-changer in the UK retail world. While loyalty schemes were nothing new, Tesco was the first retailer able to integrate loyalty card data with checkout purchase data to turn those data into profitable information, translating them into improved product assortments and personalised coupons, discounts and rewards. They did so in close partnership with Dunnhumby, hailed as the pinnacle of retail consulting because of their ability to make the data sing and dance to dissect and understand the shopper like no one else could. Tesco was their biggest customer until the retailer finally actually bought them.

This capability to analyse shopper data and turn them into useful information was one of the key reasons why Tesco could credibly argue that making the customer central was the reason for their success in the UK between 1990-2010, as their CEO, Terry Leahy, explained in his autobiography.

Now, in hindsight, it appears there were other drivers behind Tesco's success. In fact, Tesco's massive store expansion, their powerful and highly motivated army of store managers, the passive behaviour of their traditional competitors and the marginal presence of strong hard discounters in the UK were other major factors contributing to Tesco's success during that period. Tesco won the race for space, for sure, but it is having problems winning the race for differentiation, it is now clear.

Customers' concerns for privacy can have a negative impact on their willingness to purchase online, shows a study by Neslin ('Multichannel Customer Management,' *International Journal of Research in Marketing,* 2007, vol 24, pp. 129-148). Another study indicates that consumers may even be willing to pay a premium for privacy (JY Tsai, S Egelman, L Cranor, A Acquisti, 'The Effect of Online Privacy Information on Purchasing Behavior: An Experimental Study,' Information Systems Research, June 2011, pp. 254-268). Accessed at www.guanotronic.com/~serge/papers/isr10. pdf). Privacy issues are not just a concern for older generations. A very interesting study from USC's Annenberg Institute ('Is Online Privacy Over?' 2013) shows that millennials are also concerned about allowing access to their personal data or their web behavior. However, they are willing to share their specific location to receive coupons or deals from nearby businesses. Privacy versus real value offered is the key issue.

Privacy versus value offered

'I buy my meat in one store, my tomatoes in another store and my herbs on the other side of the street. Otherwise, with their statistics, they will discover my secret pasta sauce recipe.' Silly as it may be, this joke by cartoonist Philippe Geluck (Le Chat) illustrates people's awareness of the use of shoppers' data by retailers – and even more by e-tailers. There is no Big Data without…data. Will shoppers remain willing to share data on their whereabouts and their buying behavior, and what do they expect in return?

Customers' concerns for privacy can have a negative impact on their willingness to purchase online, shows a study by Neslin ('Multichannel Customer Management,' International Journal of Research in Marketing, 2007, vol 24, pp. 129-148). Another study indicates that consumers may even be willing to pay a premium for privacy (JY Tsai, S Egelman, L Cranor, A Acquisti, 'The Effect of Online Privacy Information on Purchasing Behavior: An Experimental Study,' Information Systems Research, June 2011, pp. 254-268). Accessed at www.guanotronic.com/~serge/papers/isr10. pdf). Privacy issues are not just a concern for older generations. A very interesting study from USC's Annenberg Institute ('Is Online Privacy Over?' 2013) shows that millennials are also concerned about allowing access to their personal data or their web behavior. However, they are willing to share their specific location to receive coupons or deals from nearby businesses. Privacy versus real value offered is the key issue.

In recent years, the market situation has changed dramatically. Aldi and Lidl are investing in aggressive growth, increasing price pressure on the British market. On the other side of the competitive spectrum, the other major players are getting their act together by offering better value to shoppers. Finally, their accelerated international growth syphoned off many of their top UK store management executives. Now the retailer sees its profits fall and doesn't seem capable of finding appropriate answers to these shifting market conditions. Still, Tesco uses its Club Card and has Dunnhumby going in overdrive, analysing the hell out of bigger and bigger data from shoppers and using increasingly sophisticated analytics and artificial intelligence tools. Without much in the way of results, so far… What's more, Tesco is considering selling Dunnhumby. Could it be that there is more to retail than Big Data?

Chapter Insights

1   There is tremendous hype on how the digital transformation will fundamentally change every industry. Managers should be careful not to get caught up in it, even at the risk of being seen as 'old hat'. The fact that recent research shows that good old TV advertising still has a significantly better ROI than digital communication is a good illustration.

2   Big Data opens up new sources for improving brand owners' and retailers' business models. However, this will take time, and the industry has to avoid trying to run faster than the consumer and the shopper it is trying to better satisfy. Price obfuscation at retail being a case in point of getting carried away by technical sophistication while consumers are left behind, confused.

3   The best insights, algorithms and decision rules (e.g. for price, promo, shelf space, advertising spend) based on optimised Big Data methodologies, will not be used if the manager does not understand them or if they seem counterintuitive. There will be rich pickings for organisations that manage to meld the skills of managers who feel they have the experience and marketing nous, with the insights from IT driven analysts who often dismiss these traditional managers as irrational dinosaurs.

Chapter 4
Doing Good or Doing Well – or Both?

'In ten to fifteen years, people will be making all of their choices based on "Is this good?" Is this good for my skin? Is this good for my hair? Is this good for my kids? Is this good for the planet? It will motivate the entire economy. We are moving to a place where all purchase decisions will be made based on empathy. Do I care? How does it impact me? And do these brands care about my well-being?"

Eddy Moretti, chief creative officer at Vice, the influential online media company, is convinced that brands will need to radically alter the way they do business and communicate if they want to survive the next decade. Millennials are setting new standards. In their worldview, companies need to take responsibility, and sustainability is becoming one of the reasons why they might prefer one brand over another. The conclusion seems to be that building brand penetration will require a sustainable business model. In a transparent world, trust becomes a vital asset.

It is no coincidence that Unilever recently announced a partnership with Vice, to become the launch sponsor of a new women-focused-content channel. Broadly, the FMCG multinational is a strong believer and trailblazer in corporate social responsibility (CSR). 'We are proving that there is no contradiction between sustainable and profitable growth. We are seeing increasingly how sustainability drives growth of our brands, reduces our costs and manages our risks,' says Paul Polman, Unilever's media-savvy CEO. The quote illustrates the publicly stated common stance of consumer goods multinationals regarding CSR nowadays. Most companies publish a social responsibility report as an addition to their annual report, officially embracing the well-known 'people, planet, profit' mantra coined by British sustainability expert John Elkington during the '90s. But not all of them go as far as Unilever.

Polman has positioned Unilever's Sustainable Living Plan at the heart of the company strategy and states that sustainable, equitable growth is the only acceptable business model. He acts as an evangelist on sustainability (it is said that as a young man, he toyed with the idea of becoming a priest) and speaks at all the right conferences. This approach seems to pay off, at least for Paul Polman himself, since he received a sizeable bonus from Unilever's board to reward his contribution to the performance of the group in terms of sustainable development. Clear proof that sustainable development is not incompatible with (personal) profit, one might say. And his company, Unilever, is probably one of the most rewarded multinationals in this field, leading several sustainability indexes. The question is, can a publicly quoted corporation, acting in highly competitive markets, really be consistent on social responsibility in all its aspects?

Unilever may have been leading the Food Producers sector of the Dow Jones Sustainability Indexes for years, but it is also the biggest ice cream manufacturer in the world. What about obesity – and especially child obesity? Yes, Dove has taken an unorthodox position in focusing away from 'model zeroes' and going for the 'beauty inside'. Its ambition of strengthening women's self-esteem is indeed inspirational and courageous. However, at the same time Unilever has a successful deodorant brand (Axe/Lynx) showing clips of testosterone-fuelled young men chasing women as sex objects. How consistent is that? At least Danone walked the talk when it took the decision to focus on being a healthy food company, selling their most profitable business, the brewery Kronenbourg, as well as their biscuits division.

To what extent CSR can really drive penetration remains to be seen, but at any rate, neglecting the sustainability issue may cause serious problems for brand owners. All too easily, food manufacturers come under fire from consumer organizations, food activists or even respected politicians who are not always as well informed as they are supposed to be. Recently Ségolène Royal, the current French minister of ecology, made public statements that the Ferrero company should be forbidden to sell Nutella in France because it contains palm oil. Royal said in a television interview that the use of palm oil was leading to 'massive deforestation', which was a cause of global warming. But soon she had to apologize and congratulate Nutella and Ferrero, after Greenpeace confirmed that Ferrero was using only ecologically certified sources of palm oil…

Three Attitudes Towards CSR

According to Jean Tirole, the 2014 Nobel Prize laureate in economic sciences, companies may adopt one of three attitudes with regard to corporate social responsibility:

1 They embrace CSR because they expect it to be profitable in the short term. And indeed, some consumers are prepared to pay more for 'fair trade' or ecological products, for example. Some managers are willing to accept lower wages while working for 'honest' companies or sustainable investment funds. But where is the pay-off? On the stock market, we can find multiple investment funds for 'well-behaved companies' that are environmentally friendly, sustainable, socially responsible. How do they perform? Not too well, really. Alternative energy stocks lost 50% of their value during the last 5 years, while the S&P doubled. Morgan Stanley's sustainability indices all underperform. Of course, they should underperform, given the fact that these shares are held by 'do-gooders' who ask a lower risk premium. Now compare that to the performance of so-called 'sin stocks' like the 'Seven Deadly Sins' index fund from Motif: those tend to outperform the market (see Figure 11). There seems to be no automatic link between doing good and doing well.

Figure 11. Performance of Motif's 'Seven Deadly Sins' index fund (top line) versus S&P 500 (bottom line).

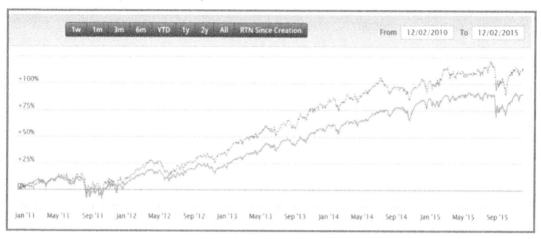

Source: Motif Investing, 2015.

Professors Hong (NYU) and Kacperczyk (Princeton), writing in *the Journal of Financial Economics, in 2009* found that investors have gained 2.5% more per year investing in sin stocks like Harrah's Entertainment and Diageo (responsible for spirits ranging from Guinness to Smirnoff) than in companies of comparable size in other sectors. The study defined sin stocks as those of companies involved in alcohol, tobacco and gaming between 1926 to 2006. One reason why sin stocks outperform is because some investors shun them outright. "Because of social norms, some investors find it unsuitable to hold certain stocks," Kacperczyk said. This reduces the demand for these stocks and thereby increases their risk. To compensate for this higher risk, these sin stocks have to produce higher returns.

2   Companies may adopt a CSR strategy because they believe consumers will leave them in the long run if they don't. This seems to be Unilever's stance, judging from Paul Polman's 2015 statement: 'We now have the opportunity to eradicate poverty and deal with the issue of climate change. What bigger opportunity do you want to see? If we don't all tackle climate change in a constructive way, global growth will be stifled.'

There is a sense by some observers that 'sinful' companies will have a hard time surviving in the long term, as society and its consumers are becoming more sensitive to social and environmental issues. Moreover, a sustainable strategy might have direct implications for the company itself: it is in the interest of fish-processing companies to keep the fish population in equilibrium; chocolate manufacturers need to ensure future cocoa sourcing.

3   A third motive for a CSR strategy may be purely philanthropic. While the first two attitudes are motivated by normal business objectives, this third motive is not based on a monetary payback. Of course, managers are free to practice philanthropy on an individual basis, with their own money, but there is no reason why they should do so with their shareholders' money.

It seems that many companies are driven by the second, long-term motive, although some seem to be closer to philanthropy altogether. But let's not be naive. It's not a bad idea to be somewhat sceptical about what companies say and do in the context of CSR. Are they doing good, or just doing well?

Take a look at Innocent, the smoothie brand that donates 10% of its profits to charity. As their website states: 'Ever since we began, we've always given some of our profits to charity. In 2004 we started the Innocent foundation, which funds projects in the UK and all over the world to alleviate hunger.' This sounds commendable and very generous indeed. Could it be, God forbid, that Innocent has done some pricing analysis to find out which price and charitable donation will maximize short-term profits? If Innocent's move were purely philanthropic, they wouldn't need to mention it at all, would they? The mere fact that they mention it will probably convince some more consumers to buy an Innocent drink rather than a competing product – which they would have bought if there were no charitable donation. And why the 10% donation, and not 5% or 15%? It is probably too cynical to think that the 10% donation maximizes profits for Innocent?

Obesity: The Elephant in the Kitchen

Corporate social responsibility can refer to many different issues: environmental, social, ethical… In the FMCG scene, one issue stands out: obesity. Even if the statistics are familiar, they are overwhelming. This is a major social problem, relevant to food brand owners but also to retailers selling food products and producing them under their private labels. The question is, can food brands be blamed for obesity? How should they react?

The Innocent Drinks case is a good starting point to explain the problem. Innocent is a relatively new brand, developed in 1999 by three young entrepreneurs and sold by them to Coca-Cola in 2013.

It all started out as a very nice and attractive story, though. The three friends were driven by a serious amount of idealism from the start. They wanted to do something good for mankind, which as a result led to something good for themselves as well. Doing good and doing well, they would offer wholesome fruit juices (smoothies) without any additives. They had many interesting and original flavours and fruits, and they used their carton packaging to tell consumers about their originality, the healthiness of their product and the fact that they donated 10% of their profits to charity. They emphasized that the product was made of wholesome fruits with nothing added – being purely natural, the products must be good. And they also focused on the motto '5 fruits a day will keep the doctor away', emphasizing that the smoothies contain all the juice and fibre of the original fruit. A great story, isn't it? So great, indeed, that the Coca-Cola company paid £320 million for the 'ethical' brand. Actually, if consumers see Innocent smoothies as a treat and drink a small glass of the stuff, it has many of the positives the brand claims. However, there is another side to the story.

Experts from the World Health Organization (WHO) assert there should be a reduction of free sugars intake to 5% of total calorie intake, translated into a recommended daily allowance (RDA) of about 25 grams of sugar per day, given a typical adult allowance of about 2000 calories per day. Following Innocent's serving suggestion of 250ml, one serving would provide 27.3 g of sugars, or 109% of the adult RDA.

Logically, Innocent labelling should include the RDA for sugars (109%). It doesn't. After repeatedly trying to confront them with this, the only response I could get was that Innocent is as natural as the fruit it is made of, that it is very healthy for humans and that it is the second best thing humans can do for their health, after giving up smoking. An Innocent employee calling himself Rio stated, 'So we think it's crazy to label fruit or fruit smoothies and juice as unhealthy.'

Well, I tend to disagree. Natural products like fruit do contain sugar and calories. It is not difficult for an adult to drink the whole carton (one litre) and thus take in four times their WHO RDA at one sitting. Drinking a carton of Innocent is equivalent to eating seven fruits, including the calories of these seven fruits. Now, nobody would sit down and peal and eat seven oranges, would they? Drinking a couple of glasses of an orange smoothie from Innocent is easy and very enjoyable, no question. But is it good for you? Only in small amounts, as a sweet treat, as a dessert.

Maybe Innocent is not as innocent as we are told to believe.

A spoonful of sugar
The obesity debate isn't new, but the nature of this debate has evolved over the past decades. For a long period of time, saturated fat was seen as the main enemy in the battle against obesity, and from the '80s on, food manufacturers started reducing the saturated fat content of their products, substituting animal fats with unsaturated, hydrogenated vegetable oils, also known as trans-fats, and considered dangerous today. On top of that, they substituted sugar for fat to enhance the taste and texture of these lower-fat foods. As a result, a large number of food products found on supermarket shelves today contain 'hidden' added sugars. Everybody realizes, of course, that there is sugar in candy bars or ice cream. But who would expect to find added sugars in soups, sauces, pizzas, ready meals, potato snacks or processed meats? A spoonful of sugar helps the medicine go down, indeed. Even health-conscious consumers trying to avoid sugar by steering clear of cakes, confectionery and soft drinks may in fact be taking in much more added sugar than they imagine through foods (such as breads or sauces) that have traditionally been low in sugar, but are now adulterated in this way.

The fat and sugar issue cannot be overestimated by food brands and retailers. An astonishing amount of evidence is against them.

First, it has been scientifically proven that fat and sugar have a well-established causal link to obesity.

Second, there is no scientific doubt that obesity leads to comorbidities including diabetes, various cancers and cardiovascular problems.

And third, there is a strong suspicion that fat and sugar are addictive. Even if this thesis hasn't been fully accepted yet, more and more research strongly points in this direction. Brain scans have shown that people who are obese have fewer dopamine receptors, just like people who are addicted to cocaine or alcohol. 'Neurological similarities exist in the response of humans to foods and to drugs,' says a study by Corin and Grigson ('Food Addiction: Fact or Fiction,' *Journal of Nutrition*, January 2009).

'The food industry obviously manipulates the qualities of its foods to maximize desirability. That's what they're in business to do. But if some foods start taking over the brain to create a biological demand, that's a problem. Both animal and human studies suggest that an addictive process is profoundly possible,' states Kelly Brownell, Director of Yale University's Rudd Center for Food Policy & Obesity.

Further proof on the addictive nature of sugars and fats would put the food industry in a very uncomfortable position. Even if food manufacturers admit there is a problem with obesity, they argue along three lines to neutralize criticism. First, they state that there are no good or bad foods, it is all about quantity and variety. Second, people don't exercise enough. You need to burn off the calories you eat. And third, people are free to choose what they eat. No food brand forces consumers to eat their products, and no government should constrain what one can and cannot eat. The last point hinges on the addictive nature of fat and sugar. If they are addictive, then we are in cigarette and alcohol territory. If they aren't, then the free will argument carries some weight.

Of course, the addiction issue is not black and white. There is a level in between where, when the stimulation is there, people have a hard time saying no. Just as Monica Lewinski was too much temptation for Bill Clinton, the omnipresent offer overwhelms their ability to resist. Some foods have this ability to override people's self-control mechanisms, creating a salty, crunchy, orgasmic pleasure that is just too yummy to reject. Is that addiction, or seduction or conditioning for intense rewards, making that person into an obsessed food rat?

Our brain on sugar and fat

Nobody choses to be an addict – or to be fat. Neurochemical reward centres in our brain override our willpower, leading to unwanted behaviour that goes against our rational, thinking self. Smokers are fully aware of the fact that tobacco will increase their risk of cancer and cardiovascular disease. Still they find it very hard to quit. Alcoholics realize that they are destroying their lives – and the lives of their loved ones – but find themselves helpless before a bottle of bourbon. This is what addiction does.

So could it be that some form of addiction prevents obese people from losing weight, even if they have a strong desire to become healthy and fit? After all, there is no reward in suffering from high blood pressure, diabetes, heart disease or arthritis; there is no pleasure in being socially excluded. But seemingly there is a lot of gratification in eating foods combining high sugar, fat and salt contents. Is this more than 'just cravings'?

Researchers from Yale's Rudd Centre have validated a Food Addiction Scale based on a survey about eating habits. Patients are asked if they agree or disagree with the following statements:

- I find that when I start eating certain foods, I end up eating much more than I had planned.
- Not eating certain types of food or cutting down on certain types of food is something I worry about.
- I spend a lot of time feeling sluggish or lethargic from overeating.
- There have been times when I consumed certain foods so often or in such large quantities that I spent time dealing with negative feelings from overeating instead of working, spending time with my family or friends, or engaging in other important activities or recreational activities I enjoy.
- I kept consuming the same types of food or the same amount of food even though I was having emotional and/or physical problems.
- Over time, I have found that I need to eat more and more to get the feeling I want, such as reduced negative emotions or increased pleasure.
- I have had withdrawal symptoms when I cut down or stopped eating certain foods (please do NOT include withdrawal symptoms caused by cutting down on caffeinated beverages such as soda pop, coffee, tea, energy drinks, etc.). For example: Developing physical symptoms, feeling agitated, or feeling anxious.
- My behaviour with respect to food and eating causes significant distress.
- I experience significant problems in my ability to function effectively (daily routine, job/school, social activities, family activities, health difficulties) because of food and eating.

Agreeing on most of these statements labels respondents as 'food addicts'. And to be clear, to this day there are no reports of people showing addiction to broccoli or kale. Sugar, fat and salt stimulate our brain's reward centres through the neurotransmitter dopamine, exactly like other addictive drugs. It is especially the technological games played with these ingredients that cause the problems. Sugar, fat and salt have been available, quite freely, for a few hundred years, and you can't blame current producers and retailers for selling these. The new problem is the industrial skill (art, trickery or genius) that takes these basic nutrients and transforms them, with the objective of ever-increasing palatability, convenience and variety. (David Kessler, 'The End of Overeating: Taking Control of Our Insatiable Appetite,' 2010).

Should one accuse the food industry of a 'hidden complot' that aims to make people excessively fat? Of course not! The industry simply responds to the consumer preferences that most strongly drive purchase, which are taste, convenience and price. We want our food tasty, cheap and at within easy reach in this order. We also prefer our food to be healthy, and for ourselves to stay slim, but health is not in the top three. Indeed, when food brands do communicate on health, many consumers tend to conclude that the food will probably be less tasty.

Consider what happened to American fast food chain Subway, when they launched a commercial starring Jared Fogle, a student who lost a lot of weight eating Subway sandwiches instead of other fast food. The story seemed to catch on and Subway sales took off, so the company went into overdrive on healthy eating. But what Subway overlooked was that 'healthiness' is just a nice extra. For the consumer it only comes fourth after taste, good value and convenience. So even if 'healthiness' is a point of differentiation, Subway quickly had to take corrective action and also stress how tasty, convenient and high-value their food was. They didn't have to be the best in those attributes, but parity was a minimum. Talking only about 'healthy fast food' was not a winner (Keller, Sternthal and Tybout, 'Three Questions You Need to Ask About Your Brand,' *Harvard Business Review*, September 2002). Consumers may endorse healthy fast food outlets in focus groups or in a questionnaire, but when it comes to their actual behaviour, it is a different thing altogether.

It is only logical that food manufacturers, wanting to maximize profit, take into account these consumer preferences. They produce very tasty food products, low priced and easily available. No problem there. The side-effect, however, is a problem. A 2014 McKinsey report, 'Overcoming Obesity,' estimated the economic impact of obesity at about $2 trillion a year, and the *Financial Times* pointed out that this represents approximately the annual global costs of war and terrorism. If the consumer does not know what is good for him or her, then the regulator has to step in, unless food companies do something about it before the regulator intervenes.

Taxation or reformulation?
We have basically turned AIDs from a terminal to a chronic disease, and we are on a similar path for many forms of cancer. Now, how can we combat the obesity epidemic? Some of the more obvious roadmaps include taxation, education, promoting longer-term health as opposed to the short-term pleasure of eating. But this is far from evident.

Various countries, including Denmark, Hungary and Israel, have been toying with a 'fat tax'. The results have been mixed. In Denmark, the tax was dropped because it increased administration costs for companies and there was union protest against job losses in the Danish food industry. It has been argued that the 'fat tax' in Denmark was too small to have a serious impact. A *British Medical Journal* study (July 2015) found that such taxes would have to increase the price of unhealthy food by as much as 20% in order to cut consumption sufficiently to reduce obesity, and they should be paired with subsidies on fruits and vegetables, to avoid that consumers would swap out one unhealthy habit for another. Other countries and cities have established a 'soda tax' on sugary soft drinks: France (2012), Mexico (2013) and Berkeley, California (2014). However, the results have not been uniformly positive, and the reason is obvious: we happen to like sweet-tasting foods from birth.

Neonatal facial expressions in infant humans show happiness after tasting sugar, but express disgust after tasting bitter tastes, as was shown by Jacob E. Steiner (Neuroscience and Biobehavioral Reviews, 2001). US President George H. W. Bush was famous for stating: 'I do not like broccoli. And I haven't liked it since I was a little kid and my mother made me eat it. And I'm President of the United States and I'm not going to eat any more broccoli.' Even with Coca-Cola's marketing budget, governments will not be able to persuade consumers that they like to eat their greens more than their carbs.

Food companies, feeling the pressure, reformulate their products, lowering fat, salt and sugar contents. This is obviously a good thing, one might think, were it not for surprisingly negative reactions by consumers. Indeed, for most people, it is hard to believe that healthy food can be tasty at all – taste being the number one factor driving food choices. Consumers might simply not buy the healthy alternative, sometimes referred to as 'Frankenfood'. This in turn leads manufacturers to launch sub-brands for healthier options, leaving their main brands unimproved, or to reformulate their products without communicating about it.

Another typical reaction, especially in overweight consumers, is to eat larger portions of the healthier products, as was shown by Brian Wansink and Pierre Chandon ('Can "Low-Fat" Nutrition Labels Lead to Obesity?', *Journal of Marketing Research*, November 2006). When offered so-called 'low-fat' M&M sweets, consumption increased by 46% for people who were overweight. The subjects wrongly assumed that low-fat meant fewer calories and that there would be no harm in eating a larger quantity. Such misassumptions are actually very common. Who would expect a can of Minute Maid apple juice without added sugars to contain 10% more calories than a can of regular Coca-Cola?

Tackling obesity

Improving the nutritional quality of food products will not suffice to fight the obesity epidemic. so how should food manufacturers handle this enormous challenge? let's have a look at a few do's and don'ts.

What companies should not do, for starters, is blame the consumer for not exercising enough. true, it wouldn't hurt most people to visit the fitness club a bit more often, but this is not the point. Lots of food products contain way too many calories and are too seductive to be left untouched by most people. When you offer supersize fatty and/or sugary foods at very low prices available 'everywhere', you can't get away with pointing your finger at your consumer.

A second no-go is minimizing the impact of your one SKU on the obesity problem. This is about the impact of all SKUs in the aggregate. People are confronted with sugary and fatty foods from breakfast until dinner. The industry has to deal with this.

Consistency is another issue. Pepsico CEO Indra Nooyi formulated the ambition for her company to focus more on healthy food categories, stating that food companies should be part of the solution. This sounds very commendable and courageous, but how credible is this coming from a publicly quoted multinational relying mostly on sugary soft drinks and salty snacks whose profit margins are considerable?

Should governments tax unhealthy foods (and subsidize healthy options)?

'Ultra-sugary drinks are arguably the tobacco of our generation.' This rather confrontational quote doesn't come from some obscure food activist who loves to harass 'big food' companies. No, this is actually an idea developed by Kenneth Rogoff, Professor of Economics and Public Policy at Harvard University and recipient of the 2011 Deutsche Bank Prize in Financial Economics, as well chief economist of the International Monetary Fund from 2001 to 2003.

Rogoff proposes a solution which is based on the fact that educating people about better diets and eating habits sounds reasonable and measured but doesn't work at all (see Table 19). The impact of Michelle Obama's well-meant efforts remains unclear. He points out that in the past, successful health-improving initiatives by governments have always supplemented education by legislation: think smoking bans, seat belt laws and speed limits. Inspired by what worked to some extent for alcohol and cigarettes, he proposes a retail tax on all processed foods – not just sugary drinks – and a subsidy for non-processed foods. If this is to be a neutral initiative for taxpayers, the subsidies can be large, as there are far more unhealthy foods than healthy foods. Subsidies are needed since obesity is most prevalent with lower-income people and since in the US, on average, eating healthy food costs $1.50 extra per person per day.

Rogoff argues convincingly, 'Prevailing prices do not reflect the true societal costs of foods. Diet-related chronic diseases account for substantial health care expenditures and indirectly may undermine the international competitiveness of the US economy. Individuals with healthy diets have not only lower health care costs but also longer, more productive lives, in turn contributing to higher tax revenue. Thus, both negative health and economic consequences of poor nutrition could be mitigated by a national system of subsides and taxes to facilitate more sensible dietary choices.' Is the food industry prepared?

Table 19. Policy proposals for 'good' and 'bad' foods

	% PRICE INCREASES	% SAME PRICES	% PRICE CUTS
WAITROSE	29	56	15
TESCO	30	50	20
ASDA	27	50	23
MORRISONS	30	46	24
SAINSBURY'S	39	35	26

Source: Mozaffarian, Rogoff and Ludwig, 'The Real Cost of Food,' Journal of the American Medical Association, September 2014.

Emphasizing that companies are merely selling what consumers want to buy, and that everybody has the right to choose whatever they want to eat, may backfire soon enough, given the potentially addictive nature of super-palatable food.

On the other hand, it wouldn't be a good idea to develop healthy products and position them as medication. Danone, for example, tried launching a 'beauty-from-the-inside yoghurt' in 2008 under the brand name Essensis, without much success. This is the danger of being too far ahead of your consumers. The same company experienced a backlash in its Actimel and Danacol sales after a change in European regulations on health claims. Though not neglecting the health benefits of fermented dairy products, Danone's focus is back on taste now,

It is often wrongly argued that what brand owners and retailers should do is invest in R&D to create product offerings the consumer likes that are also good for their health and well-being. It should be possible to produce healthy products with great taste, no? Between 1981 and 2009 in Germany, Danone reduced fat by 63%, sugar by 25% and calories by 36% in its 'FruchtZwerge' products, while keeping taste constant. However, this will not solve the problem. As was demonstrated in the Wansink and Chandon experiment mentioned above, if the newly developed food is tasty and healthy, then people will simply eat more of it. There is a risk they will compensate by overeating.

That is the real problem: food manufacturers are seducing consumers to eat more by the usual routes – producing nicer-tasting, more convenient and cheaper foods. The problem of obesity is not driven by the fact that the food is essentially unhealthy, so technology to make it more healthy but just as nice, does not face the problem head on. The real solutions, for the consumer and the food companies, need to make people pay the same but eat less. So, for example, developing a cafe/Starbucks-type hospitality concept based on tea rather than say beer or ice cream would be genuine progress. However, if an ice cream parlour opens next door to such a tea shop, which would be more successful? This is why the government will have to step in and restrict access – as with alcohol and licensing laws, banning direct sales to kids, etc. When the government does that, is your business going to be hurt? You can maybe prepare for that change, but not resist it.

An interesting path would consist of offering smaller portions, encouraging and educating consumers to enjoy tasty food without overeating. Casual dining restaurant chain TGI Friday's offers its customers a "Right Portion, Right Price" menu, which gives them the option of several smaller entrees when they dine out, at lower prices, thereby encouraging people to control their calorie intake.

The availability of healthy options is key. Some supermarkets have removed candies from the checkout section and replaced them with healthy fruit snacks. Soft drink vending machines should include mineral water next to sugary drinks; snack vending machines may offer apples.

Information and education

Education is of vital importance here. Children need to be taught healthy eating habits and shown the consequences of unhealthy diets. They need to have explained to them that the instant gratification of sugar and fat may lead to problems later, causing multiple diseases, including obesity and diabetes. Probably the best place to do so would be at school, preferably by credible teachers. Grown-ups, on the other hand, should understand that offering plenty of sugar, fat and sweets like chocolate to kids as a reward or to be liked by them is not a good idea and that there are better rewards and presents to offer.

Can education really have an impact? The results of a famous experiment seem to indicate that solid information is capable of changing behaviour. In the so-called 'marshmallow test', a series of studies on delayed gratification done in the late 1960s and early '70s by psychology professor Walter Mischel at Stanford University, children were offered a choice between one small reward (a marshmallow or a cookie) provided immediately, or two small rewards (marshmallows or cookies) if they waited for a short period, approximately 15 minutes, during which the tester left the room and then returned. In over 600 children who took part in the experiment, a minority ate the marshmallow immediately. Of those who attempted to delay, one third deferred gratification long enough to get the second marshmallow. In follow-up studies, Mischel found unexpected correlations between the results of the marshmallow test and the success of the children many years later, including scores on SAT tests, body mass index (an indicator of obesity) and drug usage in those same people, 30 years and more than 40 years later. The conclusion seemed to be that people with more self-control had a better chance of succeeding in life.

Two further insights are important here. First, professor Mischel showed in subsequent experiments that the degree of instant gratification is not an intrinsic genetic trait of a person, but a skill that can be learned and improved. Secondly, a 2012 study at the University of Rochester altered the experiment by dividing children into two groups: one group was given a broken promise before the marshmallow test was conducted – they were assured they would get a reward after performing a task, but did not get it after all. This was the unreliable tester group. The second group had a fulfilled promise before their marshmallow test. This reliable tester group waited up to four times longer (12 minutes) than the unreliable tester group for the second marshmallow to appear. The authors argue that this calls into question the original interpretation of self-control as the critical factor in children's performance. In fact, the study demonstrated that children's capability to wait for a greater reward rather than quickly taking a lesser reward is strongly influenced by the reliability and trustworthiness of the environment.

These insights, often ignored, are absolutely fundamental in finding ways of reducing obesity and its costly and horrible consequences for individuals and for the state. Indeed, reliable information on food and eating habits can have an impact on our consumption behavior, showing us that it is possible, after all, to resist the omnipresent food temptations we are confronted with every day of our lives, provided we are taught by credible and trustworthy teachers about healthy food choices from an early age.

Inspiration can also be found at Texas supermarket chain H.E. Butt, which developed a program called 'Health at H-E-B' to educate and inform its employees and customers on how to lead healthier lifestyles. The program started out as an internal workgroup for obese employees who would encourage each other, define targets and celebrate success. The idea was that H-E-B should be able sell the program to their own partners and workers, before being able to successfully sell it to the customers. As the program showed promising results, the next step was to introduce the program to its shoppers. An interesting challenge, and not without risk, given the fact that Texas is one of the most obese states in the US and that there is a lot of misinformation among consumers about all healthy foods being expensive, not tasty or difficult to prepare. H-E-B wanted to act, but without losing sales or customers, of course.

A 'Health at H-E-B' handbook, available for employees and shoppers, provided much-needed information on healthy food and lifestyles. H-E-B decided to clearly identify healthier options on its shelves and to run promotions on healthy food products. In order to motivate consumers even more, the retailer now runs an annual 'H-E-B Community Challenge', inviting communities across the state to compete to see which can demonstrate the greatest commitment to healthy living, and a 'Slim Down Showdown Challenge', an educational program helping people to adopt healthier lifestyles and achieve weight loss. The results of this remarkable program, run in close partnership with many different local organizations, can be found on the www.hebcommunitychallenge.com website, which claims to have made an impact on more than 1.2 million individuals already. H-E-B has identified the obesity problem as a major opportunity to connect with its employees and customers, building awareness and building business at the same time. Doing good *and* doing well seems possible after all.

Chapter Insights

1   If 'doing good' and 'doing well' were synergistic, all companies would have done so for a long time.
2   If the Food industry – manufacturers and retailers – does not act on the obesity issue, they will be 'cigarettized'.
3   Focusing on making food products tasty, convenient, cheap and healthy will not solve the obesity problem. Two actions that would improve the situation are (i) for the short run: substantially tax bad foods and subsidize good foods; and (ii) for the longer term: educate consumers from a very young age about healthy eating.

Part III
Improving Shelf Space

Chapter 5
The Robin Hood Syndrome

In the spring of 2009, a conflict between a retailer and a large brand owner made the world press. The Belgian supermarket chain Delhaize decided to delist more than 250 SKUs of famous Unilever brands like Knorr, Dove and Axe from the shelves, after the two parties failed to conclude price negotiations. Remarkable about this boycott was not only the large scale on which it took place, but also the fact that the retailer communicated openly about it to the press. "We refuse to pass on Unilever's proposed price increases to our shoppers," said the press release. This way, Delhaize – a retailer suffering from a weak price image – tried to present itself as a champion of low prices for consumers. Delistings are rather exceptional, it must be said. Usually only one or two SKUs are concerned, for a short period, and it is very rare for companies to communicate openly about the conflict. Retailers see delistings as a last-ditch means of pressure, threatened, for example, when the annual negotiations with brand owners have stalled. This way, delistings confirm the common belief that retailers are the dominant party in their relationships with brand suppliers. But are they?

The cost of a boycott

Ultimately, every conflict needs to get resolved, preferably without one of the concerned parties losing face. In the case of Delhaize and Unilever, details of the agreement that reversed the delistings have never been revealed, though it soon became clear that Unilever had to 'sacrifice' two senior managers. More interesting is the question of what such a conflict costs both parties. It is, probably, a 'both pay auction', but it is unclear who pays more.

If we use the above conflict as an example, for brand owner Unilever the primary cost is the difference between sales lost at Delhaize and what its brands gain at other retailers (which would be, presumably, rather little). But there may be an additional cost, and that is the risk that consumers will try out other brands, which might enter the consumers' consideration sets for the future. Moreover, the communication by Delhaize might enforce the image of a big and greedy multinational, Unilever, exploiting consumers.

For the retailer, the cost is twofold. The company may lose shoppers, people who decide to visit other retailers in order to be able to buy their preferred Unilever brands. Moreover, these shoppers may then decide to buy other products as well at the competing retailer – and decide to return more often if they liked the shopping experience. On the other hand, there may be a positive side effect on the price image of Delhaize, but everyone knows that improving price image is a rather difficult and long-term effort.

Sporadically, figures on the cost of such a boycott make the press. The British food producer Premier Foods reportedly lost £10 million in three months after Tesco delisted its Hovis, Mr Kipling and Oxo products in 2011. A year later, analysts feared for the survival of the New Covent Garden Soup Company when it was banned from Tesco stores (it is back in now). Even more recently, on March 5, 2014, French supermarket chain Carrefour delisted some SKUs of dairy giant Danone. Just a few hours later, the yogurt manufacturer agreed to lower its prices... It seems clear who is in charge.

We need to balance the story, though. Some brands are so strong that it would be very risky to delist them, and retailers know this. Ferrero, for example, is reputed to be a tough negotiator, not afraid of saying: 'Here is our offer. You don't like it? OK, kick us out!' In some countries (including Germany and Russia), the power of Ferrero brands like Nutella, Kinder, and Rocher lets them get away with this. It's all about power plays and 'realpolitik'. In January 2014, Lidl in Germany stopped selling Coca-Cola after a price dispute. This lasted no longer than a week. Even without an agreement, the discounter was quickly forced to relist Coca-Cola, as shoppers did not like the Pepsi and own brand alternatives, and competitors offered their shoppers significant Coke promotions.

Why retailers delist brands
1. It's about credibility. Sometimes, you need to show to all the other brands that your threat to delist them is not just words.
2. It's about money. Once delisted, the brand owner will typically have to pay a bit more to get back on the shelf. And this 'a bit more' will soon become the standard for all the suppliers in the category.
3. It's about competition. Even if they don't really know what a good deal is, retailers will keep squeezing their suppliers, because they know their competitors do the same and they demand a level playing field. Moreover, since retailers know that suppliers are rich, they feel justified in using heavy-handed tactics 'to make brand owners hand over more juice'.

What Makes Retailers So Powerful?

When you discuss retailer relations with brand manufacturers and farmers, you hear horror stories about retailers squeezing their suppliers like lemons. Buyers are tough negotiators who are not afraid of using borderline techniques. They allegedly abuse their buying power in order to get lower prices, better margins and higher contributions. Sometimes suppliers initiate lawsuits – but not very often, because no one benefits from a definitive break-up. Sometimes, farmers and manufacturers ask the authorities to enforce fair trading relationships. But usually the government doesn't see the problem:

competition leads to lower prices, which is good for the consumer. Case closed. Or is it? There are four solid arguments that substantiate the power of retailers, but we do need to cast some shadows on this conventional wisdom. Retailers do have considerable power, but maybe not as much as is commonly believed.

1. Retailer concentration leads to buying power

There is little doubt that major retailers exercise strong purchasing power over their suppliers. Bigger retailers will get better conditions from brand owners. In the UK, this is clearly the case for Tesco, as illustrated in Figure 12.

Figure 12. Retailer buying economies of scale. COGS=costs of goods sold. The 100% level is Tesco.

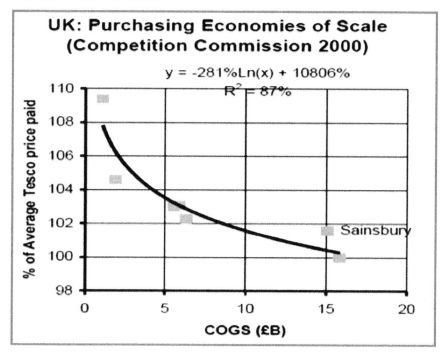

Source: Report on Grocery Retail, UK Competition Commission, 2005.

Increasing retail concentration is one of the determining factors. In many mature markets, the three largest retailers hold more than three quarters of the market (see Table 20). Moreover, major retailers unite in European purchasing alliances. Brand manufacturers who aspire to build significant market share cannot afford to miss out on one of the major retailers, which offers retailers ample opportunity to play out their dominance.

Although concentration also plays a role on the supplier's side, the proportions are asymmetric. While one retailer may represent 20% of sales for a brand manufacturer, even a strong brand usually weighs hardly a few percentage points in the turnover of the retailer. This asymmetry enables retailers to threaten to delist the brand in question.

Table 20. Retail concentration across countries

RETAILER CONCENTRATION

Finland	SOK	Kesko	Lähikauppa	95%
Denmark	COOP	Dansk SM	Supergros	89%
Switzerland	Migros	Coop	Denner	85%
Sweden	ICA	KF	Axfood	85%
Austria	REWE	Spar	Hofer	84%
Norway	NorgesGr.	Coop	Rema 1000	82%
Belgium	Colruyt	Delhaize	Carrefour	70%
Germany	Edeka	Rewe	Aldi	65%
Netherlands	AHOLD	Jumbo/C1000	Lidl	63%
Portugal	Sonae	JMR	Intermarche	63%
UK	Tesco	ASDA	Sainsbury's	61%
Spain	Carrefour	Mercadona	Eroski group	57%
Slovakia	COOP	Tesco	Billa	49%
Hungary	Tesco	Spar	Coop	45%
Greece	Carrefour	Alfa Beta	Lidl	39%
Czech rep	Tesco	Ahold	Kaufland	38%
Italy	Coop	Conad	Auchan	34%
Turkey	BIM	Migros	Carrefour	25%
Poland	Biedronka	Tesco	Lewiatan	24%

Source: AC Nielsen, 2014.

On the flip side, concentration ratios only tell part of the story. After the 'race for space' between retailers comes to an end (as it has in most developed countries), the 'race for differentiation' sets in. In other words, if in a short radius from where a shopper lives there are three reasonable options to shop for groceries, and this is replicated nationally, one would have very high concentration yet tough competition between those few retailers.

2. Retailers 'own' their shoppers

Not only do retailers have buying power, they also have sales power because they control the point of purchase. Brand manufacturers invest millions in consumer marketing, aiming to win the hearts and minds of consumers and to get on their shopping lists. But at the moment of truth, in the final minutes before they select and buy the products, consumers are in the hands of the retailer. The point of sale often has a significant impact on the final purchasing decision, and that decision frequently depends on many parameters. Is the brand or product in stock? Is it on a primary location on the shelf (eye level, end of aisle)? Is a competitor running an attractive promotion? Does the retailer offer an inexpensive store brand as an alternative? All these factors may affect the actual brand choice. As the data from the well-known annual POPAI (Point of Purchase Advertising Institute) study shows, the majority of brand decisions are made in the store (see Table 21).

Table 21. Consumer planned and unplanned purchases

	1965	1986	1995	2012
Specifically planned (brand specified)	31	34	30	24
Generally planned (category specified)	17	11	6	15
Brand Switch (as compared to planned)	2	3	4	6
Unplanned	50	53	60	55
IN STORE BRAND DECISION	69	66	70	76

Source: POPAI, Shopper Engagement Study, for the relevant years.

Convincing as they may seem, these results need to be put in perspective. In the POPAI research, for a purchase to be qualified as 'specifically planned', the shopper should have the brand written down on her shopping list. Of course, many brands are bought based on ex-ante decisions even if they do not appear on the shopping list – after all, we are dealing with routine purchases in the supermarket. No doubt there are unplanned purchases, but it depends on the product category, and the percentage is definitely not as high as POPAI would like us to believe. What else would you expect from a 'point of purchase advertising institute' except evidence supporting the idea that the point of purchase is important?

Furthermore, even if many brand-choice decisions happen in-store, manufacturers do have various possibilities to gain impact at that moment of truth. Clever brand owners invest substantial amounts of money with the retailer precisely to control the presence of their brands in the stores: they pay for having second placements, eye-level positions on the shelf and displays in the aisles, for shelf talkers and wobblers. By imposing conditional negotiated agreements focusing on the sales and sales growth of their brands, brand owners do have a major impact on what retailers actually do in their stores, keen as they are to actually satisfy these conditions to obtain the goodies from their suppliers.

3. Retailers compete directly with brand owners

What makes it all even a bit more complex is this: for the brand manufacturer, the retailer is not only a trading partner and a customer but also a competitor. In each category, retailers offer their shoppers alternatives that are typically 15% to 30% cheaper than the branded products. That price difference is made possible by the fact that retailers have lower costs in terms of product development and marketing. They copy successful concepts of the brand manufacturers and do not need to invest in expensive advertising campaigns – the store is their medium. Private-label products keep increasing their market share, and their offer is becoming more sophisticated, with low-priced basic commodities on one end of the spectrum and distinctive premium, sometimes destination, products, on the other. With their private-label offering, retailers attempt to strengthen the relationship with their shoppers and to further weaken the position of the brand manufacturers.

There is, however, a downside to this approach, as it is not a consumer-driven strategy. Shoppers do expect to find their favorite brands on the shelves. Retailers need to balance their assortments carefully. In the UK, for example, Sainsbury's became the first mainstream supermarket to have more than 50% of its turnover accounted for by private label, but this did not prevent them from losing market share in the '90s and receiving criticism from consumers. Moreover, value private labels especially had better not exceed a certain threshold share of the category, because they may dilute category profitability for their retailers due to smaller margins. Also, recent volatility in the prices of raw materials make the profitability of private labels more uncertain, as the cost of raw materials makes up a higher percentage of the cost of goods sold for the retailer than for the brand owner.

4. Information is power

The final factor that gives retailers the upper hand over their suppliers is information technology. Through their POS systems and loyalty cards, retailers have access to a mass of relevant data about shoppers and their buying behaviour. They can use this information to optimize their product range, to adjust their prices and promotions, and to efficiently organize their stores and supply chain. Moreover, they know the profile and purchase history of their individual shoppers. This enables them to present them with personalized offers tailored to their preferences. We are no longer surprised when an internet retailer like Amazon suggests products to us based on our previous purchases. Supermarkets are becoming equally adept at actively using shopper data. Their willingness to share these valuable data with their suppliers is limited – or comes with a hefty price tag.

Notwithstanding the massive hype surrounding Big Data, data analytics and artificial intelligence, we still observe among retailers relatively few credible actions based on shopper data. Though a major user of loyalty cards and data analytics via their wholly owned data analysis subsidiary, Dunnhumby, Tesco couldn't stop the rot in the last two years (they lost 50% of their market capitalization), and recent talk is that they will sell Dunnhumby and reduce their loyalty card scheme because it is very expensive. Some within Tesco even suggest that the money spent on loyalty cards could be better used for good old price cuts...

Overall, in their struggle for control over the shopper, retailers are advantaged – but not completely. To use a striking image: retailers are at the steering wheel and manufacturers are in the back of the car, where they shout and wave (and pay) to try to persuade the retailer to steer in the direction of building their profitable brands. The retailer has his eyes on a different destination – increasing his own margins, sales and profits from his own stores and store brands.

The Power and the Profits

Powerful as retailers may be, we get a very different picture when we look at their actual financial performance. Although retailers are usually larger than brand manufacturers in sales, brand manufacturers are worth significantly more than retailers. Not just today, but for many years, brand owners have significantly outperformed retailers on all standard financial parameters: sales growth, profits, market capitalization... The data in this chapter prove that over time, retailers have not been able to close the gap – on the contrary.

To compare the performance of large retailers and brand owners, I used two large data sources: DataStream and Bloomberg. Since reliable data are only available for publicly quoted companies, my sample did not include privately owned companies. This had a greater impact on the retail sample than on the manufacturers' sample. Important retail companies including Aldi, Lidl, Rewe and Leclerc were not included. On the manufacturer side, Mars was the most notable omission. This limitation is common to all empirical research in this area, and I believe the results would not have been modified substantially had I been able to include the data for major privately owned companies. The sample is wide enough to cover the full spectrum of companies operating in the industry. Similarly, I excluded smaller companies from my analysis, as their data are not continuously available for the whole time period under study.

I focused my analysis on the 25-year period from 1990 to 2013. For each year I used the data for the 10 largest retailers (grocers, discount stores, food retailers) and the 10 largest manufacturers (FMCG) in that year, based on their annual sales as expressed in US dollars, using appropriate exchange rates for non-US companies in the sample. Table 22 lists the sample of retailers, and Table 23 the manufacturers.

Table 22. Study sample of 10 largest retailers

1990	2000	2010	2013
WAL-MART	WAL-MART	WAL-MART	WAL-MART
SAFEWAY	CARREFOUR	CARREFOUR	COSTCO
CARREFOUR	AHOLD	TESCO	TESCO
TARGET	KROGER	METRO	CARREFOUR
SAINSBURY	METRO	COSTCO	KROGER
AHOLD	TARGET	KROGER	METRO
M&S	COSTCO	TARGET	AMAZON
TESCO	SAFEWAY	AEON	TARGET
CASINO	TESCO	SAFEWAY	CASINO
DELHAIZE	SAINSBURY	AHOLD	AEON

Note: Highlighted retailers made the top 10 list in all years.

Table 23. Study sample of 10 largest manufacturers

1990	2000	2010	2013
UNILEVER	NESTLE	NESTLE	NESTLE
NESTLE	UNILEVER	P&G	P&G
P&G	P&G	UNILEVER	PEPSICO
PEPSICO	COCA COLA	PEPSICO	UNILEVER
COCA COLA	PEPSICO	ANHEUSER B INBEV	COCA COLA
GENERAL MILLS	KIMBERLY CLARK	COCA COLA	ANHEUSER B INBEV
KIMBERLY CLARK	DANONE	L'OREAL	L'OREAL
CAMPBELL SOUP	HENKEL	DANONE	DANONE
COLGATE	L'OREAL	HEINEKEN	HEINEKEN
L'OREAL	COLGATE	HENKEL	HENKEL

Note: Highlighted retailers made the top 10 list in all years.

To get a comprehensive picture of the relative performance of retailers and their suppliers, I used a number of standard performance indicators: sales revenue, market capitalization, market capitalization/sales, net profit margins, return on assets and total shareholder return. The three graphs of Figure 13 indicators show that over this recent 25-year period,

1 Retailers are bigger (in terms of sales) than their suppliers.
2 Manufacturing companies are worth significantly more than retail companies.
3 Investors are willing to pay between $.30 and $.50 for every dollar of sales of a retailer, but willing to pay from 5 to almost 10 times more for every dollar of sales of a brand owner. The one retailer, Amazon, that is in manufacturer territory (market capitalization/sales=2.5) is not really a typical grocery retailer.

Grocery retailers operate on significantly lower net profit margins than brand owners (see Figure 14). To some extent, this is justified by the fact that retailers have fewer assets than brand owners (they don't have factories and research centres, etc.) and therefore fewer to pay for. However, as Figure 15 shows, even after we account for the asset intensiveness of the manufacturers' business, they still outperform retailers. Indeed, even though retailers need fewer assets to generate their sales, at the end of the day manufacturers still generate substantially more profits per dollar of assets.

Total shareholder return (TSR) is arguably the most complete corporate performance indicator, measuring the return investors get from investing in a company. TSR measures the increase in the value of the company (i.e. the change in its share price) + the annual dividend the company pays to their shareholders. Comparing TSRs confirms the picture shown by profitability. Independent of their specific time horizon (last 10 years, last 5 years, last year or last 6 months), investors would have been better off putting their money in large FMCG manufacturers than in large grocery retailers (see Figure 16).

It seems, therefore, that the brand manufacturers – at least when we consider the big players – have their business well in hand. If they are being squeezed at all, they do not seem to suffer a lot of harm from it. But the retailers' problems seem only to be getting

Figures 13a, b. Sales and market capitalization of retailers and brand owners.

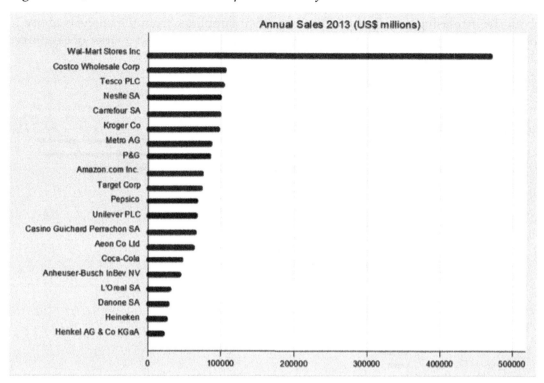

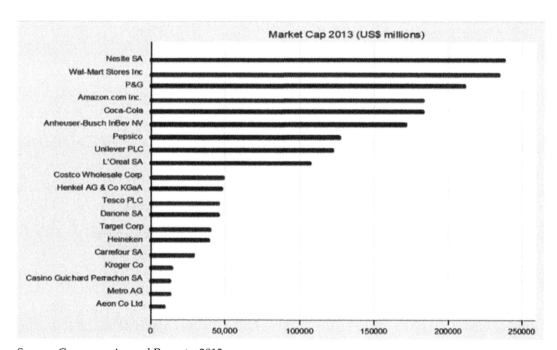

Source: Company Annual Reports, 2013.

bigger. Their sales and profitability are under pressure from price wars, increased competition and e-commerce. Although we are constantly bombarded by news stories about the increasing power of retailers over their suppliers, from the analysis above it looks like the gap in performance has not been reduced over the last quarter of a century. On the contrary...

Figure 13c. Market capitalization/sales of retailers and brand owners.

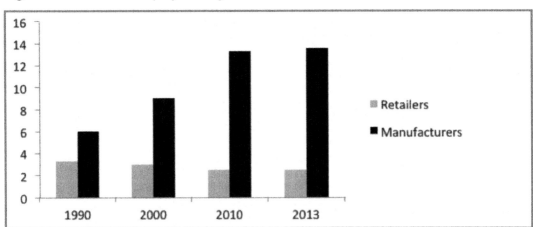

Source: Company Annual Reports, 2013.

Figure 14. Relative net profit margins.

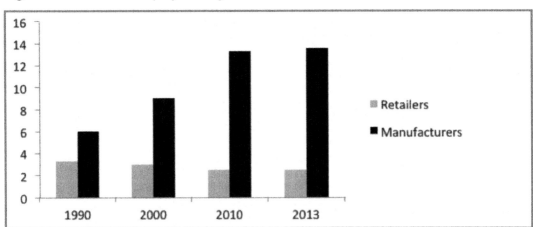

Source: Company Annual Reports 1990, 2000, 2010, 2013.

Figure 15. Relative return on assets.

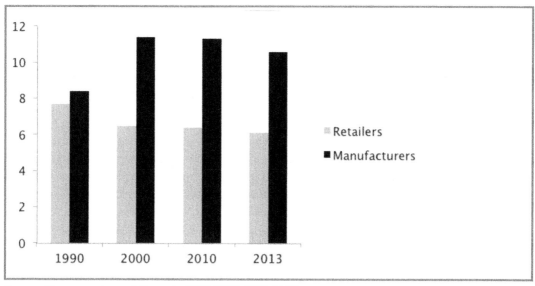

Source: Company Annual Reports, 1990, 2000, 2010, 2013.

Figure 16. Relative total shareholder return.

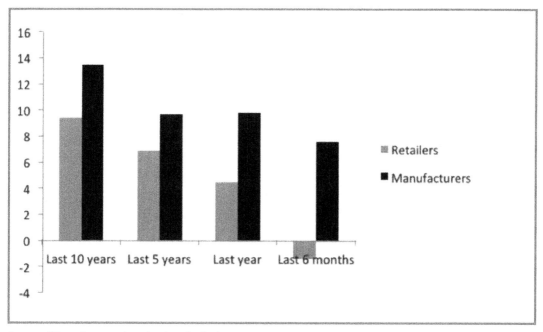

Source: Bloomberg and author's calculations.

105

Horizontal versus vertical power

If retailers are really that powerful, how is it possible that their economic performance does not reflect this?

The answer is, retailers suffer from the Robin Hood syndrome. The English folk hero Robin Hood and his men stole from the rich to give to the poor. He himself did not become wealthy from his freebooters' activities (though he did get the girl). Retailers do exactly the same (but they don't get the girl). They do obtain impressive deals from their suppliers in the form of price reductions, delays of payment and larger trade promotions budgets. But they fail to hold on to that value. What they do with the money they succeed in extracting from brand owners is simply pass it on to the final consumer in the form of lower selling prices and deeper and more frequent promotions. If you extract benefits from your suppliers and subsequently use these goodies to seduce shoppers to come to your stores, then what are you left with?

Power is not a one-dimensional concept. We must distinguish between two forms of power: vertical and horizontal. Vertical power is the power that retailers have over their suppliers, which does allow them to demand and obtain substantial benefits from them. Horizontal power, however, is the power retailers have relative to their retail competitors. This is what retailers lack. For shoppers, the cost of switching between retailers is perceived to be low. This destroys the retailers' hard-fought rents from their vertical power. A very substantial part of what they manage to extract from manufacturers, they pass on to the consumer. It is as if they negotiate on behalf of the consumer. Like Robin Hood, retailers behave like philanthropists. They are like unions working very hard to extract benefits for their members (consumers) from their employers (brand owners). If retailers did not exist, the government would have to invent them. They do exactly what government is supposed to do, protect consumers from the monopolistic powers of brand owners.

Why is competition among retailers so intense? Why do they lack horizontal power? Manufacturers compete with each other too, but that competition does not lead to value destruction. What's going on? The retailers seem to be the victims of their business model.

Prisoners of their own business model

Retailers turn to price competition out of necessity and because it is faster and cheaper than other forms of differentiation. On top of that, reducing prices does not require immediate cash outlays for the retailer. Retailers must address the broadest possible population of shoppers in the trading area of each of their stores and quickly counter initiatives by their competitors, because their business model is characterized by high fixed costs and low margins. When you operate large retail stores, it becomes difficult to focus on a specific segment of shoppers. You need as many shoppers as possible to come to your stores, because the costs of operating these large stores have a high fixed component; whether there are many or few customers coming to the store, the cost of operating the store isn't all that different. Hard discounters can afford to segment because they operate small stores, have lower fixed costs and tend to locate in areas where households are more price sensitive. High-end retailers like Waitrose cope with this problem by locating their large stores in areas that are relatively wealthy, where they can charge higher prices for their service offering. These types of stores have a much more limited geographical scope and therefore tend to be operated by smaller retail companies.

Of course, mainstream retailers do work on aspects like convenience and service. But these initiatives are often easy to copy if successful. Suppose a retailer decides to invest in helping shoppers packing their goods in bags at the checkout. There are two possibilities: either the shoppers don't care about this service, causing the retailer to lose money and time; or it does work, and then the competition will copy the concept immediately... Moreover, consumers seem to attach relatively little value to retail services. Only a minority of shoppers seem willing to pay a premium for a more agreeable shopping experience. This might be because the shopping experience is transient, and shopping is a utilitarian activity. It might be because 'value' is perceived in the physical product bought, and it is considered intelligent behaviour to find the same item at the lowest price – in many markets (estate agency, head hunters, car salesmen) the services of the middleman are seen as a cost to minimise rather than a service worth paying for. A final reason why shoppers don't value retail services highly is because they have been told by those same retailers for many years that it is all about price and promotions. Guess what? Consumers now believe them!

In order to tackle the Robin Hood syndrome, retailers will have to make radical changes in their business model and in the way they operate, so much is clear. They will need to find ways to make consumers and shoppers willing to pay for added services or they have to cut all these incremental services, focus on efficiency and offer a sustainable price advantage. Huge challenges, indeed, that we will develop further in the next chapter.

The retailing battlefields

The Robin Hood syndrome to which retailers are prone makes being a grocery retailer a very tough business. Retailers run an extremely complex business model with thousands of SKUs, many different formats, high fixed costs, and on top of everything else, low margins. No wonder they are stressed trying to generate a satisfying return for their shareholders. All over the world, mainstream grocery retailers are struggling to remain competitive in a rapidly changing market where new entrants change the rules. Below is a snapshot of what is currently happening in grocery retail in the biggest markets around the globe.

In Germany, hard discounters now account for 40% of the FMCG market. Quality supermarkets never succeeded in matching the Aldi and Lidl price levels. Metro was forced to restructure, Tengelmann sold its Kaiser's supermarket business to Edeka. Although their French CEO, Alain Caparros, learned his trade at Aldi, Rewe's hard discount chain, Penny, doesn't seem to be able to make any hay, after years of trying...

The retailing battlefields cont.

- In France, hypermarkets have suffered while hard discounters prosper. Quasi-franchise operations like Leclerc and Intermarché seem to be thriving, while Carrefour, after years of problems, is trying to get their house back in order. In spite of strict laws on trade relations and pricing, price aggressiveness is increasing and big players are joining forces in buying alliances, putting pressure on their suppliers to offer better conditions.
- For a long time, hard discounters seemed to have a hard time conquering the UK market, because supermarkets reacted by offering a no-frills, cheap value, private-label option for their shoppers and because the hard discounters didn't invest much in expanding their network of stores, as the UK was not at the top of their list of markets to conquer. But over the last few years Aldi and Lidl have gained considerable market share, while market leader Tesco got into trouble, as did Morrissons. In an attempt to defend its position, Sainsbury has signed a partnership with Danish discount retailer Netto. If you can't beat them, join them...
- The financial crisis has impacted shopping habits in Spain. The market is dominated by Mercadona, a successful, privately owned, low-cost player, while main challenger Carrefour bets on aggressive promotions and product innovation. Hard discounters have a significant market share, with both Aldi and Lidl present next to local player Dia. Traditional proximity retailers and specialists (bakeries, butchers...) are suffering.
- Local food shops and specialists are still big in Italy, where supermarket concentration is less developed. Competition is heating up as more foreign players, including discounters, enter the market: Auchan, Carrefour, Aldi, Lidl, Billa, and Penny (Rewe) are competing with aggressive local players Eurospin, MD Discount and IN's Mercato.
- In the Benelux countries, the success of hard discounters Aldi and Lidl and aggressive local players Colruyt and Jumbo has caused a loss of market share for some big names. Carrefour was forced to restructure in 2010, Delhaize in 2014-2015, and Albert Heijn is now solving Delhaize's problems by taking them over...
- For decades, the US market was largely dominated by supercenters à la Walmart and Kroger. But supermarkets and neighborhood markets are gaining share, while cheap dollar stores have managed to conquer their piece of the pie and Aldi is expanding their hard discount store penetration; Lidl is seriously considering entering the frame as well. The landscape has never been more competitive, with more options than ever available for consumers. Alongside these developments amongst established grocery retailers, new players like Amazon may cause serious havoc in the market for many traditional players, definitely in non-food but also in grocery...
- In Australia, two large retailers, Coles and Woolworths, control about 70% of the market and compete aggressively on price. Nevertheless, discounters Costco and Aldi have managed to gain considerable market share.
- The Japanese market, characterized by an important role for convenience stores, has proved very difficult for foreign operators to enter. Still, Walmart and Costco hold a strong position and force local chains 7-Eleven and Aeon to lower prices.
- Even though big international retailers like Walmart, Carrefour, Tesco and Metro have been trading in China for many years, this huge market remains fragmented and local competition is fierce, causing the foreign entrants to slow down their expansion projects. E-commerce is growing at an enormous rate.
- A growing middle class willing to pay for quality makes South Africa an interesting market. The entrance of Walmart in 2011 caused a price war, but local retailers Shoprite, Massmart, Pick'n Pay, Spar and Woolworths seem able to defend their positions so far.

Chapter Insights

1 Although retailers are powerful, they stay relatively poor
2 Retailers' vertical power is diluted by their lack of horizontal power, turning them, against their own will, into Robin Hoods.
3 Brand-owners should avoid giving more margin to retailers: it is like giving more drugs to drug addicts.

Chapter 6
The Retailers' Distinctiveness Challenge:

In the world of FMCG, brands need to constantly attract attention and stand out in order to enter and stay in the consideration set of consumers and thereby drive and sustain penetration. It takes a lot of effort to become 'top of mind' and even more to remain there, as competition is harsh and good ideas get copied quickly. But what makes Coke really different from Pepsi? Apart from a marginal difference in taste which most consumers are unable to identify in blind taste tests, both products are basically identical. This lack of substantial differences between product offerings is typical in most product categories in the FMCG industry. What is important for brands is to be salient and consistent in their communication while constantly trying to be relevant and memorable to consumers. This is what the most successful brands do best.

So what about retailers? Consumers are well aware of the stores in their trading area, but they tend to shop in the store closest to where they live (or work, or where they drop the kids off). To attract the patronage of shoppers who regularly drive by the shop closest to them, retailers have to offer the shopper something special that she values and for which she is willing to drive a bit further. Can retailers develop real differential advantages in order to stand out from their competitors?

As we have seen in the former chapter, retailers need to get out of their 'sameness' image and create a degree of distinctiveness to avoid the Robin Hood Syndrome. The fact that for the vast majority of retailers there is very little distinctiveness beyond location must mean this is not an easy task. Often mainstream retailers try to be good at all aspects of their offer, but they seem to have a problem excelling at any specific element in it. As a result shoppers will be uninspired, as they can do better with split baskets, shopping at the hard discounters for some categories and at quality retailers for others. Why go for the compromise when you can have the best of both worlds? Retailers should realise that it is just not possible to be great at everything. They need to learn to make clear choices, and with choices come consequences. In order to stand out on specific advantages, they will need to accept to be not so good (and even below par) on other aspects.

How brands differentiate

Brands try to differentiate themselves from their competitors by focusing their communication on functional or emotional features that are perceived to be unique, valuable and sustainable. Most new brands have such a feature at the time they enter the market. If it is successful, very often this valuable and unique feature will be copied, through the normal competitive forces. Then, beyond the search for new unique and valuable features, brands have to manage their consumer penetration through their marketing and sales efforts to stay top of mind and be available at every purchase occasion for the consumer.

Initially, Dove was a moisturizing soap for the skin, stating that it was milder than other soap brands thanks to its neutral pH balance. Some other brands copied them, and the brand was a middling success with sales of around $400 million. Then Dove introduced a new feature to differentiate itself: an emotional feature, based on reconsidering society's pre-set definitions of beauty. Dove proposed the notion of 'internal beauty' which culminated in its successful 'Campaign for Real Beauty'. Not many brands can claim such differentiation, and Dove became a $4 billion brand.

Is this remarkable success story an example of what happens when consumers fall in love with a brand and experience a deep emotional connection with it? Of course not. What the 'Real Beauty' theme has done for Unilever is provide them with a platform to communicate with consumers and keep telling inspirational stories in order to stay salient, top of mind and memorable. This is the crux of the matter, and it explains why a company like Unilever spends about seven times as much on advertising as on R&D.

For a long time, laundry detergent brand Persil kept conveying functional messages such as 'washes whiter', 'smells better', 'makes clothes feel softer' – just like all the other laundry detergent brands. But then it took a different option with its emotional 'Dirt Is Good' campaign, showing children getting dirty while playing. The message stated that getting dirty is a good thing for kids, as playing games is crucial for their development as human beings, and that parents shouldn't worry about the clothes, because Persil would take care of the dirt. Again, an inspired platform for Unilever to talk about the brand and maintain top-of-mind awareness and thereby consumer penetration.

In many FMCG categories, the idea of a competitive advantage is ambiguous, at best. When Coke says that they are 'the real thing', does this really make them better/different from Pepsi? Probably not, but the baseline provides Coca-Cola with a communications platform on which to build many different, linked stories in campaigns over time, to develop a consistent, familiar and memorable image of the brand which occupies a robust position in the consumers' consideration set. Such a platform should be unique, appreciated and hopefully difficult to copy. This is what the 'internal beauty' theme does for Dove, or what the image of the three frogs did for Budweiser. Heineken used to have a campaign that explicitly made fun of competitive advantages, claiming that it 'Refreshes the parts that other beers cannot reach'… Again, it gave them a platform to communicate.

Actually, although brand managers probably feel strongly about the degree of uniqueness of their brands, in the consumers' mind the perceived differences between brands are less pronounced. Below are two illustrations of how consumers' perceptions of various brand attributes tend to the mean (see tables 24 and 25).

Table 24. *Performance indicators of toothpaste brands*

BRANDS IN DECREASING ORDER OF MARKET SHARE	% AGREEING PROMOTES STRONG & HEALTHY TEETH	AVERAGE % AGREEING ON 12 ATTRIBUTES
COLGATE DC	55	54
MACLEANS	68	59
CREST	70	60
COLGATE BMF	57	55
AQUAFRESH	47	52
GIBBS	62	53
MENTADENT	65	58
ULTRABRITE	57	55
AVERAGE	60	56

Source: Wiemer Snijder, 'Dreams of Differentiation,' Slide Share, March 2013, slide 52.

Table 25. *Performance indicators of car brands*

	% BRAND USERS	UP-TO-DATE	TOUGH	ENERGETIC	AVERAGE OF ALL 28 ATTRIBUTES
FORD	19	23	14	5	12
VAUXHALL/OPEL	13	20	16	5	12
ROVER	10	11	21	6	14
PEUGEOT	6	19	23	7	12
VW	6	16	16	8	12
RENAULT	5	33	22	19	11
AVERAGE	10	20	19	8	12

Source: Wiemer Snijder, Dreams of Differentiation, Slide Share, March 2013, slide 65.

Differences in perceptions between leading brands tend to be small, as illustrated in table 26 for carbonated soft drinks (UK) and for retail banks (Australia).

Table 26. *Difference and uniqueness of CSD and bank brands*

CSD	DIFFERENT	UNIQUE	EITHER	BANKS	DIFFERENT	UNIQUE	EITHER
COKE	8*	13	19	ANZ	12	4	15
DIET COKE	9	8	15	CBA	12	12	19
PEPSI	7	10	15	NAB	8	12	12
FANTA	8	5	12	WESTPAC	9	6	11
PEPSI MAX	9	10	19	ST GEORGE	26	16	32
SCHWEPPES	6	9	13				
CANADA DRY	10	9	17				
AVERAGE	9	9	16				

*8% of consumers feel that Coke is different from other carbonated soft drinks (CSDs). Source: J Romanuik, B Sharp, and A Ehrenberg, 'Evidence Concerning the Importance of Perceived Brand Differentiation,' Australasian Marketing Journal, 2007.

That is not to say that marketing should not try to differentiate – on the contrary. However, marketers should be realistic in their ambitions. What they can and should achieve is to create a degree of salience for their brands in the mind of the consumer (see Table 27). And by salience I mean the ability of a brand to get switched on in the mind of the consumer in buying situations. Being in the consumer's consideration set is perhaps the simplest single conceptualization of salience. Salience is not the same as differentiation in terms of the brand's attributes, but it is the essence of the brand derived from its degree of availability and point of sales presence, its intensity of communication, its sales and promotional efforts, and the memorability of its communication platform.

Table 27. Salience of CSD, whisky and toothpaste brands

CSD	SALIENCE		WISKY	SALIENCE		TOOTHPASTE	SALIENCE
Coke	23		J walker	18		Crest	36
Fanta	12		J&B	17		Colgate	30
Diet Coke	10		Jameson	15		Aquafresh	14
Pepsi	9		TFG	13		A & H	9
Dr Pepper	9		Balantine's	13		Sensodyne	7

Brands in decreasing order of market share. CSD=carbonated soft drink.
Source: source Wiemer Snijder, Dreams of Differentiation, Slide Share, March 2013, slide 74 .

This salience should be constantly developed to make sure the brand remains prominent in the consumers' consideration set of brands at every purchase occasion. It seems as if retailers have a single platform they all use: 'We are cheaper'! Whereas brands develop non-price platforms to communicate and position themselves, retailers seem to constantly (over time as well as geographically) gravitate to the price (and price promotion) platform. Most retailers and the grocery retail sector overall pay a heavy price for this short-term price focus.

Why grocery retailers get caught in the low-price syndrome

It is remarkable to see how retailers are still pretty much stuck in the world of functional differentiation, price. Why is it that retailer differentiation lags behind manufacturer differentiation? The issue needs some explanation.

For starters, manufacturers set off much earlier, investing heavily in their brands in order to create some form of saliency in the mind of the consumer. Of course, retailing is a very old profession as well, but for a very long time it remained a local family business based on the functional advantage of location and the emotional advantage of trust, as shop owners knew every single shopper personally. All this has changed since modern, large-scale retailers came to market. While for manufacturers it is all about having a strong brand, in retail the focus is on having the best location.

Most retailers rely on a very broad, all-inclusive positioning, using slogans nobody would disagree with, like 'Every little helps' at Tesco; 'J'optimisme' at Carrefour; 'Save money – live better' at Walmart; 'Good neighbours, great prices' at Food Lion; 'Ein M besser' at Migros; 'Bien acheter, bien manger' at Delhaize... Most of the messages are functional and price driven. It is often argued that retailers' positioning should be more edgy and specific. However, they cannot do so because of the economics of their business model. As we explained in Chapter 5, once retailers get caught in the high fixed-cost, low-margin catch-22, differentiation beyond location becomes difficult – except with lower prices. Building substantial non-price advantages requires two things retailers don't have: time and money. It takes time for consumers to grasp and buy into a non-price positioning, and in the meantime competitors will simply cut prices to attract shoppers. Differentiation takes money as well, because if a successful differential advantage is not expensive to develop and does not require a long time to implement, then it will be copied immediately, leaving the retailers back where they started: undifferentiated, but with higher costs.

This is why retailers have been telling consumers for a long time that it is all about price: 'We have the lowest prices', 'We offer the biggest price promotions', et cetera… Thus, retailers have convinced consumers that this is what retail is all about: creating value for consumers by offering the lowest possible prices. As a result, the consumer doesn't see the retailer as a service provider but rather as an institution providing grocery products at low prices. Compare that to manufacturer brands; how many of them compete on price as their platform in their communication?

The fact that typical large supermarket or hypermarket stores need to generate considerable sales in order to attain break-even means that they have a hard time selecting specific segments of shoppers. Retailers need to attract shoppers from all segments to their store to generate sufficient sales volumes. This is not the case for hard discounters, who can focus on low-price-driven shoppers because they have lower operating costs and less fixed costs (due to smaller stores in cheaper areas and with smaller assortments). They don't need to attract all shopper segments, and tend to locate in areas that are highly populated by lower-income households. Neither is it the case for high-end retailers like Waitrose in the UK, who can target the more affluent consumers, to a large degree by locating in high-income trading areas.

Manufacturers, on the other hand, not limited by the high fixed-costs/low-margin constraints, can have many brands, even in the same category, with very different communication platforms. Moreover, a brand has a much higher shopper exposure than a retail store; even a smallish brand is probably on the shelves at all retailers all over the country. This exposure creates scale even for brands that focus on a limited consumer segment. It is a level of exposure retailers can never reach.

The evolution of competition in the retail sector in a given trading area can be characterized as a sequence of two races. First retailers get involved in a 'race for space', where the key competitive weapon is location – or selling space, as virtual locations like online shops also have their race for space. Hence the famous saying that retailing is about three things: location, location and location. As soon as competing retailers have occupied the terrain and the consumer has the choice between several options for their shopping trips, then the second race starts, the 'race for distinctiveness'. From now on, retailers will have to give the consumer good reasons to come to their store instead of one closer to home (or the office, or the children's school), which is a challenge. In general, retailers are pretty good at the first, the race for space, and predominantly poor at the second, the race for differentiation. Often, they think they are still in the first race when the second race has already started. Even more often, they opt for a very predictable approach to become attractive to shoppers: price competition. Let's have a closer look at both races.

The Race for Space: Building Penetration

Retailers aiming for a considerable market share in a given geography will need to open the necessary number of stores, at the 'best' locations. Since shoppers tend to shop in the stores located nearest to them, retailers have to open stores where the consumers are, and preferably do so before their competitors do. This is what we call the race for space, and it is terribly important because it determines the retailers' market share potential. So if you win that race, and you don't mess up afterwards, you have a solid advantage over your competitors.

Figure 17. Distance to stores and % grocery spend.

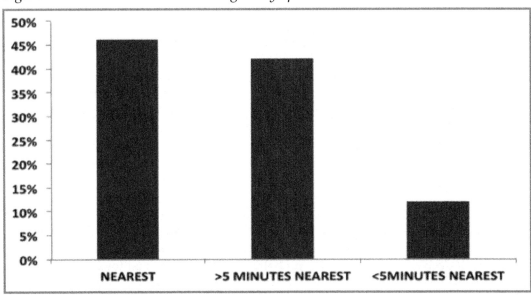

Source: Kantar Research UK, 2013.

To illustrate the importance of the race for space, data by Kantar Research in the UK show that stores located more than 5 minutes away from a shopper only get on average just over 10% of that shopper's grocery expenditures (Figure 17). What's more, having a local monopoly (a store with no competitors within 10 minutes) enables retailers to enjoy a 3% EBIT 'monopoly rent' (Figure 18).

Figure 18. Store competition and EBIT margin.

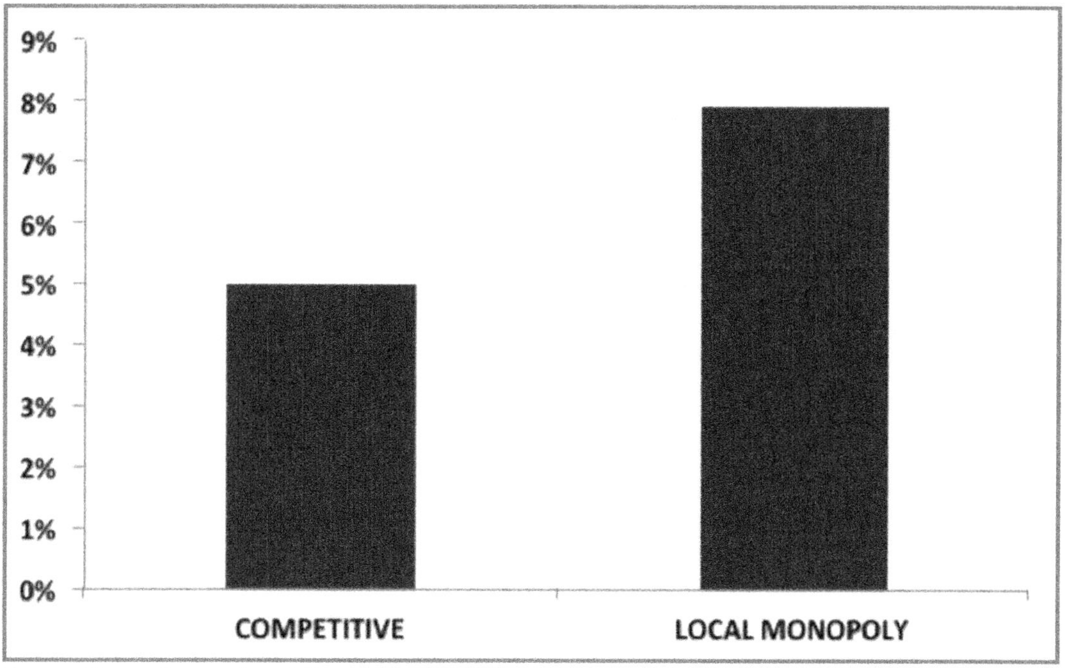

Source: Kantar Research and Bernstein, 2013 UK.

Today's largest international retailers are proven winners in the race for space. They have managed to gain a dominant position through rapid expansion before their competitors. Opening more and larger stores more quickly than their competitors is what made Walmart stand out in the US, or Tesco in the UK. Figure 19 clearly illustrates how Tesco has outperformed its competitors in the UK over the last fifteen years.

For Asda, Sainsbury, Morrison and Waitrose, it is too late to catch up now, as the market has become saturated with brick and mortar stores, with 83% of the population having access to at least three supermarket banners and spatial planning legislation becoming stricter.

During the race for space, speed is key. Winning the race is vital for two reasons:

(1) the first entrant in a trading area will capture monopoly rents and

(2) the winner of the space race will have the most stores and therefore will also capture economies of scale from larger networks of locations (supply chain, buying,…).

Once the space race starts to reach its end and consumers have plenty of alternative locations to shop, profitability starts to suffer.

Figure 19. Race for space in UK super/hypermarkets retail.

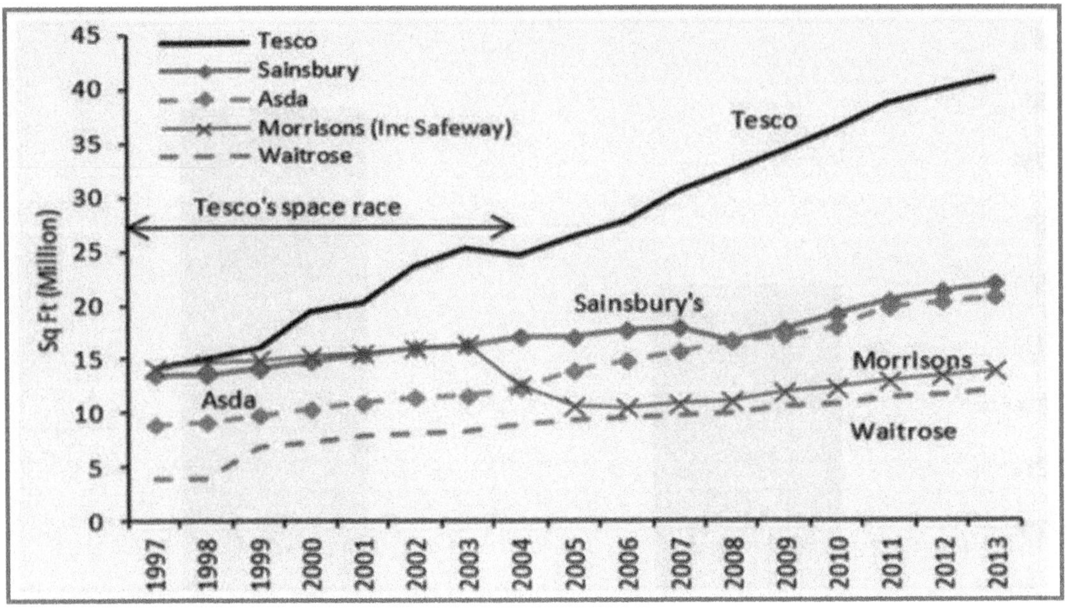

Source: Bernstein Analysis, 2014.

It is important to note however, that every race for space is related to a specific type of shopping trip and/or retail format. So, while the UK market is currently at the point where shoppers have sufficient choice for their main shopping trip, there are still other races going on. There is, for example, a space race for convenience stores, as well as for online grocery shopping. We see all players participating frantically in both races. Recently, there is a fourth race for space taking place in the UK for hard discounters, with Aldi, Lidl and the Sainsbury-Netto combination opening hard discount stores at accelerated pace.

As Figure 20 shows, markets do not develop at the same rhythm. While the race for space for super/hypermarkets is nearing its conclusion in most Western European countries and the US, there is still a huge expansion potential in emerging markets.

The race for space will follow different scenarios in various markets, depending on shopper density, the cost of real estate and planning permission constraints. Some towns may be too small to support more than two supermarkets, for example, and will not leave room for a third entrant. As a consequence, in countries with many small towns, this can lead to a very high retailer concentration, but not necessarily to less competition, which is often even more intense. In Australia, for example, the market is dominated by two large grocery chains, Woolworths and Coles, who are engaged in a fierce rivalry despite their combined 72% market share. On top of this, some towns do have room for a smaller-scale competitor, like a convenience store or a hard discounter, creating potential for players like 7-Eleven or Aldi. A comparable situation can be observed in several Scandinavian countries.

Figure 20. Number of stores per 35,000 capita.

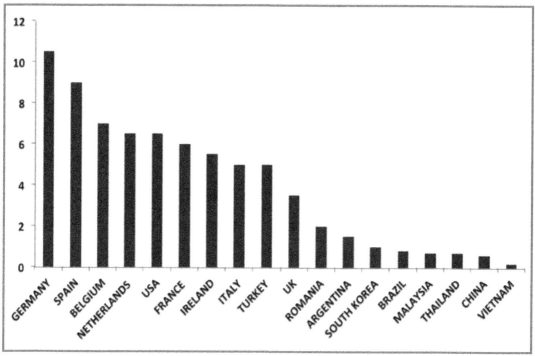

Source: Kantar Worldpanel, 2014.

Why is the race for space so important for retailers? The first chapter showed how essential penetration is for brands: Andrew Ehrenberg clearly demonstrated that consumer penetration is the key driver for organic growth of brands, much more so than loyalty or purchase frequency. Actually, the same law applies to retailers. The key variable driving sales and market share for retailers is shopper penetration: the number of shoppers visiting their stores; or the number of stores a retailer has in a country. It is rather difficult for a retailer to sustainably increase the number of trips (per year) or the size of the basket (per shopper) unless they increase penetration. Figures 21 and 22, for a small European country, illustrate the role household penetration plays in building shopper store trips as well as their basket sizes.

Since a retailer's market share is driven by household penetration, which is driven by the number of stores the retailer operates, it isn't hard to see that the race for space can be quite decisive in establishing the balance of power between retailers. Even if the race for space is not the only race retailers need to win, it is the most important. As the race for space determines the market share potential of a retailer, it dominates the race for differentiation, which determines how much of this potential is actually realized.

Figure 21. Household penetration and trip frequency in grocery retail in a small European country, 2011.
The dots on the graphs represent specific retailers. For confidentiality reasons their names cannot be revealed.

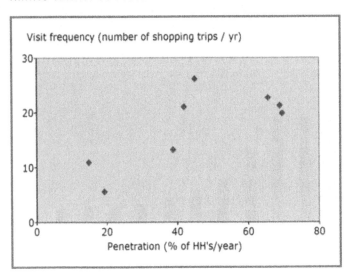

Source: Bain analysis, 2012.

Figure 22. Household penetration and basket size in grocery retail, small European country, 2011.
The dots on the graphs represent specific retailers. For confidentiality reasons their names cannot be revealed.

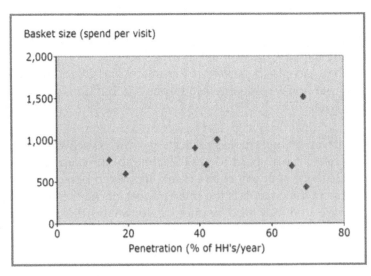

Source: Bain analysis, 2012.

They won the race for space

- Wal-Mart is probably the best example of a clear winner in the race for space. Sam Walton's innovative idea was to build stores in smaller towns, where other retailers were not present, and then expand quickly to as many towns as possible.
- In the UK, Tesco became number one thanks to its aggressive store expansion strategy. Former CEO Terry Leahy bought as much constructible land as he could and put a lot of effort into obtaining building permits for large stores, leaving the other players behind him. Actually, with hindsight, maybe Tesco went ahead a bit too fast, as it was announced in 2015 that they would have to write down about £2 billion worth of overvalued constructible land which they will not use as the race for large out-of-town big box stores is over. Other competitors were too slow. It was the biggest mistake former CEO Archie Norman made with Asda: they did not open enough locations when it was still possible, and now that there are fewer opportunities, the race for differentiation has started for large stores. In the UK there are currently three other races for space going on: for convenience stores, for e-commerce capacity and for hard discounters. Morrison's seems to be the clear loser, so far, in the race for convenience stores and online retail. Note that Amazon is obviously doing very well in the race for e-commerce space.
- Magnit in Russia has become extremely successful by expanding into regions where there is little competition. In a way they reproduce what Walmart did in the US many years ago.
- In Poland, Biedronka managed to acquire a strong position by rapidly expanding the number of stores in areas where there was less competition for their discount concept.
- Winning the race for space is also what Albert Heijn did in the Netherlands. They are present in every town – almost literally.

The Race for Differentiation: Wooing the Shopper

Winning the race for space doesn't end the competitive game. At some point in time, the consumer has the choice between several competing stores in a trading area, and a new race starts: the race for distinctiveness. Here, location is less crucial and other discriminating variables become vital: price, promotions, service, assortment, store design, communication – using these variables, retailers will try to convince shoppers to be included in the consideration set for their shopping needs.

This illustrates the importance of a clear banner positioning for retailers. Decisive as it may be, penetration is not exclusively driven by the number of stores a retailer has. It is also important for the retailer to enter into the consideration set of a majority of shoppers for a specific shopping trip – or for more than one type of shopping trip. Shoppers may turn to one retailer for their weekly stock-up trip, to another one for top-up trips and yet another one for shopping on-the-go. Or they may consider the same retailer for a number of different shopping missions.

The hard discounter Lidl, for example, was predominantly considered for bulk purchases for a limited number of product categories. By expanding its offer with fresh produce, chilled products, bakery and some well-known brands, it is now trying to get into the consideration set for weekly shopping trips, which seems to work to some extent in several European markets. On the other hand, Asda in the UK is not only stuck with locations that are typically aimed at weekly shopping trips, but as a consequence of their positioning as a big box, low-service, low-price retailer, with a large assortment biased towards cheaper products, attracting poorer and ethnically diverse shoppers, it remains problematic for them to enter and sustain their position in the consideration set of middle-class shoppers.

While retailers have a plethora of variables at their disposition to make themselves different from their rivals, they tend to overemphasize a very obvious factor: price. The question here is, how many retailers can distinguish themselves as the lowest-price retailer? The problem with retailers continuously convincing their shoppers that price is key is that shoppers gradually start to believe them, and this invariably leads to these retailers becoming Robin Hoods.

If retailers really aim to woo shoppers into deliberately passing other stores by to shop at their store, it seems only logical that at least some of these retailers will need to be known for something more than just low prices. Retailers in search of making themselves distinct in the eyes of potential shoppers will have to learn to make choices.

How winning the race for space doesn't guarantee long-term success

In retail, as in sports, you are only as good as your last race. It is still possible for a retailer to win the race for space by a large margin and subsequently lose this advantage because of poor performance in the race for differentiation. This is what happened, remarkably, to GB (the acronym refers to 'Grand Bazar'), a European forerunner in the supermarket industry and Belgium's grocery market leader from the 1960s until the '90s.

GB was nothing less than a retail pioneer when it opened its first Belgian supermarket in 1958 and the very first European hypermarket in 1961 (two years before Carrefour, to be precise). In the following years, the chain kept opening large stores at the very best locations, making use of a first-mover advantage to rapidly build market share. GB became and remained the undisputed market leader for decades, with a market share of more than 30% at their peak in the '80s, operating hypermarkets, supermarkets, and convenience stores; running a successful franchising division for independent-store owners; and building a retail empire in non-food markets as well. They had it all. What could possibly go wrong?

Well, almost everything went wrong. Today, you won't find a single GB store in the country. The banner has completely disappeared. What happened is probably a typical case of the arrogance that sometimes arises when companies begin to assume that success is self-evident. The retailer became self-sufficient, started lacking innovation power and commercial strength, handed over decision power to the trade unions and basically just fell asleep. What was once a dynamic commercial innovator became a conservative administrative Moloch, a fossilized business that was mockingly referred to in Belgium as the 'Ministry of Retail'. They completely lost sight of the consumer and the shopper.

Needless to say, this opened perspectives for challengers offering superior quality and service (Delhaize) or far lower prices (Colruyt). In spite of their great locations and their leadership in terms of number of stores and selling space in Belgium, GB saw its market share decline, and kept piling up losses until the shareholders saw no other option than to sell the retail business to Carrefour (in 2000) and their outstanding real estate portfolio to Redevco (in 2001), today one of Europe's largest commercial real estate investors. Colruyt and Delhaize became the respective numbers one and two in the Belgian grocery market, while Carrefour was forced to undertake painful restructuring. This case shows that latecomers can still catch up if the market leader drops the ball. Even if the race for space is dominant, retailers have to do a good job in the differentiation game to be distinct enough to retain a strong position in shoppers' consideration set of stores to visit.

Three Avenues for Building a Distinct Grocery Retailer

In the race for distinctiveness, retailers need to make choices, just like brands do. This is far from evident. Making a grocery store distinct and attractive beyond its location is very tough, not just because retailers have not developed the core competencies needed to do so, or because they don't have the time or margins needed to build non-location, non-price differentiation, but also because it means convincing a shopper to go (or drive) past a store to reach another store they prefer more. This is hard – much harder than for brands, as these brands are physically available for all shoppers in virtually every store they visit, on the same shelf as all the other brands in the same product category.

Typically, mainstream retailers are terribly afraid of disappointing part of their customer base. They are so afraid, actually, that they stock lots of unpopular SKUs just to avoid a shopper being disappointed by the offer. It is amazing to see how many SKUs in a supermarket do not even pass the checkout once a week. The table in the 'Innovation for Brands' chapter is revealing. So even if retailers could become a lot more efficient and profitable if they reduced their assortment by 50%, they refuse to do so out of fear that a mere handful of shoppers might go to another store for their regular shopping.

Retailers want to keep everyone happy, which is obviously impossible given the large heterogeneity of their customer base. In order to stand out, companies must make choices. It is unrealistic to try to be excellent in every dimension of the retail offer: price, range, service, promotions, nice shops, friendly staff and so on. This inevitably leads to mediocrity. Pick your arena.

Even the biggest retailers in this world, Tesco and recently even Wal-Mart, have to face this hard reality. By wanting to be good at everything, they end up being dominated by other retailers who have made explicit choices. For all their might and their economies of scale and scope, both icons, Tesco and Wal-Mart, are hurting badly: Tesco has lost 50% of its market value over the last years and Walmart was forced to announce two profit warnings in the second half of 2015. Although the two also have some idiosyncratic problems, they are in similar boats: they are losing shoppers and their offer is dominated by the offer of competitors in their key home market. Food shoppers know they can get cheaper prices with better quality from hard discounters (like Aldi and Lidl,) and shoppers for non-food products know the same is true with Amazon's dominant offer. On the other end of the spectrum, shoppers prefer the quality, the assortment and the retailer brands from well-run service/quality differentiated supermarkets such as Wegmans, Trader Joe's, Whole Foods, and Waitrose, to name a few.

In order to differentiate themselves sustainably, retailers must shape their offerings into a credible profile, with some outstanding differentiating attributes and some below average. Only when economising on certain dimensions of the offer can one invest to excel in other – relevant – areas. Obviously retailers have to respect hygiene standards, and they will always have to have reasonable prices, but they must recognize that you cannot be the best in everything. To excel on a few relevant dimensions, retailers should dare to be below par on other dimensions... This may seem very reasonable to most business executives, but tell this to senior grocery retail executives and they will roll their eyes and cry anathema, blaming you for not understanding the essence of their business. In their view, they cannot publicly admit being poor on some dimension, as it would give shoppers a reason not to shop at their store.

In any case, retailers must consider with care which additional services they will offer their shoppers. The risk for any service is that it permanently increases the cost of doing business without creating a sustainable advantage. Offering a new service isn't meaningful unless three conditions are met: (1) the shopper perceives the service as valuable; (2) it should be hard to copy by competitors; and (3) break-even should be reached in a short period of time. If these conditions are not satisfied, the retailer will find himself back where he started, but with a higher cost base.

Three differentiation avenues are open for retailers – and to a large extent they are mutually exclusive:

1 The price-driven approach, which is mainly the territory of hard discounters.
2 The service-driven approach, basically for retailers aiming at smaller target market.
3 The shopper-driven approach, focused on winning locally.

The price avenue
Poor people need them, rich people love them: low prices will always be hard to resist for shoppers, but the question is, how can retailers hold on to a sustainable price advantage in the medium-to-long term? It is no coincidence if low price seems to be the territory of the hard discounters. Price can only be a prime differentiator for the player with the lowest cost structure. It requires a lean and extremely disciplined organization

Making a retailer distinct is possible

- Aldi and Lidl, the successful German hard discounters, offer unbeatable value for money, a consistent shopping experience and convenience. But the range is limited; the shopping environment is bleak, without whistles and bells.
- The British supermarket chain Waitrose tempts shoppers with a rich assortment and a high-quality private-label range. On the other hand, prices are higher and shopping convenience is limited because they have a limited number of locations.
- Trader Joe's, a US chain owned by Aldi but completely different in concept and run independently, stands out with a unique assortment at great prices. Its product offer is totally different from other grocery retailers. In these tropical-themed grocery stores where employees wear Hawaiian shirts, shoppers can discover delicious food products sourced from around the globe. Trader Joe's is renowned for specific 'star' products, like the cheap but good quality 'Two Buck Chuck' wines sourced specifically for them from Charles Shaw.
- Wegmans, a relatively small, family-owned supermarket chain operating in the eastern US, makes the difference with a particular assortment, friendly and competent staff, and an exceptional customer experience. But Wegmans does not offer the lowest prices, nor the best locations.
- When Juan Roig took over the steering wheel at Spanish retailer Mercadona in 1981, they had eight shops in the Valencia area. Today they are the biggest grocery retailer in Spain, with about 1,400 stores. How did they do it? The company vision says the shopper is the boss and the first thing the boss wants is low prices, so Mercadona has a business model that allows them to offer these low prices. Their assortment is smaller than that of other supermarkets, because Mercadona buys what the shopper wants to find in their stores rather than what suppliers want to sell to Mercadona. Their own employees are thoroughly trained and paid well, including some profit sharing

with an appropriate portfolio of small stores, a limited assortment, little service, simplicity in operations, and motivated employees to execute the strategy flawlessly (typically, hard discounters pay their employees pretty well).

A low price positioning can work anywhere, because in every market there is a significant proportion of consumers interested in this proposition, not for their full shopping needs but certainly for part of their total basket. The concept works best when there is a high price umbrella in the market, held up by mainstream retailers. Therefore, hard discounters don't enter markets early. They need a higher reference point...

As there seems to be a market in every country in the world for the hard discount format and since Aldi and Lidl cannot be everywhere at the same time, there are plenty of opportunities around the globe for entrepreneurs to copy them. The key for a successful entry as an Aldi or Lidl copy is timing. There has to be a sufficiently strong presence of mainstream retailers in the market to make sure the hard discount proposition really 'bites', in relation to the higher-priced 'normal' retailers.

Biedronka in Poland and BIM in Turkey are successful examples of retailers adopting the Aldi/Lidl hard discounter approach and to win the race for space in their respective countries. Ironically, both players, clearly copycats, have outdone the Aldi and Lidl originals by managing to make their copies very 'country specific'. Both Biedronka (although owned by a Portuguese retailer, they kept the Polish name meaning 'ladybird') and BIM emphasize their localness, in part by their communication about the very high share of local suppliers in the assortment they propose to their shoppers.

Apart from hard discounters, which bet on the lowest prices combined with a small assortment and minimal service, we can distinguish retailers that play with something more than just price. Sometimes they are called 'soft' discounters. On top of relatively low prices, they offer choice, a larger assortment that includes national brands. Amazon, currently especially in the non-food area, is a notable exception in that they do offer a huge assortment and home-delivery service, as well as very low prices. Their offer is sustainable because they are in a unique position. They are very big and have therefore significant economies of scale. Their pure play e-tailer business model reduces their real estate investments and their Marketplace business generates significant profits to subsidize the low prices in the rest of their Amazon business. Add to that the fact that their shareholders are very accommodating by tolerating a zero dividend policy.

But do you have to be huge to be successful as a soft discounter? Well, it certainly helps, but it is not necessary. A remarkable case in point is Colruyt, Belgium's market leader despite fierce competition from international heavyweights like Carrefour, Aldi, Lidl, and Metro. Because they became successful before Aldi and Lidl became big in the Belgian market, a first-mover advantage helped them act – at least temporarily – as a local buffer against hard discounter growth. What is their secret? A credible and enforced lowest-price guarantee is at the core of Colruyt's positioning, even though they offer a complete assortment including national brands, fresh produce and chilled food in stores that are twice as large as the average hard discounter. They are able to do this thanks to their surprisingly lean, cost-conscious organization, thanks to a smart local pricing system, and thanks to a local scale advantage over Aldi and Lidl – food being predominantly local, especially in a market like Belgium where quality-conscious consumers won't accept pale compromises. Moreover, Colruyt mainly sells branded products, as they allow for transparent price comparisons with competitors selling the same SKUs.

What characterizes each of these hard and soft discounters is that they have thoroughly grasped the irresistible nature of low prices. 'There are two kinds of companies, those that work to try to charge more and those that work to charge less. We will be the second,' said Jeff Bezos, CEO of Amazon.

Although this sounds almost trite and obvious, it is actually insightful and far from obvious. Economists would tend to have a different view, and even mathematically prove it, but of course, they are not retailers. Suppose you are a retailer and you are able to buy some products a lot cheaper than your competitors, what do you do? Do you charge just a little bit less than your competitors, or do you sell them really cheaply? Economic theory would argue for the first option, because it's a double win: you can offer the shopper a good deal and at the same time make a juicy margin. Why give away margin if the consumer is already happy with the attractive price you offer and you don't get more volume by lowering the price further? What could be better? But Sam Walton and Jeff Bezos would disagree. They would fully pass on the advantage to the shopper. Not out of philanthropic motives, but because in their minds, the shopper will be delighted, have a good price image of that retailer and come back to the store in the future, allowing the retailer to sell larger volumes, which will ultimately lead to bigger profits.

However, one should never forget that competing on price can only be a sound strategy for retailers with the lowest cost structure. Look at it this way: competing on price is like making a fire – it can create a lot of warmth but it will constantly need more wood. Competing on non-price factors is like a river: as long as the source is higher than the sea, the water will flow… But if you have a lot of wood, and if you want to work hard and there is no river in sight…

Why price will remain at the top of the list

'[Amazon has] done price elasticity studies, and the answer is always that we should raise prices. We don't do that, because we believe – and we have to take this as an article of faith – that by keeping our prices very, very low, we earn trust with customers over time, and that that actually does maximize free cash flow over the long term.'

'I very frequently get the question: "What's going to change in the next 10 years?" And that is a very interesting question; it's a very common one. I almost never get the question: "What's not going to change in the next 10 years?" And I submit to you that that second question is actually the more important of the two – because you can build a business strategy around the things that are stable in time….[I]n our retail business, we know that customers want low prices, and I know that's going to be true 10 years from now. They want fast delivery; they want vast selection. It's impossible to imagine a future 10 years from now where a customer comes up and says, 'Jeff, I love Amazon; I just wish the prices were a little higher,' [or] 'I love Amazon; I just wish you'd deliver a little more slowly.' Impossible. And so the effort we put into those things, spinning those things up, we know the energy we put into it today will still be paying off dividends for our customers 10 years from now. When you have something that you know is true, even over the long term, you can afford to put a lot of energy into it.'
— Jeff Bezos, CEO of Amazon

The service avenue

Is it possible for retailers to offer a specific service which is difficult to copy and for which the consumer is willing to make a detour and/or to pay a little bit more? Success stories of retailers who actually know how to differentiate themselves seem to confirm this, although examples are rather scarce. The point seems to be that a service positioning in grocery retailing cannot be the heart of the total market. Retailers known for a truly distinctive service approach are seldom total market leaders: think of Waitrose, Whole Foods, Trader Joe's, Wegmans, and on a broader scale than grocery, Harrod's, Rob, and Fauchon.

Distinctive services may include offering a large or exceptional assortment, high-value fresh products, a quality private label, loyalty programs, special shopper services, store atmosphere... Actually, if your ambition as a grocery retailer is not to have the largest market share, one does not have to shake the world to its foundations to figure out a way to create a unique retail proposition for shoppers. Being special in some relevant aspect for the shopper may do the job. Super Inter in Colombia, for example, is a pretty average retailer. Its stores are not particularly nice and their service is mediocre, but they are unique in their meat assortment: a phenomenal choice at attractive prices, resulting in a terrific offer for the shopper. They can do this because they sell a massive amount of meat and can therefore get good deals from their meat suppliers. What's more, over time they have developed an unprecedented know-how and expertise in the world of Colombian meat, which makes their competitive advantage reasonably sustainable. The shopper goes to Super Inter for the meat, and then does the rest of their shopping (or at least part of it) in the same store.

Making a difference is what Whole Foods does with organic food or Marks & Spencer does with chilled convenience food products and ready meals. A retailer should ask himself, 'What can I be known for by my shoppers?', or 'What can I develop as a destination category or product?'

The difficulty for retailers differentiating on service is staying ahead of the competition. Successful initiatives will inevitably be copied. Terry Leahy's motto for Tesco, 'Every little helps', demonstrates how Tesco has to constantly add new little improvements for their shoppers, because successful new features will be copied quickly. It is striking to see that hard discounters all over Europe have begun expanding their assortment over the past decade, introducing fresh produce, ready meals, and organic and fair trade products at significantly lower prices than the mainstream supermarkets. It will be a challenge for service retailers to keep the lead in their service advantage without losing themselves in extravagant sophistication. It will equally be a challenge for the hard discounters, given their expanded offer, to keep their costs low enough to make a sustainable difference in the market with low prices. Or, is the upgrading movement we see – especially by Lidl – a striking example of the wheel of retailing, whereby they are in the process of losing their cost advantage by becoming a 'normal' supermarket retail format?

As price remains a factor of importance even for service-driven supermarkets, maybe retailers should have the courage to turn the question around. Instead of thinking about what services they should add in order to woo more shoppers to their stores, retailers could ask themselves: 'Which service to the shopper can we drop, in exchange for offering lower prices?' We know shoppers do not value the typical services offered by retailers very highly. The shopper may be happily willing to perform specific services herself if she gets paid for them in the form of lower prices. Alternatively, dropping one service may release budgets for developing another, more relevant service for shoppers. So the art of retailing may be in finding new exchange rates between what the shopper is prepared to pay for a service and what the service costs the retailer.

Is e-commerce a differentiating service?

The study of the evolution of grocery retailing over time leads to the conclusion that most of its innovation has come from retailers passing on specific activities to their shoppers in return for lower prices. It started with Clarence Saunders' Piggly Wiggly self-service concept in Memphis, Tennessee, in 1916, and it culminates today in the appearance of self-scanning and self-checkouts. Similar developments have happened in other service industries like the travel and hotel business. It seems like an adequate process of transferring activities to where they can be performed most efficiently, and it characterizes the move from mom-and-pop stores to self-service supermarkets to hypermarkets to hard discounters. In this process the emphasis of the retailers' communication to the shoppers was always that their format was cheaper. The consumer has bought into this way of thinking, and as a result shoppers have difficulty paying for any service that retailers offer.

At the same time, we now see the reverse movement of 'home delivery' in its various forms, from pick-up points and drives to actual delivery at the front door. These recent e-commerce developments seem to go against the normal evolution mentioned above: the retailer takes over more activities traditionally done by consumers. In grocery retail, however, only a small segment of above-average-income consumers seem willing to pay for this service, which probably explains the slow progress of e-commerce and home delivery in grocery retail. This leads to some very interesting questions.

Has the continued reduction of services offered by retail contributed to increased price competition to such an extent that any service offered by retailers is not appreciated by shoppers – except for small pockets of well-off consumers? Should we see the rise of e-commerce in food retail as just another differentiation of retail services, aimed strictly at those who can afford it? If so, we might compare it to the differentiation between first class and business class in airlines, and conclude that e-commerce has a limited potential in FMCG.

Or, are we witnessing an actual trend reversal in retail, and will this added service take over when more and more consumers, and in particular millennials, become familiar with home shopping? Will technology changes make added services acceptable to the masses? In this case, home delivery may well become the new normal in grocery retail.

Anyway, this leads to a difficult choice for retailers: should they focus on how to reduce service and pass on more activities to the consumer in exchange for lower prices, or invest in technology to find a new business model and a new cost structure that will make e-commerce the dominant retail channel? As retailers don't really know which one will prevail, they hesitate to make pronounced choices – as usual – so they do both: they set up ways of offering the low-prices option and simultaneously invest in setting up a home-delivery service. Today we see most, if not all, retailers offering home delivery – even the hard discounters are testing the waters – as well as a hard discount option.

A further negative side effect of offering less and less service in addition to accentuating low prices and promotions is that it leads to a lack of understanding of consumer and shopper behaviour by retailers. An advantage of adding services (like home delivery) is that it brings retailers closer to shoppers, enabling them to better understand their shoppers' behaviour and maybe become a bigger part of their lives.

The local-shoppers avenue

A third option for creating a distinctive grocery retail proposition is based on satisfying local shoppers better than your competitors do. In a nutshell, grocery retail is a local business, and to win, you need to win locally – in every store! This path is fundamentally different from the previous two in that it is less driven by a central positioning of the store network. The underlying philosophy is that shoppers choose the store in which they shop locally, and that the banner image of the grocer on a national scale is relatively unimportant to them. Of course, there is the notion that the grocer has to inspire trust in shoppers, but who would argue that this cannot be achieved by local communication and local store management? Of course, a retailer needs economies of scale in buying, communications, et cetera, but these are still possible when you build an intelligent network of stores with sufficient degrees of freedom for local store management.

This shopper-driven approach can be fueled by store managers, by Big Data or by a combination of both.

Shopper-driven differentiation fueled by the store manager is based on the insight that if competition between stores is always local, every store needs to adapt to its local shoppers and the local manager is the best-placed person to manage this local fine-tuning of the retail offer. Therefore, store managers should be allowed to adapt their offer to the demands of their local shoppers, within reasonable limits. Retailers simply cannot have totally different assortments or unique layouts and merchandising in every single store in the network. But what central management should do is offer store managers a menu of options in terms of pricing, promotions, assortment and merchandising, from which they can choose the option that best fits local shoppers and the local competitive situation. To avoid wild inconsistencies within the store network and to make sure economies of scale are properly leveraged, such a menu should be constructed by headquarters, but with sufficient flexibility to allow store managers to adjust to their specific environment of shoppers and competitors. To make this approach viable, it is imperative that store managers are well trained, strongly incentivized, and paid for their local performance with stretched targets. At the same time, there needs to be a strict and fair system of checks and balances. Detailed information on essential KPIs at the store level should be generated on a daily basis and acted upon centrally, in order to make sure errors are picked up and corrected stante pede and successes in specific stores are communicated throughout the network and leveraged within the complete network. Things that get measured tend to improve.

Big Data–driven differentiation doesn't focus on every local store, but goes one step further: it is aimed at each individual shopper at each store. The aim is to offer 'one-to-one' propositions to every shopper. This is sustainable because competing retailers don't have the same data on the focal retailer's shoppers or the same systems to leverage those available data. Store managers are not as central in this approach, but they do need to be fully integrated to execute the strategy, making sure that the store is clean, the shelves are filled, their personnel is well managed and motivated, the parking lot is well maintained, and that promises made to individual shoppers via Big Data are kept when they actually come to the store. Both options pose their own problems and challenges, but in combination, they may provide an interesting and actually untried pathway. Let's have a look at them in turn.

Empowering the Store Manager

Four years ago, while preparing a management development program for senior executives from a large international retailer – let's call them 'Walfour' – I spent a few days visiting about ten stores with a regional director responsible for about 50 large stores. The store visits mostly repeated the following obviously well-rehearsed scenario. When we met the manager of the first store we entered, a hypermarket format, the director asked him: 'What is the name of this store?' Surprised, the store manager answered: 'It is Warfour, of course – you know that.' Upon which the director responded: 'Are you sure? I got the impression that it's called John's store', John being the first name of the manager. Then the director went on to explain that every store manager had received a note from headquarters the previous month, telling them that confectionary was banned from the checkout area until further notice. So why were there still chocolate bars at the checkout? The store manager argued that confectionary was very profitable in his store, which was located in an area with many large households with children. 'Not allowed,' the director insisted. Then we went from product category to product category in the store, repeating the same plot: every time the rules decided by headquarters had not been followed, the director would comment and urge the store manager to get in line by his next visit.

In one store, the regional director asked why there were no promotions for a big beer brand in the store, when the store manager had been informed, together with all his colleagues, that heavy promotions were part of an important deal the retailer had negotiated with a large beer brand owner. The store manager explained that in her store, situated in a wealthier area, wine was a more appropriate category to promote than beer. Of course the regional director disagreed: it had to be beer!

Isn't it striking? Every large retailer will assure you that they are shopper driven, and that customer-centricity is of the utmost importance in retail. Each will confirm that winning means you win locally in every single store, because competition is always local. All will assert how important the impact of the store manager is on the performance of a store. Yet, they constrain store managers and limit the parameters they can play with. Headquarters will make most decisions on assortment, planograms, pricing, promotions, merchandising, and so forth. Why? It is obvious they don't trust their store managers. Too many of them are poor performers. Retailers often end up with mediocre store managers because the really bad ones get dismissed and the best ones are promoted to more senior roles. The bigwigs are also worried that if they hand over the keys to the store managers, the chain will be all over the place and many inconsistencies will show up that are difficult to justify. Which, of course, is understandable.

Moreover, when you discuss the importance of store managers with top retail people, they all agree that store managers have a significant impact on sales and profitability of their stores, but they have no idea how big this impact really is. They tend to agree that the impact is asymmetric: the negative impact of a poor store manager is bigger than the positive impact of a good store manager. But there is no consensus at all on the figures. It is amazing that they don't know how big a store manager's impact is. Or maybe it isn't? When I was on the point of studying this issue for a large German retailer, I was stopped from doing so under union pressure. The unions (who sit on the board of large German companies) were afraid the results of the study would provide management with ammunition to fire underperforming store managers...

Still, I would suggest that retailers are able to win by unleashing the power of their store managers. I do realize this is a matter of degree and balance. You can't let store managers make all the decisions they see fit for their area. There are company imperatives to be dealt with, economies of scale and a necessary degree of consistency within the chain. Proof that it is nevertheless possible to assign some decision power to store managers can be found in the many franchising concepts that seem to work well in the grocery area. Big players like Carrefour, E.Leclerc, Delhaize and Albert Heijn have an important part of their store portfolio run by independent store managers, local businesspeople who sign a franchising contract with the retailer and manage one or more local stores for them (sometimes owning the store, but mostly renting it from the retailers' real estate division). While these entrepreneurs have to respect the store concept defined by headquarters, they do have some freedom in the management of their business. Thus, a local entrepreneur with a butcher diploma would be able to offer a unique meat assortment, another may have completed a wine course that allows him to select and advise on exceptional chateaux, while an IT enthusiast may develop a targeted local marketing program for his store. These entrepreneurs typically outperform company-operated stores but are a source of concern as well, since some of them do not always follow HQ's dictates, which might jeopardize company morale. And there is of course the risk that they might defect to a competitor...

Still, it is clear that a number of caveats have to be dealt with before handing more power to store managers.

1. **You cannot let every store manager do something totally different**. Retailers need economies of scale, for example in buying and logistics. Headquarters will need to define the parameters with which store managers can play locally. For example, in terms of assortment one could envisage a 'must have' set of SKUs, and then a set of SKUs that individual store managers can manage to fit their environment. In a more affluent location, wine might be more prominent than in a blue-collar area, where beer might be more important. There might also be, in the fresh area, an opportunity for the store manager to source more locally and use that to appeal to the shopper base.

2. How do you **identify good store managers**? Objective analysis is needed. One could gather all the data available in the company on individual store managers and the performances of their store managers overall and use statistical analysis to objectively identify the profile of 'good' store managers.

3   How do you **avoid ending up with mediocre store managers**? As it goes, poor managers are dismissed or moved sideways, and good ones tend to be ambitious and want to be promoted. Retailers will need to develop incentive schemes to motivate store managers to stay in their job. Should retailers actively go after good store managers from competitors? Probably not, as this may create a bad competitive environment. Try to prepare the next generation of store managers from your new talent.

4   How do you **leverage your best store managers** and use them to train and coach the best people from the next level in the hierarchy? Retailers should make a big effort to create a 'store manager academy' in the company to (i) explain and teach what store managers should do; (ii) create a store manager culture in the company; and (iii) add prestige to the store managers constituency. Don't forget that many of these people lack higher formal education and would be very pleased to have the opportunity to catch up. Bring the know-how of your good store managers into the curriculum and the teaching in this 'store managers academy'.

5   How do you **attract the best future store managers**? Once you have figured out what the desired characteristics are of good store managers, use this info in your recruitment efforts of new talent. Offer them an exciting job, with more decision power, great financial remuneration (pay for performance) and a clear career path. Create a culture where you are seen as the Goldman Sachs or the P&G or the Google of store management.

A new role for the grocery store

In local communities in many developed countries, there may be a need for a 'local champion', a business that can act as a resource for the people in the community. In the old days, the church, the pub, the post office or the local shopkeeper played that role. Could a grocery retailer fill this gap and become a crucial part of the local fabric? The store manager would become the conduit, knowing what's cooking in his community and getting involved. This is what I like to call 'weightless brand ownership': extending the grocery retail equity into other services that would help the retailer in achieving non-price differentiation.

Getting the Most out of Big Data

Retailers have long dreamt of being able to identify what makes every individual shopper tick and to formulate tailor-made propositions accordingly. The possibilities for data acquisition and data analytics have grown exponentially over the years and will continue to do so. In Chapter 3, 'Marketing in a Digital World,' we discussed the opportunities created by Big Data. There is a definite first-mover advantage here for retailers grasping this opportunity to offer shoppers a distinctive retail offer. But one has to remain realistic about the benefits of Big Data. Notwithstanding all the hype, keep in mind that although Tesco certainly benefited from its early venture into a Big Data type of approach, this has not prevented the retailer from losing many shoppers over the past few years, and no single retailer – not even Amazon or Alibaba – has even come close to predicting what you or I would like to buy next time around. We'll get there, but not yet!

The winning combination

Big data does have a major advantage, though: it is an objective counterweight against biased decision-making by inconsistent managers who sometimes think they are right even when they might simply be wrong. We are, after all, human beings with bounded rationality. Even top notch specialists miss the ball sometimes. Take this example: In a serious scientific study, the identical detailed profile of a patient was sent to 100 general practitioners in the New England region of the US. Their diagnosis varied from 'No problem, aspirin will do the job' to 'Urgent, needs to be sent to the hospital for surgical treatment'. This is scary, really. If intelligent and well-trained medical professionals fail to agree on serious medical problems, what should we expect from average store managers if we give them carte blanche? This is why the combination of store managers and Big Data, where the latter can help test and generate ideas from the hands-on store managers, is probably the way to go.

Chapter Insights

1 Location and penetration are still key in retail. They are not everything, but they are a pretty powerful start.
2 The race for distinctiveness is the Achilles' heel for retailers: they try to be good at everything that could possibly make them distinctive and therefore end up as mediocre and blurred. They have to have the guts to dare to be bad on some dimensions to generate the necessary resources to be outstanding on specific, chosen dimensions that count for the shopper.
3 Creating a distinctive retail proposition based on a business model driven by the store manager and by excelling locally is too often dismissed or overlooked by retailers.

Chapter 7
What Drives Your Trade Partner?

When I talk to brand owners and ask them what their challenges are for the years to come, invariably one of their top three concerns is the increasing demands from their customers, the retailers. In fact, so they assure me, these large retailers must be getting rich as a result of demanding ever more from them. Just look at the richest people in a number of countries: invariably retailers top the list. Think of the Walton family (Walmart stores) in the US; the Albrecht family (Aldi) in Germany; the Mulliez family (many retail businesses, the biggest of which is Auchan) in France; Juan Roig (Mercadona) in Spain; and Mikhail Fridman (X5) and Sergey Galitsky (Magnit) in Russia, to name just a few.

'How do you think they got there? From us financing their business,' the brand owners tell me. In France, for example, they explain that in 2015, the large retailers imposed a 4% list price reduction on suppliers of the top 1,600 brands, yet the same retailers in 2014 significantly increased the prices of their private-label products in the categories where these 1,600 brands operated. Brand owners even go a step further and show me an article from the respected weekly *Le Nouvel Observateur*, which based on an in-depth analysis shows that the family Jaud, who own several Leclerc hypermarkets (for a total of 100,000 square meters) is richer than the Michelin family, owners of the top brand in the tire industry. These brand owners operating in France go on about the continuously increasing concentration of buying power in the hands of fewer and fewer French retailers: 2014 alone saw the birth of joint buying alliances between Auchan and Système U, Intermarché and Casino, and Carrefour and Cora, while Carrefour also bought back the French Dia operations. This increased buying power leads to tougher interactions, where retailers draw more and more blood.

When I talk to senior executives in the retail industry, they invariably tell me: 'This is nonsense – brand owners are much better off than we are. Just open the *Financial Times* or the *Wall Street Journal* and read about their growth in terms of both sales and profits. If that doesn't convince you, look at their share price evolution and compare it to ours. There is no doubt they are far richer than we are. We need to fight like crazy to achieve their imposed targets in order to get some goodies from them, and often these hard-fought terms are just like Monopoly money.'

Monopoly money? 'Yes,' they explain, 'the brand owners raise the list price (for one of twenty reasons they make up) and then give a discount on an artificially high list price. Believe me, they are running circles around us, and they keep complaining about how unfair we are to them, crying all the way to the bank. We retailers run a tough business: there is always another store close by available for the shopper. We have very high costs to run our operations and our margins are razor thin because of the competitive pressure we have to deal with. And if all this still does not persuade you, just go have a look at their offices and then visit ours. Compare the shiny palaces of Unilever at Blackfriars in London, Coca-Cola in Atlanta, Nestlé in Vevey (Switzerland), P&G in Cincinnati or l'Oréal in Clichy, and then have a look at the humble headquarters of Wal-Mart in Bentonville, Metro in Düsseldorf or Tesco in Cheshunt (UK). It's not complicated, really – just bare facts.'

So who is right, the brand owners or the retailers?

A marriage of convenience
The relationship between FMCG manufacturers and retailers is invariably described as 'difficult'. While both parties are supposed to collaborate intensely in order to better serve the final consumer, conflicting interests cause recurring discussions over trade conditions, pricing and promotions, payment delays and so on. Still, sales people on the brand-owner side often emphasize the importance of maintaining 'good relations' with their business partners. Even in an environment that has become more fact based over the years, the human factor remains important and social skills make a difference, they argue.

But contrary to what some think, love is a concept that does not exist in business. Brand owners and retailers that cooperate might try to move their interactions from transactional to relational, but they both have shareholders, and their interests are not served by, for example, a retailer helping a supplier who is having a hard time. Maybe a John Lennon and Paul McCartney kind of relationship is the best one can hope for, a partnership between two strong parties who can work well together in spite of contrasting views, opposite interests or even clashing personalities. Lennon and McCartney did not particularly like each other on a personal level, but each respected the other's talent and realized that the output of their collaboration was greater than the sum of its parts. It was only after the balance between the two was lost, and John got frustrated with the feeling that Paul was claiming too much control, that the end of the band was near. This shows that such a partnership implies mutual trust, which takes time to build and may dissolve in a second. But love? No, the relationship will never be unconditional. The preferred word to use in this relationship is 'respect', not 'love'. A marriage of convenience, if you will.

The quality of the relationship between a retailer and a manufacturer depends largely on two critical factors: the degree of information available at the level of both trade partners and the market conditions in which they operate. Let's explain.

The better a player knows what he wants from his trade partner, and the better he understands the economics of his own business model as well as that of his trade partner,

138

the higher the probability that he will realize what's feasible to obtain. Therefore, he will have a pretty good idea if the deal that is achieved is a good deal or not. Conversely, less prepared and less informed trade partners will be more in the dark as to the degree to which the deal agreed on was beneficial for them or not. This can sometimes lead to more aggressive behaviour, compensating for the lack of information. Consensus has it that Aldi and Lidl, like Wal-Mart, are tough but fair negotiators with their trade partners; they tend to be well informed and know what they want.

The more competitive the market, the tougher the relationship will be. France and Germany are often characterized as very difficult markets as far as the interaction between retailers and manufacturers is concerned. Why? Both markets are very price competitive at the retailer level. In Germany, Aldi and Lidl occupy a very strong market position and put strong price pressure on the other retailers. In France, the dominance of large franchise retailers like E.Leclerc and Intermarché, in combination with discounters Aldi and Lidl, make for a similarly price-competitive retail scene. For many years, the retailer–manufacturer interaction in the UK was considered more collaborative, less aggressive or conflictual. At the same time, Tesco was seen as aggressive in their dealings with their suppliers in Poland, a more competitive retail scene at that time. Over the years, the UK market has become more aggressive due to the presence and growing success of price-driven hard discounters Aldi and Lidl, and suppliers find this reflected in more challenging interactions with their retailers.

But why do retailers get aggressive with their suppliers? The key point is that they demand to have, at least, a 'level playing field'. If retailers have to compete for shoppers, they cannot afford to be disadvantaged in the prices their suppliers charge them. However, in most cases retailers can't be sure if their competitors are getting a better deal or not. Retailers in price-competitive markets see no other option than to squeeze their suppliers till the juice runs out, and then squeeze even a bit more. This makes them feel more comfortable about the deals they get – because, after all, they know very well that their competitors are squeezing their suppliers equally hard.

At the core of the conflicting relationship between retailers and manufacturers is a clear lack of understanding of each other's business models. Can companies really cooperate in a sustainable way if they don't understand exactly how the other party makes money? In order to be able to work together constructively, manufacturers should thoroughly comprehend the retailers' business model – and vice-versa. This is crucial. This chapter will try to explain the fundamentally different economics of both parties and offer suggestions on how to engage in productive, collaborative business relationships.

Two Fundamentally Different Business Models

Manufacturers and retailers have very different ways of generating their profitability. There are many ways of measuring value creation and each generates different insights. We need to compare different ratios, because profitability is a multidimensional concept;

there are many ways to look at it. Take a simple example comparing two companies that most people would say are at opposite ends of a profitability spectrum: pharmaceuticals giant Pfizer and no-frills cut-price airline operator Ryanair. Who is actually more profitable? Well, that depends on how you look at it. Let's compare some key 'performance indicators for 2014:

1 *Absolute net profits after tax*
Pfizer: €8.1 billion
Ryanair: €0.5 billion
Clearly Pfizer generates far more profits, but are they therefore more profitable than Ryanair?

2 *Net profit margin after tax (NPAT/sales)*
Pfizer: 18%
Ryanair: 10%
Again Pfizer has the upper hand...

3 *Return on assets (NPAT/Sales)*
Pfizer: 5.4%
Ryanair: 5.7%
Here the balance is reversed. Pfizer needs a massive amount of assets (€151 billion) to generate their profits, a lot more than Ryanair (€9 billion).

4 *Shareholder return on equity (NPAT/Equity)*
Pfizer: 13%
Ryanair: 15%
Ryanair generates more returns from shareholders' invested equity than Pfizer does.

5 *Total shareholder return (change in share price + dividends) over last 5 years*
Pfizer: +130%
Ryanair: +280%
Again, for an investor on the stock market, Ryanair has been a far better option than Pfizer, notwithstanding Pfizer's amazing absolute profits and profit margin.

Now, in the same way, we can compare retailers and manufacturers. What do we learn from Table 28?

Return on equity (ROE) is an elegant performance indicator, as it not only goes to the essence of the rationale for a business (measuring the return for shareholders' invested capital), but also because it can neatly be decomposed in the three critical levers a company can use to improve its profitability: margin (Net Profit after Tax/ Sales), efficiency (Sales/Assets) and financial leverage (Assets/Equity) (Table 29).

Table 28. Comparing brand owners and retailers on various performance indicators

	NET PROFIT MARGIN average 2010-13 (1)	RETURN ON ASSETS average 2010-13 (2)	WORKING CAPITAL/SALES (3)	ROE (4)
RETAILERS				
CARREFOUR	1.1	1.9	-3.0%	14%
METRO	1.0	2.0	-0.7%	4%
TARGET	5.0	7.5	0%	18%
WAL-MART	4.0	9.3	-1.3%	21%
BRANDOWNERS				
COCA-COLA	18.2	9.2	+3.0%	24%
NESTLE	10.8	8.3	+1.0%	13%
P&G	14.8	8.8	+4.0%	17%
UNILEVER	10.2	11.1	-9.6%	39%

(1) NET OPERATING PROFITS AFTER TAX / SALES, Source Bloomberg
(2) NET OPERATING PROFITS AFTER TAX/ ASSETS, Source Bloomberg
(3) ((RECEIVABLES + INVENTORIES)- PAYABLES) / Sales, Source Bloomberg
(4) NET OPERATING PROFITS AFTER TAX / EQUITY, Source Bloomberg

Table 29. Economics of retailers

	NPAT/SALES	SALES/ASSETS	ASSETS/EQUITY
HOW?	• DISTINCTIVENESS • SIZE	• WORKING CAPITAL • EFFICIENT OPERATIONS	• DEBT/EQUITY BALANCE

Profit margins

As expected, retailers' margins are a lot smaller than manufacturers'. Notwithstanding the fact that retailers presumably get better deals from their suppliers each year, their profit margins don't increase (the figures over time on net profit margins in the Robin Hood Chapter 5 illustrate this). So if we ask how brand owners can add value to retailers, giving them more margin seems a not so effective approach. Retailers have an incontinence problem; they simply compete this increased margin away.

Over time, manufacturers have done a very effective job in improving their own profit margins. They have, for example, shut down factories, laid off people and cut overheads, as well as getting rid of lower-margin businesses, acquiring better-margin businesses and introducing new products with better margins. At the same time they have managed to weather the storms from their demanding retailers: in part they pay with real money and in part they pay with 'funny money' by increasing list prices.

Retailers have been unable to increase their margins because shoppers see them as very similar and therefore easily substitutable once they are conveniently located and price differences become significant. On top of that, they are stuck with high fixed costs (a big store with a lot of shoppers has about the same cost to operate as the same store with few shoppers). These high fixed costs force retailers to maximize their sales (i.e. to attract as many shoppers to their stores as possible). The fastest way to do this is by lowering prices and offering promotions. Once a competing retailer starts doing this, all the competing retailers get locked into a prisoners' dilemma of following the first, reinforcing lowering prices and increasing promotional activities.

So how can brand owners help *retailers* improve *their* margins?

It seems a good idea to try to give the retailer something he can hold on to, rather than just more margin. Don't give more drugs to a junkie. What can brand owners offer? There are many things:

- Exclusive and differentiated products (with different packaging, formats, varieties…). This may cost the supplier more, but the retailer will appreciate it
- Unique promotions
- Support to help the retailer understand shoppers better (with sophisticated analytics on joint Big Data)
- On-time delivery
- Flawless invoicing
- Support in reducing out-of-stocks
- Support in creating in-store excitement

These things all sound traditional and to some extent seem 'boring', but they illustrate the direction in which to go to collaborate more effectively. Let me single out one element: reducing out-of-stocks. They are a huge problem, even bigger for the supplier than for the retailer. Yet, current collaboration on this matter often focuses on logistics somewhere in the supply chain, when the real problem is about in-store management of the shelf and shelf replenishment.

Take another example: on-time delivery and correct invoicing. Many times, suppliers talk to retailers about sophisticated new analyses and tools, but basic service levels are poor and inconsistent. This is something to work on that will produce tangible results. Furthermore, these improvements will contribute to building stronger trust between both parties.

Return on assets (ROA)

Brand owners often argue they need bigger profit margins because they have heavier investments in factories and equipment than retailers. If this were true, the ROA for retailers and manufacturers would be similar. Well, it is not. Manufacturers have significantly better ROA – with one exception. Wal-Mart actually performs within brand-owner territory thanks to their huge economies of scale (they are almost five times bigger than the number two retailer in the world) as well as their legendary efficient operations, both in-store and upstream in their supply chain.

What can brand owners do to help retailers improve their ROA?

ROA is about efficiency combined with margin. How can retailers generate more sales with less assets? A dimension many retailers have focused on is the working capital they use. Basically, working capital is a measure of the capital needed to run the business: accounts receivable + inventories – accounts payable. Essentially it is the difference between investments (in credit given to customers + capital tied up in inventories) minus the money due to suppliers as a result of an agreed delay of payment (DOP). In Table 30 we observe a great variance across retailers in the effectiveness with which they manage their use of capital. Most retailers have negative working capital. A -3% working capital/sales ratio for a company means that for every €100 of sales, the company collects €103 in cash. This incremental cash can be reinvested in growth (more stores, other CapEx, mergers and acquisitions) or to improve cash returns to shareholders (dividends, share buybacks). Of course, retailers do not have a monopoly on generating negative working capital; some suppliers, like Unilever, have very strong negative working capital.

Table 30. Working capital as a percentage of sales, selected retailers and brand owners

RETAILERS		BRANDOWNERS	
CASINO	-18%	UNILEVER	-9%
METRO	-10%	DANONE	-6%
CARREFOUR	-9%	PEPSICO	-5%
WALMART	-3%	NESTLE	1%
KROGER	-3%	BEIERSDORF	9%

Source: Company Annual Reports, 2014, and author's calculations.

Brand owners can contribute to improving retailers' working capital needs by helping them improve their inventory management and, depending on their own cost of capital, by granting them more DOP. Minimizing inventory, while avoiding out-of-stocks, is absolutely vital for retailers. Brand owners can make themselves very valuable to their retail customers by offering an in-depth understanding of the way shoppers behave in case of an out-of-stock – and subsequently act on it together.

Please note: Often the notion of having negative working capital is mentioned as a strong advantage for retailers. However, one should not overestimate the importance of having negative working capital. The advantage is crucial in an economic environment with high interest rates. But in the current climate of very low interest rates in most developed countries, the negative working capital advantage is less powerful. Just image how the discussions on DOP evolved between Migros and their suppliers when interest rates turned negative in Switzerland.

Financial leverage

Often the largest number on retailers' balance sheets is the amount of money they owe their suppliers through the DOP they obtain. European retailers tend to be highly leveraged as they have high cost of capital and often originate from family ownership. Suppliers, who often have lower cost of capital than their retailer customers, might oblige, but they are reluctant to do so and typically don't give their sales organization free reign to manage the DOP negotiation tool. Why? They feel that DOP will be difficult to reverse in the future and tends to create a domino effect (if one retailer gets longer 'days', others might want the same when they find out). Finally, there are other levers brand owners can use, such as bonuses and quantity discounts, that are more easily used as conditional 'goodies' than DOP.

Margin is the key

Manufacturers should understand that retailers are running precarious businesses. They are constrained by low margins and at the same time have to cope with high fixed costs – just like airline companies, actually. When you walk into a large store you can immediately see that the cost of operating it is not very different if the store is full of shoppers or half empty. This leads to retailers' profits being very sensitive to small changes in volume. In the realistic profit and loss statement example of a retailer shown in Table 31, a small change (2%) in sales leads to a huge change (15%) in net profits! This result is driven by the retailers' fixed cost component. Volume is an amazing multiplier for retailers. Unfortunately, it works in both directions.

Table 31. Volatility of retailer profitability

	STARTING POSITION	SALES INCREASE 2%	SALES DECREASE 2%
SALES	100,000	102,000	98,000
COST GOODS SOLD	78,000	79,600	76,400
GROSS MARGIN	22,000	22,400	21,600
FIXED COSTS	16,000	16,000	16,000
VARIABLE COSTS	4,000	4,100	3,900
NET PROFITS	2,000	2,300	1,700

Source: Based on retailers' annual reports and author's calculations.

Understanding the differing business models of retailers and manufacturers can help smooth some typical discussion points in a negotiation process. For example, when a retailer realizes a supplier has much bigger margins and reproaches him for driving a tough bargain when he is far more profitable, the manufacturer can explain that his company has far more assets than the retailer and needs more working capital that has to be financed by higher margins. On the other hand, when a manufacturer tells a retailer that he is so powerful and that each year he wants more margins and lower prices, the retailer can show the manufacturer that actually, on the whole, manufacturers get better returns on their investments than retailers. Manufacturers should understand why retailers demand such long DOPs. And both need to understand that a retailer's business is more precarious, because of low margins and high fixed costs. Retailers have only one way to deal with this: increase their margins, through making their offer more distinctive and by making their operations extremely efficient. Reducing retailers' fixed costs could be another option. However, the latter is hard to do given the intrinsic nature of the retail business.

Table 32 shows a realistic example of the economics of a successful retailer and a successful brand owner. For the sake of explaining the fundamental economic differences between retailers and brand owners, we keep in this example the total ROE of both players identical (15%).

Table 32. Profitability of a typical retailer and a typical brand owner

	NET PROFIT MARGIN	ASSET TURNOVER	FINANCIAL LEVERAGE	RETURN ON EQUITY
RETAILERS	1.5%	2.0	5	15
BRANDOWNERS	12.5%	0.6	2	15

Source: Author's calculations.

Here is the question: If this retailer were asked to improve his ROE, which lever would be most impactful: net profit margin (NPM, better margins); asset turnover (more efficiency); or financial leverage (longer DOP)?

Some people would think increasing DOP. Think again! Margin is the key, as it is the biggest multiplier: increase NPM by one percentage point (to 2.5%) and ROE increases by 66% (from 15% to 25%). A one percentage point improvement is small for a business running 20,000 SKUs or more. The second most impactful lever is efficiency, and in last position is DOP (the smallest multiplier). Astute observers will see that to actually increase NPM as well as efficiency, sales (or sales volume) is a key variable to play with, as it improves both NPM and asset turnover. The other key parameter to improve the retailer's ROE is making the retail offer distinct (other than in price), which will improve the retailer's margin. Notice how, on the contrary, a one percentage point increase in the NPM only improves the brand owner's ROE by 8% (from 15% to 16.2%). Manufacturers do have a more comfortable business because the higher margins provide them with a cushion to dampen the effects of negative exogenous events.

A quiz
Let's have a quiz just to check if the beginning of the chapter was well understood. Table 33 shows five important financial indicators for nine well-known big brand owners and retailers (Carrefour, Magnit, BIM, Wal-Mart, Metro, P&G, Nestle, Coca-Cola and Kroger). Can you figure out which company is which?

Table 33. Who Is Who?

COMPANY	NPM	AT	FL	ROE	MCAP/SALES
A	5.6	2.2	2.2	24	1.2
B	15.4	0.5	3.1	24	4.0
C	3.8	2.3	2.7	23	0.5
D	1.3	1.8	5.4	13	0.3
E	9.9	0.7	1.9	13	2.6
F	3.4	4.4	2.7	40	1.3
G	0.15	1.9	5.8	2	0.2
H	14.5	0.6	2.1	17	2.8
I	1.5	3.3	5.3	28	0.4

NPM=net profit margin; AT=asset turnover; FL=financial leverage; ROE=return on equity; MCap/Sales= market capitalization/sales.

How should one proceed in trying to identify who is who? Here are some key insights to help.

First of all, let's use two facts everybody is aware of. Retailers have lower net profit margins than brand owners, and non-food brand owners tend to have higher margins than food brand owners.

Second, it is clear that retailers have less assets (factories, machineries) and therefore they tend to have higher asset turnover (sales/assets), i.e. they need less assets to produce sales than brand owners.

Third, because of the perceived higher risk of investing in retailers, on average they tend to be less trusted by financial markets, and as a result have a higher cost of capital. This leads to longer DOPs, as other sources to attract money (banks, equity markets) to finance the business are more expensive.

And fourth, retailers are not valued as highly as brand owners. They are more vulnerable because of their low margins. Price wars lead to value destruction. Typically, one can buy a retailer for about 50% of their annual sales. For Coca-Cola, one has to pay 400% of their annual sales.

So, have you identified the nine companies? The following are the correct answers:

A: Magnit. This relatively young but impressive Russian retailer is applying the original Wal-Mart strategy in Russia, building new stores in areas where modern trade is not well developed yet. They have outstanding logistics operations, as originally they were a logistics company. Their strategy leads to relatively high margins (due to less competition and low operating costs), a situation that cannot last when they start to hit more competition. The exceptional market capitalization over sales ratio for a retailer is due to the fact that the financial markets seem to trust this company. This leads to a relatively low cost of capital and less debt. The company is driven by a strong personality (Sergey

Galitsky), something frequently observed with successful retailers: Gotlieb Duttweiler at Migros, Sam Walton at Wal-Mart, Terry Leahy at Tesco, Juan Roig at Mercadona…

B: Coca-Cola Company. The great profit margins speak for themselves. The asset turnover is low because they have high assets, in part because they have bought back their bottling operation in the US and because they have been purchasing new brands – buying brands implies paying goodwill, which enters as an asset on the balance sheet.

C: Wal-Mart. For a retailer, the margins are impressive, especially given their low prices. This is thanks to their enormous buying power and their great economies of scale in how they run their operations, particularly in the US, Mexico and Canada. They have relatively low debt because financial markets trust them and therefore they have comparatively low cost of capital.

D: Carrefour. This is the typical profile of a large European grocery retailer: low margins, not so efficient and a high cost of capital because financial markets perceive them as a risky investment. This leads to longer DOP and therefore high financial leverage.

E: Nestlé. This multinational has great margins for a food company, the consequence of a smart acquisition and sell-off strategy over time where they disposed of products in lower-margin categories and acquired businesses in higher-margin categories. The overall low ROE is due to their low financial leverage and a high asset base. Their outstanding performance is all the more impressive as their home base (Switzerland) is tiny.

F: BIM. This is a successful Aldi copy in Turkey. An interesting case, as it gives us a glimpse of what Aldi's financials should look like: good margins notwithstanding low prices, driven by low operating costs (a small assortment, little service and small, cheap real estate). Great efficiency, equally thanks to the limited assortment, everyday low price (EDLP) and very efficient operations. They do not have high debt levels. They are very efficient in their negotiations, offering huge volumes to the suppliers they select.

G: Metro. The ratios are not untypical for European large-scale players. Actually, the economics of most European retailers are somewhere in between Metro and Carrefour (D). The very poor margins are a result of a lack of differentiation in a home market (Germany) that is extremely price driven. Their efficiency is OK, but not great as compared to, for example, Kroger (I). The high financial leverage is driven by long DOPs as a result of their high cost of capital.

H: P&G. The high margins are typical of non-food FMCG manufacturers, and the efficiency is average. They are well perceived by financial markets and have therefore a low cost of capital, resulting in a conservative financial leverage.

I: Kroger. This is an excellent US supermarket retailer. They are large ($100 billion sales) and have performed well in recent years. They are efficient and are relatively highly leveraged, with very efficient operations.

The Strategic Trade Marketing Triangle

Now that we understand the fundamentally different economics driving both trade partners, what are the practical implications for the retailer–manufacturer relationship? How should suppliers interact with their retailers and vice-versa? Brand owners used to have key account managers whose job it was to achieve specific objectives with critical retail accounts, in terms of sales, shelf space, listing of new products, etc. But this is changing now. Because of the increased sophistication and complexity of retailers and multiplicity of sales channels, brand owners need to balance three objectives across their portfolio of 'go to market' options:

1　They need to provide value for the retailer.
2　They need to make sure retailers, and not just brands, are profitable for brand owners.
3　It is not good enough to have just a couple of large retailers to whom they offer good value and that are profitable for them. Manufacturers should avoid becoming too dependent on a handful of intermediaries that control the route to the consumer of their brands.

Clearly the brand owner needs to make trade-offs between these three objectives as they are not complementary to each other. They cannot give away all the value they create to their retailer customers. The more routes to market the brand owner manages to use, the less dependency he will have on a few powerful customers. Yet, satisfying such a diversified set of routes to the consumer has a heavy ongoing cost. Similarly, it will become harder and more costly to offer great value to all the intermediaries operating all those routes to the final consumer. In other words, manufacturers face the challenge of a difficult balancing act. Let's have a look at the three corners of what we shall call the strategic trade marketing triangle (Figure 23).

Figure 23. The strategic trade marketing triangle.

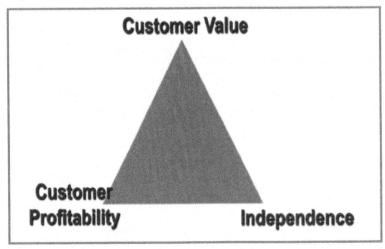

Providing customer value

What can a supplier do to ensure that retailers do their utmost to do justice to his brand offer? Why should the retailer list specific brands? Understanding retailer economics provides a good angle from which to approach these issues.

For starters, some brands are just unavoidable. They have such a strong position in the minds of the consumer that retailers simply cannot do without them. Several supermarket retailers have tried to do business without Coca-Cola, for example, but in most cases this led to a loss of shoppers, unless they had a very specific positioning and business model like Aldi, for instance. Brands that are winning the battle for mind space have a definite advantage in the battle for shelf space.

A well-rehearsed way of providing value to retailers is through efficient logistics. Retailers are cost sensitive, and every initiative allowing them to reduce costs while keeping the service intact will be warmly welcomed.

Similarly, reducing out-of-stocks and improving on-shelf availability is a strong mechanism to increase sales and retain shoppers. Note that an out-of-stock is more costly for suppliers than for retailers (the consumer can still switch to another brand in the store). Suppliers' logistic responsibility should not stop at the retailers' distribution centre, as out-of-stock situations are often caused by poor shelf management in the store. This may create opportunities for brand owners offering assistance at the point of sales, during important promotional activities, for example.

Helping retailers offer a better in-store shopping experience may prove beneficial. A nice example is the 'Perfect Store' program developed by Unilever to assist smaller retailers in emerging markets, among others. The program was designed to help retailers improve store and shelf layout. Other suppliers offer similar support, sometimes exclusively in their own category, sometimes for the whole store.

A product offer differentiated for the retailer can help her alleviate price pressure. Reducing transparency for the shopper across retailers will prevent price comparisons. However, this will probably increase logistic costs for the brand owner, and can also become expensive as it may undermine brand equity.

As mentioned elsewhere, many retailers are typically not so great at marketing. Even though they have access to enormous amounts of shopper data, they find it hard to translate those into actionable shopper insights. Brand owners have more and better data analysis power and should use this methodological advantage in combination with retailer data as a useful path to create value for their retail customers. Investing in useful shopper insights may contribute to retailer profitability and strengthen the brand owners' position. Since many could offer this capability, first-mover advantages might be important here.

There is no doubt that category management services are a value-creating tool that brand owners can offer their retail customers by offering neutral advice on growing the category to everyone's benefit. Provided the advice is neutral and based on solid market information and insights, category management is a valuable asset that brand owners and retailers should capitalize on.

However, one has to be careful not to fall into category management traps. Here is one example among many. Put yourself in the position of detergents buyer Pedro Soares at retailer Pingo. When the P&G team presents their insights and recommendations, based on consumer and shopper panel data as well as Pingo's own data, they proudly announce an amazing insight: shoppers buying P&G detergent brands leave the store with a higher total ticket than did shoppers who did not buy P&G detergents. This, of course, should be music to Pedro's ears, and he should offer more shelf space to P&G brands. Great, everyone is a winner.

But Pedro soon finds out that Unilever, Henkel and Colgate are each delivering the same truths. He is not sure he can believe all of them. Actually, P&G's insight is correct, but not for the reason Pedro was led to believe. The insight is true not because less price-sensitive shoppers buy P&G detergents, but because shoppers buy detergents on 'big trips'. Category management is a powerful and robust tool to improve collaboration between brand owners and retailers when properly applied, but not when category management is driven by the slogan 'Let's beat the data till it confesses'.

Similarly, in the context of category management, suppliers keep coming up with the promise that they will grow the category. There was even an approach called JAG (Jointly Agreed Growth), developed in collaboration with McKinsey, to formalize brand owners' and retailers' joint efforts to generate growth by boosting win-win opportunities. How effective are such approaches? Promised growth will effectively be possible in some cases – in particular, in emerging and developing markets, though this growth may be the result of cannibalizing traditional channels. But it is doubtful that all suppliers will be able to grow the category at every major retail customer every year. Still, one has to admit that Colgate was successful at all retailers, building on the message that people should brush their teeth twice a day.

There is much to be said in favour of a fact-based analysis of categories, where brand owners and retailers pool their considerable and complementary knowledge of shopper behaviour, but if category management is used by the supplier as just another myopic sales tool, the only conclusion for retailers has to be that they themselves, and nobody else, should be the 'category captain'.

Improving customer profitability

It is all very fine for brand owners to create value for the retailer, but they must also keep some for themselves and not give everything away. To make sure that retailers remain profitable customers, brand owners should thoroughly understand the cost drivers of their route to market. Activity-based costing (ABC) identifies cost drivers and helps the brand owner find out the relative profitability of his various distribution channels and retailers. Once cost drivers are established and relative retailer profitability is derived, brand owners can then incentivise their retailers and their channels in a way that will improve their profitability for the brand owner. One should keep in mind that the key cost driver is not always size. Other factors such as bespoke services provided to retailers can be a major determinant of customer profitability.

Brand owners have management and accounting systems that provide them with deep and detailed information about the profitability of their brands. However, many have a much more limited grasp of the profitability of their retailers and their channels. When asked about this, many tell me this is old hat, they do know the relative profitability of their retailers and their channels. Probing a bit deeper often reveals that they have an understanding of their gross margins but lack ABC-driven understanding of the profitability of their retailers and what the drivers of this profitability are. What is needed is a profit and loss statement per important retailer and per relevant distribution channel.

A solid understanding of customer cost drivers also opens the door for making non-price negotiations between brand owners and retailers more tangible. An interesting option is the use of price menus. The idea is that suppliers offer discounts depending on the service offered to their retail customers. This approach brings non-price elements into negotiations and may also improve efficient solutions. Assume for example that via an ABC exercise, the supplier has established the two critical customer profitability drivers are delivery time and pallet SKU configuration. The brand owner may then offer a 25% discount if the retailer accepts a factory pallet three days after order, but only a 5% discount if he wants tailor-made pallets per store, 24 hours after ordering (see Table 34). Retailers can then decide which service option they prefer, thereby also improving the overall efficiency of the supply chain.

Table 34. Sample price menu of discounts by delivery time and pallet configuration

	3 days after order	2 days after order	24 hours after order
Factory Pallet	25%	20%	10%
DC Pallet	19%	17%	13%
Store Pallet	14%	10%	5%

DC=distribution center

Brand owners who take customer profitability seriously will drive their interaction with their retailers from a Turkish bazaar haggling culture towards a more fact-based 'pay for performance' philosophy, where they consider their retail and channel partners as service providers and pay them for services provided. They can pay for outputs (e.g. sales growth), or for inputs (e.g. shelf space, POS activities). Typically, suppliers pay for a mixture, but for strong brands, paying for inputs is more sensible, while weaker brands should prefer to pay for outputs. The advantage of this more fact-based approach is that 'things that get measured tend to improve'. Unfortunately, few manufacturers and retailers are equipped to understand the true costs and benefits of what they can offer (retailers) and what they can buy (manufacturers). How much should Kellogg's be willing to pay to Tesco for a secondary display of their Special K product in Tesco's UK stores?

Probably, neither party really knows, so the haggling starts with Tesco trying to jack up the price per unit of shelf space offered and Kellogg's trying to bring it down. There is little doubt Big Data has a lot to offer in this area for all parties.

In an international environment with many routes to market, it is crucial to be fair and consistent in compensating retailers. Brand owners should establish transparent rules to avoid getting caught out with diverging conditions for different key retailers. The latter will find out when they merge or when buyers switch between retailers or when retailers meet each other at events organized by their friendly suppliers. For example, imagine the turbulence created by the exchange of negotiation details when players such as Colruyt and Swiss COOP from the Core buying group joined Alidis the buying group comprised of Edeka , Intermarche and Eroski. Differences need to be justifiable, and consistent across retailers and across countries. Maybe suppliers should even consider posting the set of conditions and options they offer their retailers on the internet, accessible to all. If possible, it might improve the trust between parties. If not possible – for example, because it will take time to harmonize conditions – brand owners should centralize conditions and have at the very least 'ex-ante justifiable differences' rather than having to make up forced explanations of why one retailer gets more favourable terms than a competitor even though the brand owner has been pontificating about 'partnership' and 'preferred customer' to all its important retailers.

Divide and Conquer

In most markets in the developed world, grocery retail concentration is strong. Often, in a particular market, three to five big retailers account for more than 75% of brand owners' turnover, leaving suppliers in a vulnerable position. How can they secure their independence? One way of ensuring a superior bargaining position is to develop unavoidable brands and unique and valuable services. Another is to explore alternative distribution channels. Divide and conquer: food brands could look into food-service channels, for example, while cosmetics brands could turn to specialist retailers, hairdressers, etc. With the emergence of e-commerce, new and interesting routes to market come into view, including third-party webshops or even direct sales to consumers.

Brand owners have a wide variety of partners in their 'route to the consumer', ranging from big international and mom-and-pop retailers to TV shopping network channels such as Shakti, which Unilever uses in emerging markets. It is therefore hard for them to have a detailed analysis for each and every one. Typically, suppliers segment customers by considering two dimensions: i) the future importance of the retailer in a given market (size, current growth, future potential); and ii) what the retailer represents for the supplier in terms of target consumers, profitability, win-win attitude…

This simple analysis leads to the identification of four types of retail customers: bullies, stars, losers and mates (see Table 35). Depending on where their retail customers sit in this matrix, brand owners will commit more or less resources to them and develop appropriate strategies for them, depending on where they fit into the 'route to market' portfolio.

Table 35. Customer segmentation

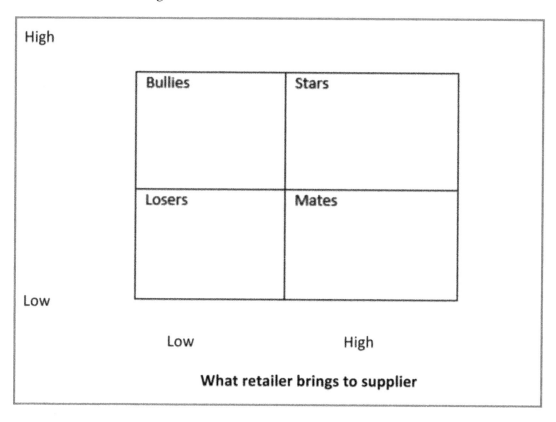

Stars, of course, deserve a dedicated team, involving top management. With bullies, one has two options: if it seems possible to migrate them to the stars segment, have a dedicated team and get top management involved; if not, have a small team focus on customer profitability and avoid disruptions. Losers should be managed by automation; one cannot afford to invest in them. Mates are often a source of inefficiency. Some of them are actually 'mates' of the sales people. Maybe they have lost importance over the years, but still get intensive care from the sales organization. This should be avoided. They can probably be managed more efficiently if one gradually scales down the team and moves freed resources to more important customer targets.

Collaborative Winning in Negotiations

By the end of each year, key account managers face the mission of entering negotiations with their buyers, in order to define next year's business terms. These negotiations may take several weeks or even months, often involve specific rituals, including psychological warfare, and in the end, often, nobody is really pleased with the outcome. Nevertheless, the same game resumes one year later, following the same rules. Is a more productive negotiation model for the FMCG sector attainable?

Why brand owners should or should not produce private labels

Should a brand owner produce private label for its retail customers? Not infrequently, manufacturers are faced with this delicate question. There are, of course, well-rehearsed arguments in favour of doing so. The manufacturer may have excess factory capacity. If the manufacturer refuses, the retailer will ask a competitor. Private label may provide additional sales and margin. And not least, a private-label partnership may contribute to building a better relationship with the retailer.

On the other hand, maybe a supplier should not 'dance with the devil', due to the risk of becoming more dependent on that retailer. Moreover, producing private labels requires a different business model than commercializing branded products. Can one be successful running two cultures in one company when competing with players who focus everything on just one business model? It will be a challenge to do properly. Moreover, it is likely the private label will cannibalize the branded business. The retailer will ask for a private-label copy of the brands' latest innovations, which makes the brand-owner vulnerable. And if consumers find out the brand owner is the private-label producer, it may hurt brand equity.

A few suggestions may help a supplier decide whether stepping into the private-label business is a good idea.

1 Don't be emotional about the issue. Look at it as a business proposition. How do the numbers stack up? What is the ROI? The answer can be positive or negative.
2 If you decide to get involved in supplying private label, insist on organizing it as a separate business. This means a separate production capacity, a separate sales organization, and so on. Certainly don't use average costs for the brands and marginal costs for the private label. Don't let the branded business subsidize the your private label business.
3 Don't do it to build better relationships with the retailer. You will become more dependent.
4 Do you have the competences? Brand owners often think they can do the private-label business with their left hand. False!
5. If you do private label, make sure you diversify. Work for several retailers, favouring multi-year contracts.
6. Do not shout about it. Never state you do or do not produce private label. You don't know what might happen in the future. Actually, stating you don't do private label already gives credibility to private label products; why else would you have to deny it?
7. After all these principles, stay opportunistic and capitalize on opportunities when they occur. Actually, sometimes you might not have a choice.

In repeated negotiations, both parties should aim for 'win-win' deals, deals where both parties are better off (although brand owners sometimes joke that if retailers want win-win deals, they mean they want to win twice). Avoid neglecting options where at least one party could be better off without the other party being worse off. In reality, most negotiations do not succeed in optimizing the outcome for both parties. Why? One should understand that a negotiation has two components: building the cake and dividing the cake, and the process needs to be managed in that order. The problem is that trade partners are often obsessed with their own share of the cake and care less about any proposal to increase its size, because they don't trust each other. If a proposition comes from the brand owner, the retailer automatically assumes it is bad for him…and vice-versa. Consequently, the second stage of dividing the cake often dominates a negotiation.

Figure 24 shows the 'negotiations opportunity set', depicting the collection of all possible deals negotiators can generate, measured in terms of retailer and manufacturer profits. The collection of deals that satisfies the win-win condition, – i.e. the set of Pareto optimal deals – is characterized by the curve at the border of the negotiation opportunity set. This is the possibility frontier: the best both trading partners can do in terms of building as large a cake as possible, if they are trusting, creative, open minded and thoughtful. Every proposal, at first, should aim at moving in the north-east direction, making both parties better off. In real life, although it is a useful concept, the possibility frontier will probably never be reached.

A typical deal often ends up at the round dot near the centre of the graph. It is clear that the deal is inefficient, because each party could have been better off without making the other party worse off. In fact, *any* outcome in the dark area in the graph would be better. Still, in reality, negotiations often get stuck at the round dot position, leaving both trade partners frustrated with a suboptimal outcome.

Figure 24. The core of the negotiations game.

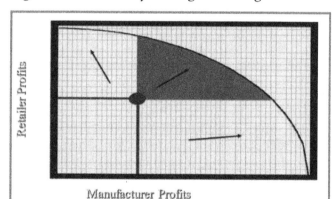

(Actually, the graph should be three-dimensional, with the shopper as the third axis. Now, the objective will become 'win cubed'. Indeed, if win-win means that both manufacturer and retailer are getting better off by exploiting the consumer, it is not only unsustainable in the long run, but also illegal and similar to collusion.)

If negotiations keep getting stuck at the round dot in the graph, should we conclude that a win-win outcome is an elegant academic concept, but not feasible in real manufacturer–retailer relations? The fundamental problem is an enormous lack of trust between both negotiating parties. Often, they will feel hard done by. For example, in some countries and with some retailers, brand owners feel they are not treated with respect and that retailers are only interested in one thing: having more discounts or other monetary goods (listing fees, anniversary presents, promotional funds, etc.), if possible, unconditionally. Similarly, in the same countries, retailers feel as if they are doing all the heavy lifting, and at the end of the day getting very little in return. Yes, they see themselves as slaves of the brand owners, especially when they start comparing relative profit margins and other financial parameters.

The remedies are obvious. First, both parties should try to understand each other more objectively, especially the economics of their respective business models. As we showed in the chapters on the Robin Hood syndrome and on the differing economics of retailers and brand owners, both parties are driven by fundamentally different business models. Second, brand owners should become more transparent in the deals they offer, going as far as posting them on the web, and they should move towards the concept of 'preferred customer' rather than getting stuck in the 'preferred supplier' stereotype.

How far can you go?
A crucial concept that every negotiator should be familiar with is 'best alternative to a negotiated agreement' (BATNA). The concept is particularly relevant when considering delistings, for both the manufacturer and the retailer. Both need to have a plan B (the BATNA) in the back of their mind at every point in the negotiation process. Suppose the retailer is prepared to delist your brand – what is the next best thing you can propose? The BATNA determines how far the brand owner should be willing to go to avoid the delisting. Each player should also give some thought to the other player's BATNA to get an idea of how far he can go.

How differences create opportunities
It is amazing: when you ask a group of executives if manufacturers and retailers can both win simultaneously, you usually get a variety of answers: The tough guys say no ('Let's be honest, we know win-win isn't true in the real world, it's just impossible'). The other group says yes, arguing that both parties can win because they need each other and share common interests (the shopper), or because they both give in a bit to come to a deal, or because they are in the same boat and have to get on, there is no choice. All these arguments are deeply flawed.

Take a look at Ferrero, a strong brand owner known for standing tall against the tough and ever-more-demanding retailers in Germany. When retailers want more benefits from them, Ferrero answers, 'What part of "no" don't you understand?' In other words, Ferrero thinks their BATNA is far better than the retailer's and eventually the retailer will give in, because Ferrero's assumption is right: shoppers want Nutella in Germany. So does Ferrero

156

win? I would argue no, they could have done even better. By understanding what Ferrero really values, Ferrero may give in a bit to the retailer and get in return something more that they really value.

It is true that most people, including seasoned sales executives and retail buyers, don't fully understand how both parties can win in a negotiation. Actually, it is pretty simple. There are at least two situations that allow for a realistic win-win; the first is self-evident for many people, the second is less well understood.

First, both parties can win if they can grow the market. If actions by the brand owner can increase the size of the cake (the total size of the category), then both retailers and manufacturers can win simultaneously. Colgate used to play this scenario over and over: 'We make people brush their teeth more frequently' was their mantra. For a while that type of strategy can work. But how credible are brand owners when all of them promise the retailer year after year that they will increase the size of the category, especially in the mature economies of Western Europe and the US?

Second, and most importantly, negotiators should understand that differences, not similarities, create opportunities for both parties to win. Often, executives will explain that retailers and manufactures need each other and that they both want the same thing, they share a common interest (the most gullible will say: to satisfy the consumer or shopper). Think again! Win-win is possible precisely because both parties want different things: they have different preferences and/or costs and/or benefits. This is what any trade is based on: differences. It is in this case that both can win. The manufacturer can offer the retailer something that costs him less than it benefits the retailer, and vice-versa. After all, why do people buy or sell stuff? Well, it must be that the buyer thinks the object is worth more to him than the money he has to pay for it, and for the seller, vice-versa. A lack of understanding of this concept is one of the root causes of the continued conflict between retailers and manufacturers.

Suppose Frank and Jack have a nectarine and a coconut to share between them. It would seem fair to give them each half a nectarine and half a coconut. However, if Jack prefers nectarines over coconuts and Frank prefers coconuts over nectarines, it would be better for both to give the nectarine to Jack and the coconut to Frank. Of course, after Jack says he prefers nectarines, Frank might say, 'What a pity – me too,' and propose to let Jack have ¾ of the nectarine if Frank can have the whole coconut and the remaining ¼ of the nectarine... Negotiators need to be very careful indeed in properly gauging the other party's preferences and costs and benefits and in revealing their own.

If differences are so important to get to win-win, negotiators need to ask questions to find out what the other party wants, and then listen to the answers – which seems obvious, but... Good negotiators don't argue, certainly not in the beginning of a negotiation. For a good negotiator, the ratio of questions asked to number of arguments initiated should be infinity. For a poor negotiator, who continuously argues, does not ask questions and certainly does not listen to answers, the ratio is zero.

Furthermore, a negotiation is certainly not a place to show how clever you are. Acting a bit naïve, like Colombo, may be to your advantage, especially early on in the process. The other party will open up more and you will have a better chance of getting the relevant info. If you are seen by the other party as very clever, the other party will be far more cautious and reluctant to give you the information you are looking for. Make sure you get the necessary information first, by being soft. Only when you have the data you were looking for can you be hard. Poor negotiators are hard from the beginning, trying to intimidate their counterpart, and then later they give in. Which is totally wrong, as the other party knows for next time.

Conditionality is essential. Brand owners should avoid offering any benefits to retailers that are not conditional on the retailer doing something specific for the brand. Actually, this is how brand owners effectively try to control the retailer's point of sale and run the store. Paying for shelf space is a good example.

If the brand owner offers discounts, he should make them conditional on reaching a specific ambitious sales target. The retailer wants the discount and will work to reach the sales target, provided the proposed discount is juicy. Even better, when the manufacturer offers progressive discounts for increased volumes, the retailer will have a tendency to go for the higher volumes to obtain the higher discounts. This is partly because the retailer assumes his competitors will equally go for the higher discounts and request at least a level playing field. At the end of the day, the retailer gets locked into high volumes and will do everything possible to sell the products to the consumer, especially if the quantity conditionality is on volume sold rather than volume bought. *Et voilà le travail* – for the brand owner! *C'est un métier!*

The way forward
Sometimes retailers and manufacturers get along fine and even reward each other with fancy titles and ugly trophies. But beware. When a brand owner is being voted 'supplier of the year' by a retailer, one should always ask why. Is it because the supplier gave away a lot of goodies to the retailer? Or is it because they are the most professional or have the best brands? Brand owners, especially their sales and account management organization, tend to overvalue the importance of being voted 'best supplier' or 'category captain'. At the end of the day, a brand owner should aim, first and foremost, to be the preferred brand for the final consumer. If in the process they are also 'supplier of the year' to the retailer, that's a nice feather in their cap.

The mirror image of 'preferred supplier', a title assigned by retailers, is the title of 'preferred customer', conferred by brand owners to their retail customers. What does it mean when a brand owner tells a retailer they are a brand owner's 'preferred customer'? It definitely does not imply that this specific retailer gets superior conditions from the brand owner than other, competing retailers. That would be short sighted and suicidal from the point of view of the brand owner. What it means is that 'no other retailer gets better conditions from this brand owner'. Which does not mean that this retailer is the

What drives delay of payment (DOP)?

It is not surprising that the negotiation of DOP is mostly not in the hands of salespeople, but of those at a higher echelon in the company, often in finance. Three major factors are at play here: size (power), cost of capital and equity structure.

- *Size:* The bigger the company, the more power it has. Most managers understand this. But if so, why does Wal-Mart have a fewer days' DOP than, say, Metro?
- *Cost of capital:* This is the cost for a company to attract money. The better a company performs, the lower their cost of capital, because capital markets will see them as less risky and capital cost is a measure of this risk premium.

Table 36. Cost of equity for retailers

	Currency Risk	Country Risk Premium	Beta Unlevered	Leverage Excl Op. Leases	Leverage Incl Op. Leases	Beta Levered	Cost Eq. Levered
AH	0.0%	0.0%	0.60	29%	43%	0.71	7.6%
MRW	0.0%	0.0%	0.60	32%	38%	0.69	7.7%
SBRY	0.0%	0.0%	0.60	34%	58%	0.81	8.6%
TSCO	0.1%	0.6%	0.63	30%	51%	0.82	9.2%
CO	1.9%	0.9%	0.60	45%	53%	0.75	10.2%
CA	1.7%	1.1%	0.65	40%	46%	0.79	10.4%
MEO	1.1%	1.5%	0.62	46%	62%	0.87	10.9%

Source: Bloomberg, company reports, and Bernstein Analysis, 2014.

Table 36 shows the cost of capital for Ahold, Morrisons, Sainsbury's, Tesco, Casino, Carrefour and Metro. Metro has a high cost of capital because it is exposed to many international markets, some risky. For example, one of Metro's biggest businesses is Russia, and recently that has brought huge financial risks. Wal-Mart has a low cost of capital and can therefore attract money more cheaply from the stock market and banks than from their suppliers. Of course, they demand other goodies from manufacturers (discounts, etc.) in return for paying them earlier.

- *Equity structure:* This refers to a company's ownership. In the past, many European retailers were family owned. They preferred to get their financing from thousands of suppliers rather than from banks and the stock market. The former will not demand a say in how the family business is run, whereas the latter demand quarterly reports, seats on the board, etc. In a way, this is still reflected in of the DOPs of the Carrefours, Aholds, Metros and a few others, even though the ownership structure has changed. Some habits and traditions change slowly, so sometimes DOP is longer or shorter depending on what happened in the past.

only one to get this; all retailers are 'preferred customers'. Does it mean that all retailers end up with the same conditions? No, but they all should get the same options.

This is crucial because retailers, at a minimum, want a level playing field. Of course they end up with different deals, because not all retailers can buy 1 zillion units, for example. The concept of 'preferred customer' is a useful vehicle to generate trust between retailers and manufacturers. Three conditions need to be fulfilled here:

1. Transparency
In the limit, brand owners should consider posting their conditions on the web, open and transparent for everybody. This may sound like a revolutionary idea but it is necessary to avoid being seen as unfair or having favourites. It is important to note that this does not mean that every retailer will obtain the same conditions. Some retailers are bigger than others, some retailers will prefer other items from the menu, but they do get the same options to choose from. It's like brand owners offering a buffet dinner to retailers rather than offering only 'a la carte'. The buffet is there to be seen by every retail customer (which will inspire trust) and they will understand that some items on the buffet (say lobster, or big discounts for large orders) have an extra cost for the customer.

Radical transparency can only work if it is done industry wide. The 'best customer' approach is not sustainable if some players don't buy into it, and go on wheeling and dealing and bad-mouthing the transparent brand owners. In this context it should be emphasized once more that manufacturers should aim for 'respect' and not 'love' from their retail customers. What should bring 'wheeling and dealing' brand owners to a more sensible approach is the fact that they might get caught out with inconsistencies in their offerings to competing retailers.

2. Pay for performance
The retailer should be seen by the brand owner as a service provider. It is only just to pay a fair price for the services provided. It implies that both parties do measure the value of services to be negotiated. Big Data will be a strong driver to transform the negotiations between brand owners and retailers into the domain of objective measurement of cause and effect, to push the interactions between the parties in a more fact-based direction.

3. Segmentation
Brand owners have limited resources and need to make choices. Retailers don't all want the same things either. This might be seen as contradicting the transparency condition, but it does not. Brand owners should construct a menu of options that the retailer can choose from. The aviation industry can offer inspiration here: airlines don't tell anybody where to sit and what comfort level they must pay for; instead, they construct conditions such that various segments of passengers actually chose the options which make the airlines most profitable while making passengers happy as well.
Buyers are incentivised to extract as many benefits as possible from their suppliers. Every year, they enter into tough negotiations with brand manufacturers. But is this really more than a game? Retailers would be extremely naive to assume that they can negotiate better

160

deals than their competitors. It is in the interest of suppliers to offer similar benefits to every similar (especially in size) retailer. And you cannot assume that the best buyers work for one retailer and the dummies work for a competitor. So unless retailers can offer a truly unique service to their supplier, in normal circumstances, they will receive a similar package as their competitors. Of course, size does matter here, as large retailers can offer economies of scale to their suppliers, for which they get compensated by bigger benefits.

The problem with retail buyers

Traditionally, retailers bought bulk goods in large quantities at a low price to resell in smaller packages and with a margin to the consumer – that's where the term 'retail' comes from: from the French word tailler, which means 'to cut off, clip, pare, divide'. This means that retailers were logistics organizations for whom purchasing was the dominant function; after all, even today, costs of goods sold account for anywhere from 75% and to 80% of retail sales. To date, the purchasing department plays a dominant role in many retail organizations. And that can be a serious problem.

A perverse consequence of this focus on purchasing, however, is that to a large extent, retailers end up selling the juicy deals brand owners have offered to them instead of selling what the consumer demands. Indeed, suppliers have the resources to offer retail buyers attractive goodies in exchange for including brands or products that are not necessarily in line with what the shopper really wants. The result can be seen on the shelves of every supermarket: on average some 20,000 SKUs or more lie waiting there for the consumer, and half of them are selling less than one item per week... The cost of this ineffective stock is mind boggling.

Successful hard discounters such as Aldi and Lidl take a very different approach. Instead of 20,000 SKUs, they offer less than 10% of that, which is much more cost effective. They look closely at what the shopper really expects in their stores, and they constantly adjust their offering. When new items arrive in the range, others must disappear. And every week they surprise their customers with extremely attractive temporary offers. There is a lot to be said for the idea that next to low prices, this limited and manageable assortment is an important success factor for hard discounters.

Consider this interesting story by Dieter Brandes, once a high-level manager at Aldi, who was asked to help set up a new discount retail business in Turkey, inspired by Aldi. When he came to Turkey and visited the stores, he was unhappy with the assortment, which was far too large. So he asked his head office managers to stay home on Monday and go through their fridges and cupboards with their wives, listing all the FMCG items present in their homes. They were all surprised, but they did what was asked. Based on their lists, Dieter Brandes and his team set up a small but complete assortment of nothing but high-rotation SKUs. Very quickly, BIM – for that is the retailer we are talking about – became a remarkably successful business.

To get an idea of the economic, financial and negotiation advantages an Aldi type player has, just take a look at a back-of-the-envelope calculation in Table 37.

Table 37. Assortment economics of Wal-Mart versus Aldi

	Wal-Mart	Aldi
Number of SKU's	120.000	1.800
Annual Worldwide Sales (billion USD)	450	80
Sales/SKU (million USD)	3,75	44

Source: Company reports and author's calculations.

Table 38 provides another example, at a more micro level, this time from Colombia (here I promised not to disclose the names of the companies).

Table 38. Economics of Nestle products for retailers

	No of SKUs from Nestlé	Purchasing value monthly	Average per item
Super/Hypermarket market leader	400	3,375,000 USD	8,437 USD
Hard discounter	13	580,000 USD	44,615 USD

Source: Private and confidential information.

Apart from the fact that large assortments are difficult and expensive to manage, there is also a consumer side to this, the point being that consumers tend to be overwhelmed when they are offered too many choice options. Of course, consumers go on different shopping trips. For some trips, they want plenty of choice and for others, they don't. Horses for courses. But today, even when choice is important, supermarkets and hypermarkets offer a selection that far exceeds most shoppers' expectations. As discussed in Chapter 2, the American psychologist Barry Schwarz described the paradox of choice this way: although we assume that more choice leads to more freedom and happiness, in practice after a certain point there are decreasing marginal utilities for choice. Too much choice can paralyze us, and that's exactly what happens today when supermarket shoppers face 20 different types/brands of mayonnaise or 75 shampoo variants. It is no coincidence that Tesco, the struggling British retailer, recently decided to cut one third of its huge assortment. In that respect, a visit to Aldi is a relief.

Chapter Insights

1 The root cause of the conflict between retailers and manufacturers is not the lack of trust between them but the lack of distinctiveness between retailers.
2 To improve the way retailers and manufacturers interact, both parties must make an effort to deeply understand how the other party generates its profits. This will reveal the levers to use to bring the interaction to a more productive level.
3 Yes, win-win is possible, but it is not enough. Why is it possible? Because manufacturers and retailers want different things. Why is it not enough? Because optimally we need win-win-win – the consumer/shopper also has to win.

Part IV
Last but *Not* Least

Chapter 8
Getting the Job Done

A famous proverb says, 'Strategy without execution is just a dream, but execution without strategy is a nightmare.' In fact, strategy and execution form an inseparable couple, reinforcing one another exponentially when both are strong, but annihilating each other when one of them is weak.

The importance of execution dawned on me again a couple of years ago when I was directing a 'company-specific program' for Tesco at INSEAD. The program was aimed at store directors, executives responsible for all stores in a region (as opposed to store managers, responsible for one store). These people, who had worked their way up 'from the floor', were hands-on managers with great social skills and emotional intelligence, but many had limited formal education, having not passed what the English call 'A levels'. Tesco felt this lack of academic background prevented them from taking up executive jobs in the retailers' expanding geographical network. Because these store directors felt academically inferior, they were often uncomfortable expressing themselves in management meetings, which limited their future development – and as Tesco was growing rapidly, they needed home-grown experienced talent to play a strong role in their international organization.

Therefore, I was asked to put together a two-week program to give the store directors a grounding in finance, accounting, marketing and organizational behaviour. On top of that, the program had to include some cultural activities to raise the confidence and worldliness of these street-smart people. Now that was a challenge: I couldn't imagine visiting the Picasso Museum in Paris with them, let alone attending a ballet performance. So we settled for a musical evening, inviting a string quartet to play some compositions, with an introduction on the piece and the composer, and a chance to discuss the music afterwards. The quartet suggested four unknown Baroque pieces, as this was their specialization, but I insisted on some better-known, more accessible material. A difficult discussion followed… As a compromise we finally agreed on three famous compositions (by Mozart, Shostakovich and Mendelssohn) followed by a Baroque piece of their choice. The evening turned out a success, and to my surprise, what the participants liked most was the unknown Baroque piece. It made me wonder why. Was the Baroque piece a better composition? No, on the contrary. But the musicians really put their hearts and souls into that piece and were probably somewhat more lethargic while performing the three other compositions. I think it is a great illustration of the importance of execution.

Everybody wants to be a strategist

Discussions about the idea of dividing the management job into 'strategy' and 'execution' go a long way back. Some argue that the functions cannot be separated, others argue that a division is needed, since specialization is necessary to excel – and different competencies are needed for these two tasks. But either way, both jobs have to be done. Companies need to make choices, need to allocate scarce resources and define where they want to play and how they are going to win. That's what I call strategy. Then, they need to actually go out and do it. That's the execution part.

Every manager will tell you how important execution is: someone has to bring home the bacon. But many prefer, if they have a choice, to be seen as strategists. Following the strategy route is often the most assured way to get to the top in a company. Strategy consultants are usually the most expensive ones. In many companies, strategy is perceived as the clever stuff. It is the elegant and sophisticated process driven by the intellectual excellence of senior management. Strategists are those who decide where the business is going and how the company's scarce resources will be allocated over all the various investment opportunities: whether to get out of this market, focus on those market segments, build up such-and-such organizational capability. All these conclusions are supported by very professional looking PowerPoint presentations and Excel spreadsheets. Once the plan is complete and its conclusions have found buy-in from the board, senior management's job is pretty much done. But if that is true, why is the person who runs the company called the chief executive officer?

When implementation starts, this often means trouble with a capital T, as the suave logic of strategy gets confronted by the irregularities of the real world. Meeting objectives and timelines is a job reserved for another level of management, whose success will depend on the team's agility, compromise, emotional intelligence, muscle and motivation. Getting the job done is far less angelical than the strategy's high-minded helicopter view of the world. It involves getting your hands dirty. Some managers have a problem with that…

It is clear that strategists and executors must learn to collaborate more productively, but the strategists' attitude can often be summarized as 'We're the visionary people – it's up to the executors to implement the plan.' They aren't concerned about understanding what it takes to execute the plan. They don't take into account the opportunities and challenges created by practical, market-specific situations. The executors come with their own problems as well, not truly understanding or caring too much about the strategy. The outcome is easily predictable: when the results don't meet the targets, both parties play the blame game.

The inseparable couple

If strategy and execution form an inseparable couple, can one be more important than the other? There are actually two ways of looking at the relation between the two. One is to see them working additively. In this view, a weaker strategy can be compensated for by a great execution plan – and vice-versa – as they both add up. In my view, however, strategy and execution work more like a multiplication problem. In a multiplication problem, the outcome is determined by the smallest number in the multiplication set. If one of the two components is weak, the final outcome will be weak; there is no possibility of one compensating for the other. Put bluntly, great execution of a lousy strategy is no better than poor execution of a great strategy. But a good strategy, executed well, will give the company an enormous head start over its competitors. Table 39 illustrates this thesis, with three examples.

Table 39. The strategy/execution spectrum

	POOR STRATEGY	GOOD STRATEGY
POOR EXECUTION	HOPELESS	LOYALTY PROGRAMS AT RETAIL
GOOD EXECUTION	TESCO UNDER CLARKE	CANONIZE RBENCKISER

Why most retail loyalty programs fail: Good strategy, poor execution

Consider loyalty programs for retailers. In principle, they are a sound strategic concept, based on serious theoretic research by game theorists and mathematicians. The core strategic idea is to create switching costs for shoppers if and when they shop at other retailers. These switching costs can be expressed in monetary value or in valuable services for shoppers that the retailer has figured out those shoppers desire, from their past store data. The goal is to sell more to the retailer's existing shoppers. In reality, however, shoppers haven't been very sensitive to these retailer loyalty programs. Oh yes, they are really loyal shoppers: they carry loyalty cards from five different retailers... Why do retailer loyalty programs fail to produce significant results? Poor execution turns out to be the main reason.

A fundamental problem for retailers using a loyalty system to change shoppers' behaviour is that they cannot offer the shopper a big enough incentive to make a real difference. The reward grocery retailers offer cardholders is usually between 1% and 2% of the total spent, much too small to stop people from shopping at competing retailers, especially since most competitors offer the same kinds of rewards anyway. As Tesco's former CEO, Terry Leahy, put it in his 2012 book, the 1% loyalty discount 'was a thank you, pure and simple' (*Management in 10 Words,* p. 64). If they want to be able to offer more significant discounts, retailers need someone else to finance the loyalty system. Enter sugar daddy, the rich brand owner... But why would brand owners be willing to fork out additional funds to help the retailer? There must be something in it for them. For example, the retailer may have great shopper data that are of interest to the brand owner. Suppose a retailer could offer Coke the coordinates of all shoppers who have switched away from the brand in the last six months. This might be valuable enough for Coke to offer those switchers a significant coupon (maybe 20% off) in order to win them back in the short term. This would be interesting for Coke because targeting the promotion will make it more efficient, and interesting for the retailer because they can offer an attractive and exclusive coupon that is paid for by the brand. In other words, this is truly a win-win-win solution, for the shopper, the retailer and the brand owner. However, it can only work for retailers who have the capabilities to turn shopper data into shopper-specific propositions and who understand

The eternal battle between marketing and sales

The dichotomy between strategy and interaction is remarkably comparable to the interaction (or lack thereof) between marketing and sales in many FMCG organizations. The former is all about defining target markets, unique selling propositions (USPs), communication, product and brand portfolio, new product development (NPD). The latter is about local activation and dealing with the trade, often at the local level, sometimes at an international level for the largest accounts. The mismatches between both areas of expertise are the stuff of legend.

Consider this example – a true story – of an FMCG company in one of the BRIC markets, whose sales organization was trying to cope with the changing retail landscape. They had a great position in their traditional channels, built up over time, for a portfolio of well-known brands in the chocolate and candy categories, and their logistics system was well oiled to deal with these outlets. But their position with newer, larger retail chains (many of them international organizations) was not as strong. Note that chocolate is an impulse purchase item and therefore the point of sale is very important. With the modern retail channel growing very rapidly, the sales people wanted to improve this situation, so they launched the idea that their organization had to become more customer-(meaning retailer-) centric. Typically, marketing didn't like the idea too much. Whenever you try to make a brand- and consumer-focused company more retail customer–centric, there will be an issue: what the retailer wants is not necessarily what the consumer wants, from the point of view of the person responsible for the brand and the brand portfolio. The disagreement didn't get any better when marketing came up with the idea of developing tablet versions of their chocolate bar products. A bad idea, according to sales, as their contacts at the big retailers had explained to them ad nauseam that they needed more tablet chocolate like a hole in the head: it might cause some shifting of market share between brands, but it would not help retailers' sales or profits from the category. Marketing came back arguing that market research had discovered that the consumer wanted it, and as a result, the large modern retailers would have to stock and sell it. They would grow to like it.

I was called in to help the company deal with this issue. Now how can one resolve such a conflict? Honestly, I wasn't really supported by the general manager, who was not decisive and didn't take a position. Still, the company ended up agreeing on a procedure that seemed to have some appeal for everyone. Henceforth, at the beginning of the NPD funnel, all options would be considered. R&D, marketing and sales would be encouraged to submit ideas for NPD based on the needs of and opportunities from their constituencies. At the end of the funnel, both sales and marketing would have the opportunity to bring in their point of view (positive or negative) on what the new product would do for them, and if a problem of conflictual interests arose between consumers and retailers, specific options for resolving them would need to be proposed. These options would then be considered by the heads of marketing and sales, and a proposal made to the executive committee. It seems to have worked so far.

what their brand owner–suppliers might be interested in. For all the others, loyalty programs are no more than an expensive gadget with a disappointing outcome. So why do they continue them? To match their competitors – they can't all be wrong, can they?

So far, only a few retailers have stopped the loyalty card altogether and invested the cost in straight price cuts and promotions. The problem is that most retailers want to do everything simultaneously. Besides a loyalty program, they want to develop a private label, develop services, have impactful promotions, offer the largest choice and so on. The lack of focus and resources inevitably leads to mediocrity on all fronts. It is not enough to have a loyalty card, an IT system and the know-how to turn Big Data into insights and actions. You need employees who are in touch with shoppers and fully understand what the loyalty program wants to achieve and how they can contribute to achieving that. In reality, most retailers fail to deliver on this aspect. That's what you get with good strategy and poor execution.

How Tesco lost control of its steering wheel: Poor strategy, good execution

So what about good implementation of a poor strategy? In 2002, in the aftermath of the dot-com bubble, Jamie Dimon, now CEO of JPMorgan Chase, opined, 'I'd rather have a first-rate execution and second-rate strategy any time than a brilliant idea and mediocre management.'

But was he right? Let's look once more at Tesco, the British retailer that was turned into a high-performing organization by legendary CEO Terry Leahy during the '90s. In ten years' time, the company went from a poorly run fourth player in the UK to number one by a mile. A great strategy was at the base of this remarkable success story. When UK retailers were still in the middle of a race for space, Leahy bought more land with construction permits than any other company. He installed a shopper-centric vision at the company, introduced the famous slogan *Every little helps*, improved Tesco's relative prices and therefore its price image, and was a first mover on effectively using the information from their loyalty cards. But what made Tesco really stand out among other retailers was an unrelenting focus on execution in the stores. Driven by the company's motto 'Better, simpler, cheaper', Tesco's managers at the coalface had three key principles:

1 'Just do it' (few generals, many soldiers).
2 'Things that get measured tend to improve.'
3 'Get paid for performance.'

These principles were put into operation by the 'Steering Wheel', a balanced scorecard showing the key parameters on which employees would be evaluated at each level and every function in the organization (see Figure 25). The Steering Wheel was composed of four quadrants – operations, people, finance and customers – that consisted of further segments, each having their own KPIs which varied by function and hierarchical level. This Steering Wheel was the glue that held everything together, ensuring everyone in the company was singing from the same hymn sheet.

Figure 25. The famous Tesco Steering Wheel, integrating Tesco's key execution parameters. A fifth segment, 'Community', was added later.

Source: D Bell, 'Case study: Tesco Plc,' Harvard Business School, Dec. 2002.

All this was very well orchestrated by one boss: God Terry. The results were extraordinary, thanks to the multiplication effect of good execution. Then God retired and his successor, Philip Clarke, running out of ideas, made some wrong strategic turns, the biggest of which was to let Tesco's relative prices increase, in order to keep margins up under higher costs. In the UK Tesco still had the same exceptional set of stores, the same Tesco Direct channel, the same implementation principles, the same people executing them (except the many who had been promoted to Tesco's international business). However, Tesco's market share in their home market dropped, employees got frustrated because targets became harder to achieve and therefore their bonuses evaporated, and the whole thing started to unravel, until Clarke was fired.

Should Reckitt Benckiser be canonized? Good strategy, good execution

Probably the best illustration of what exceptional execution can do for a company is provided by Reckitt Benckiser, a relatively small player that is highly underestimated and sometimes looked down upon by people working for the big FMCG names such as Unilever, P&G and l'Oréal. Actually, all three could learn a great deal from Reckitt Benckiser. Just look at Figure 26, comparing its share price to that of its main competitors, those three companies, over the last fifteen years. Impressive is the least one can say. What is their secret?

Figure 26. Reckitt-Benckiser (top line) outperforms Unilever, P&G and L'Oréal.

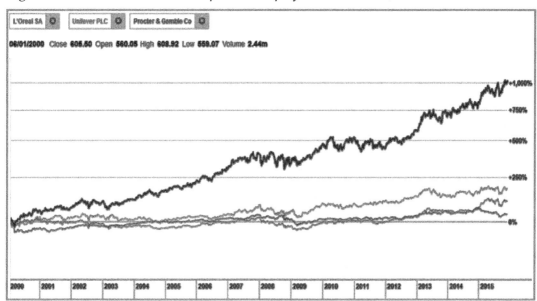

Source: Financial Times, 2015.

One of the main drivers behind Reckitt Benckiser's success story is Bart Becht, a man trained in the P&G school of hard knocks, who was CEO from 1999 to 2011. He made the company focus on fast incremental innovation, comparing innovation with baseball. He said: 'People think that it's about hitting home runs, but it's not. Innovation is about getting many base hits and occasionally hitting a home run. You very rarely win a baseball game just by hitting a home run. And the objective is to win the game.'

As discussed in Chapter 2, 'Innovation for Brands', Reckitt Benckiser excels in continuously introducing small product improvements to their existing power brands. Each of these improvements is based on insights about consumer concerns and problems with products on the market. The product improvements are only considered if they drive growth and profitability. Successive innovations on their dishwasher detergent power brand, Finish, illustrate their approach. After the original Finish, which was a pure detergent product, they entered Finish 2-in-1, which added a rinse agent; this was followed a few years later by Finish 3-in-1, which added a salt component, and then by their current 4-in-1 Finish, which added a glass-protection component. Each of these 'small' improvements grew volume as well as margin.

Becht installed a high-performance culture of incessant innovation at the company. From the CEO down, everyone is focused on innovation that drives growth. The major emphasis is on execution. People are rewarded on a 'pay for performance' basis. It is the ideal environment for managers with an outspoken 'go-getter' attitude. Reckitt Benckiser shows that execution is what separates the men from the boys.

It is worthwhile to observe that Reckitt Benckiser's approach, begun years ago, still works. Execution can be a core competency, not just a short-run advantage that depends on one or a few managers. Becht's successor Rakesh Kapoor continued going from success to success using the same approach of constant innovation and outstanding execution. Notice, by the way, how some companies talk about 'flawless' execution and others about 'outstanding' execution. The former is about not making mistakes; the latter is about using execution to take performance to the next level.

How corporate culture determines execution

If execution is the core competency that makes Reckitt Benckiser stand out among reputed competitors like Unilever or l'Oréal, we should conclude that it's about more than resources and capabilities. After all, you would think the likes of Unilever and l'Oréal have the necessary financial resources and competent managers to do the job, wouldn't you? Still, the reality is that in many companies, there is a giant gap between what needs to be done to execute a strategy successfully and the potential of the organization to actually make it happen. Can there be any other explanation? In my opinion, it's about culture. Existing cultural norms in a corporation can make execution far more challenging than it needs to be. At Tesco and Reckitt Benckiser, there was and is no room for complication. Along with Nike, they adhere to a very simple motto: 'Just do it'. But for many companies, this is just not the case. Here are some examples of successes and failures that were driven by the compatibility – or lack thereof – between corporate culture and the execution needed to implement a strategy successfully.

Snapple, in its many ups and downs, is a telling illustration of how corporate culture influences the quality of execution. The quirky fruit drink manufacturer, founded in New York in 1972, became a success in the 1980s after they developed 'the first ready-to-drink iced tea that didn't taste like battery acid,' to quote cofounder Arnold Greenberg. The growing company attracted the attention of the Thomas H. Lee Company of Boston, who successfully proposed a leveraged buy-out in 1992, renaming it "Snapple" and rolling out a national publicity campaign starring employee Wendy Kaufman. Her friendly 'Greetings from Snapple!' salute, pronounced with a heavy New York accent, helped build the company's unconventional positioning. Snapple was sold through small distributors instead of big supermarket chains, and the company was known for its people-focused management style, approaching its distribution and employee relationships with a respectful attitude, thus earning tremendous internal and operational loyalty.

This all changed when Quaker Oats bought them in 1993 for $1.7 billion. Talk about cultural incompatibility… Quaker Oats was a very corporate type of company that saw a great opportunity to make a big brand out of Snapple by applying the success formula of Gatorade, a serious brand, with a thirst-quenching positioning, distributed via supermarkets, run by a well-drilled corporate organization. Oh, they were so self-assured: 'We have an excellent sales and marketing team here at Gatorade. We believe we do know how to build brands, we do know how to advance businesses. And our expectation is that we will do the same as we take Snapple as well as Gatorade to the next level,' said Don Uzzi, President of the Quaker Oats Beverage Company.

Of course they fired Wendy and did away with the unconventional management style. Guess what? It didn't work at all. Eventually, top management got fired and Quaker Oats sold Snapple in 1997 at a great loss (for $300 million, to be exact) to Triarc, an investor company run by the famous Nelson Pelz, a rather nonconformist businessman. He and his 'crazy but clever' CEO Michael Weinstein succeeded in getting the brand on track again by refocusing on the quirky brand image, the unconventional HR policy, the alternative distribution channels… It worked like magic! In 2000 Triarc sold Snapple to Cadbury Schweppes for $1 billion.

What had happened? In an analysis of the case, John Deighton in the *Harvard Business Review* wrote: 'There is a vital interplay between the challenge a brand faces and the culture of the corporation that owns it. When brand and culture fall out of alignment, both brand and corporate owner are likely to suffer' ('How Snapple Got Its Juice Back,' January 2002). Indeed, this is what successful corporate culture does: it attracts certain kinds of employees that 'fit' with the brand and do the right things to help it flourish. In other words, corporate culture is an important determinant of successful execution. Note that when Cadbury Schweppes bought Snapple they made sure to also hire the somewhat eccentric CEO, Michael Weinstein.

Different brands, different culture

What should FMCG multinationals do with brands that don't seem to be completely in line with the general corporate culture? Selling them is certainly not the only solution. On the contrary, it can be very enriching for companies to foster brands that really stand out in their portfolio. A 'special treatment' for these exceptional brands seems only logical. Big corporations like Nestlé and Unilever have shown the way.

Take Nespresso, the successful coffee brand that has more in common with lifestyle and luxury goods than with the mass-market products you find in your average supermarket, which are the bread and butter of Nestlé. The Nespresso Club idea, distribution through exclusive boutiques and a dedicated webshop, helped Nespresso stand out from other coffee brands. But would it have been possible to execute this strategy to the limit if the Nespresso team had been sharing an office with the Nescafé and Kit Kat people? The great thing Nestlé did for Nespresso was to keep it separate from the rest of the business – and give it time and loads of funds to succeed. Nespresso's culture is closer to LVMH's, which is not your mainstream Nestlé. In order to execute its strategy, it needs different people, other KPIs. The results are undeniable, and execution played a major part in these achievements.

A comparably sensible decision was taken by Unilever when it acquired Ben & Jerry's in 2001. The unorthodox ice cream brand was driven by sustainability and CSR long before it became fashionable, and its marketing was topped by tons of humour. How could Unilever make sure these unique brand characteristics would be protected after the acquisition? Well, through a particular acquisition agreement, an independent board of directors was created to preserve and expand Ben & Jerry's social mission, brand integrity and product quality. In other words, the company was clever enough to leave them on their own to do their thing. Employees at Ben & Jerry's – be they workers or senior managers – are really hooked on what the brand stands for and love working for the company. It's a people thing. Actually, there is a lot to say for the statement that Ben & Jerry's changed Unilever more than Unilever changed Ben & Jerry's.

You don't even need separate offices in order to install a distinctive culture. Dove's core narrative of self-esteem and real beauty has touched people inside and outside of Unilever, motivating talented women to come and work for the brand because they believe in the mission and the values Dove stands for. As mentioned in Chapter 4, which discussed CSR, companies that want to 'do good' can sometimes achieve commercial success because consumers are willing to pay more for their 'honest' products and because some people are prepared to work for them for lower wages. In the case of Dove, Unilever has managed to obtain great execution because they have people working for them who are inspired by the brand.

Investing in employees pays off for retailers

Does the same logic apply to retailers? It certainly does, as retail is a service business where people are pivotal for success. In her 2014 book, *The Good Jobs Strategy: How the Smartest Companies Invest in Employees to Lower Costs and Boost Profits*, Zeynep Ton of MIT's Sloan School of Management shows how low-price retailers operate in a virtuous cycle of 'good quality and quantity of labour, helping to achieve good operational execution, which in turn leads to high sales and profits'. This seems counterintuitive, indeed, as retail managers may be tempted to lower labour costs in order to increase profits. In reality, cutting employees generates short-term financial benefits but backfires in the long run. When Home Depot's CEO Robert Nardelli cut staffing levels and increased the percentage of part-timers in 2000, he immediately managed to reduce costs and boost profits. But soon the retailer saw the adverse effects of this move: customer service suffered, customer satisfaction plunged and same-store sales dropped. Several studies and cases confirm that investing in payroll can lead to increased profit margins.

Illustrative is the case of Wegmans, a family-owned retail chain that runs 86 huge supermarkets on the East Coast in the United States. The company pays its workers extremely well compared to another similarly huge all-in-one supermarket chain, Walmart. It offers scholarships to its employees and generous benefits such as health insurance. Wegmans also offers their employees a better work/life balance than most retail jobs. Why? The Wegmans model is simple: 'A happy, knowledgeable and superbly trained employee creates a better experience for customers. When you think about employees first, the bottom line is better,' Kevin Stickles, the company's vice-president for human resources, told *The Atlantic* magazine in its March 2012 issue. 'Our employees are our number one asset, period.' Wegmans boasts a 5% turnover rate among full-time employees, compared to a 27% rate for the industry. Its benefits and work culture have put it on *Fortune*'s '100 Best Companies to Work For" list every year since the list started in 1998, reliably in the top five.

Another example of great execution by motivated staff in the retail area is Mercadona, the Spanish discount grocery store chain. At Mercadona, stores are staffed by people cross-trained to handle many positions: they manage cash registers, stock shelves, rearrange the store, develop promotions and manage others. The company pays higher wages than other retailers, and workers have opportunities to score bonuses. Moreover, according to the *Wall Street Journal(23 October 2012)* the company invests about $6,500 and four weeks of training in each newly hired employee – plus an additional 20 hours annually thereafter. As with Wegmans, this results in above-average retention and engagement rates of their employees. The underlying logic is the same: happy and confident employees make for a pleasant shopping experience that encourages shoppers to come back and spend more. Both retailers demonstrate how corporate culture can be a key determinant of successful execution.

'Pay for performance' in retail :
Getting away with poor execution?

One important part of a company's corporate culture is its remuneration policy. Excessive executive compensation and 'reward for failure' are frequent topics in the press when companies have their general annual meeting. With the very divergent trading fortunes of the UK food retailers and their recently published annual reports, Bernstein's top retail analyst Bruno Monteyne decided to dig a bit deeper.

While people can justifiably have very different opinions about the future growth potential of the three UK food retailers, one can't deny the fact that Sainsbury's management team delivered in the last year (2014) by far the best numbers in terms of sales, profits and market share. However, looking at Monteyne's report about their total pay packets and, more particularly, their total bonuses, you get to understand why Sainsbury's senior executives might feel a bit glum (Table 40). They had the lowest bonuses (and incidentally, no long-term incentive plan), while underperforming Tesco paid out handsome bonuses or golden handshakes to their remaining and departing executives. Could it be that those incentive schemes work? Maybe truly stretching bonus targets help to explain Sainsbury's relative outperformance: after all, if you pick up more than half your maximum bonus pay-out by delivering a 50% profit drop, like the managers at Tesco and Morrison's, why would you aim high?

On the other hand, stretched 'pay for performance' schemes might be a strong stimulant for improving management. Consider AB InBev and Reckitt Benckiser, two consumer goods companies known to pay their management very well. Not surprisingly, these are companies that emphasize heavily the crucial influence of outstanding execution, and what characterizes them is that they don't pay for meeting targets, but for exceeding stretched objectives.

Table 40. Compensation (in million £) UK retail top executives (CEO+CFO), 2014.

	TOTAL EXECUTIVE PAY	SALARY	BONUS	DELTA SALES	DELTA MARGIN
TESCO	9.6	2.0	7.6	-2%	-3%
SAINSBURY'S	3.0	1.5	1.5	-0.7%	-0.4%
MORRISON	3.3	1.4	1.9	-4.9%	-1.4%

Source: Bernstein, 2015

Are investment firms taking execution to the next level?

A lot has been written and told about the recent daring endeavours of the Brazilian multibillion-dollar global investment firm 3G capital and Warren Buffet's Berkshire Hathaway in the food industry, buying Heinz and merging it with Kraft Foods to create the world's fifth-largest food company. No doubt competitors are petrified by the sequence of events, wondering what the next move will bring. Typically, investment funds have a relentless focus on execution, x-raying the companies they acquire in order to strip off any superfluous cost, function, division or service, with only one goal in mind: optimizing profitability. They do so unreservedly, without taboos. One can imagine the pressure this brings to competitors, especially in the case of such a large player as the Heinz-Kraft combination.

Still, the corporate philosophy of private equity groups like 3G capital is very different from your typical ruthless hedge fund, which buys companies in trouble; gets the house in order by cutting costs, selling off businesses and squeezing the employees; and then cashes in just a few years later by selling the company or launching an IPO that greatly benefits the hedge fund partners. Now, we are actually observing a new generation of investors whose ambition it is to run extremely successful businesses for the medium to long run, and not to opportunistically sell them off. We see a distinct type of ownership emerging in the world of branded FMCG companies that actually has some of its roots in Reckitt Benckiser. There seems to be a group of well-educated, financially savvy and like-minded people who share common views on how to run FMCG companies and who know each other very well, as they meet regularly on the boards of a selection of outstanding companies: think Jorge Paulo Lemann and Marcel Herrmann Telles (two of the people behind 3G Capital); Alex Behring (Burger King, AB InBev, Kraft-Heinz); Alexandre Van Damme (AB InBev); Peter Harf (Reckitt Benckiser, Coty, Calvin Klein, D.E. Master Blenders); Olivier Goudet (Coty, Reckitt Benckiser, Jimmy Choo)…

These people may be changing the rules in FMCG management, driven by some interesting key ideas. In their view, the board decides on strategy (allocation of resources, setting goals for the company, establishing risk levels for their companies, deciding on mergers and acquisitions), while heavily incentivized management is responsible for execution. There is a clear division of tasks and a great belief in a 'pay for performance' management culture. In their view, execution of strategy is as important as strategy itself. There is a notion that this small group of individuals 'know' how to run branded goods FMCG companies better than current managements, thanks to their rich experience and, of course, their considerable financial muscle. There is no denying that their approach is very different from classic FMCG multinationals like Unilever, Nestlé or P&G, and that they seem to be on the winning side, scaring the hell out of their more traditional competitors.

Index of Terms

CPSIA information can be obtained
at www.ICGtesting.com
Printed in the USA
LVOW02s1141260216

476829LV00004B/4/P